The Reconstruction of
American History

hARPER ⚜ ᴛORChBOOKS

A reference-list of Harper Torchbooks, classified
by subjects, is printed at the end of this volume.

The Reconstruction of
American History

EDITED BY

JOHN HIGHAM

Professor of History in the University of Michigan

HARPER TORCHBOOKS ❦ THE ACADEMY LIBRARY

HARPER & ROW, PUBLISHERS

New York

The Reconstruction of American History

© Hutchinson & Co. (*Publishers*) Ltd. 1962

Printed in the United States of America

★

First published 1962

CONTENTS

ACKNOWLEDGMENT

This book has grown out of a series of short radio broadcasts which five of the authors prepared for the Voice of America in 1959.

1

THE CONSTRUCTION OF AMERICAN HISTORY

BY JOHN HIGHAM

THERE is a fairly common view, particularly among European intellectuals, that American history is not very interesting and the achievement of American historians not very important. For these disparaging opinions perhaps more can be said than an American scholar likes to admit. Spanning a mere three and a half centuries, American history has no antiquity, few ruins, and little mystery. Moving in a fairly straight line from primitive settlements to triumphant power and plenty, it looks superficially simple. Its complexity lies below the surface and therefore makes a special demand on the historical imagination.

Americans themselves have too often taken their history for granted, not having had to live continuously on intimate terms with it. In the eighteenth and nineteenth centuries ever-widening opportunities kept most American eyes fixed expectantly upon the future. A pragmatic cast of mind put more emphasis on results than on antecedents. Physical separation from Europe, and repeated declarations of intellectual independence from it, ratified a sense of emancipation from the past. Although history has served almost all Americans as an inspiring chronicle of pride, most of them have undoubtedly turned more readily to other kinds of knowledge to enlarge their range of experience.

One can concede this much but still feel that such easy generalizations tell less than half of the truth. The historical spirit has never lacked sources of strength in American culture, and the alleged 'lessons' of history have often made themselves powerfully felt in public affairs. (The Constitution itself was framed with the most scrupulous attention to the experience of earlier republics.) Americans have been writing their own history with uninterrupted enthusiasm since it began. In sheer bulk the product equals or surpasses the historical literature on any other modern nation. Since no part of the American past is really remote from the current scene, American history has to an unusual degree a personal and contemporary relevance. Moreover, in almost every generation one or more historians have been among the leading lights of American culture, and their books have exemplified some of its most pronounced characteristics. The writing of American history has always had, therefore, an intimate relation to history in the making. To examine the two together is to see America in terms of its evolving consciousness of itself.

This book deals with the most recent phase of the American attempt to understand its past. We are concerned here with the rethinking that American history has undergone in recent years. How and why have scholars in the middle decades of the twentieth century recast the main chapters in the story? Such is our question. Each of the following essays tells how a standard topic in American history was understood a generation ago and how its interpretation has altered since that time. In virtually every instance, however, the 'orthodoxy' of a generation ago was itself a revision of preceding formulations. Consequently, to see the recent changes in a large perspective, it will be helpful first to glance backward at the earlier foundations of American historiography.

Historical writing in America falls into three large periods. It began in the seventeenth century as the function of clergymen and of magistrates associated with them in executing the will of God; this was the period of Puritan history. From the early eighteenth to the late nineteenth century, the best history came from the pens of independent gentlemen, who did not write in the service of a church or from any other institutional incentive. They had a high respect for the dignity of history, in the writing of which they exhibited a generalized sense of responsibility to society. Theirs was the period of patrician history. Around the end of the nineteenth century, gentlemen-historians yielded predominance to the growing host of university professors, for whom historical activity became a corporate task and specialized career. These men made history once more an institutional product, and such it remains in this century of professional history.

The Puritan fathers of New England deserve the credit for implanting an historical consciousness in the American wilderness. They were neither the first English colonists nor the first to publicize the exploits of Englishmen in the New World. The Elizabethan adventurers who established a foot-hold in Virginia preceded them, and Captain John Smith's exuberant tract about his first year at Jamestown, *A True Relation* (1608), is probably the earliest English chronicle composed on American soil. But in the Southern and Middle colonies history seemed useful only as a casual introduction to descriptions of the current scene; until the middle of the eighteenth century, the recording of the past never emerged as a task important in its own right. For New England, however, history supplied an essential vehicle of self-analysis and—after the sermon—one of the principal modes of public discourse.

'It is our great duty,' enjoined a Massachusetts clergyman, 'to be the Lord's remembrancers or recorders.' History told not merely the doings of men; it set forth the actions of God. His will directed every event. The history recorded in scripture and unfolded in subsequent happenings offered the principal clue to His otherwise inscrutable design. To ignore history was to remain in heathen darkness, and to distort or delimit its fullness was self-deceiving. (In their passion to tell all, Puritan historians touched on the weather, the state of the crops, crimes, fashions, and business transactions, as well as public events.) Their own history in the New World held a special fascination for the Puritans. God had called them to this remote place to complete the Protestant Reformation and thus to lead the way for all mankind. In the grand strategy of history they were enacting the crucial modern chapter. The outcome was uncertain, the record equivocal. They searched it proudly for evidence of their faithfulness and anxiously for signs of their failings.

The most memorable achievements of the Puritan historians were William Bradford's *Of Plymouth Plantation* and Cotton Mather's *Magnalia Christi Americana*. The first, written piecemeal in the 1630's and 1640's, told the story of the little group of Pilgrims who fled to Holland in 1608 and then settled permanently at Plymouth in 1620. The second, published in 1702, put into a great omnium-gatherum the history of the New England churches and settlements throughout the seventeenth century. Bradford, a plain, self-taught man, was Plymouth's governor for thirty-three years; he took no initiative to publish his writings, and his history remained in manuscript for two centuries. Mather, writing fifty years after Bradford, was Boston's pre-eminent minister and the most learned American of his day; his printed works included 444 known titles. Bradford set down a straightforward narrative of shared and remembered experience. Mather erected a monument of laborious scholarship to remind a faltering generation of the greatness of its forebears. Bradford combined the simplicity of John Bunyan and the cadence of the English Bible with an effortless grasp of human motivation. Mather united antiquarian fussiness with a pompous delight in classical allusions and metaphysical conceits. But, for all their differences, both books embodied the Puritan's deeply historical sense of destiny and responsibility.

Diffused and secularized, this Puritan legacy persisted after the Church lost its controlling importance in American intellectual life. Throughout the eighteenth and nineteenth centuries the great majority of America's leading historians derived from New England. Some of them—Francis Parkman, George Bancroft, and Richard Hildreth, for example—were sons of New England clergymen. Others, in the New England colleges, got an education steeped in the moral earnestness and cultural traditions of the region. Significantly, New England produced only one major political theorist, John Adams, and he an historical theorist; it produced only one major novelist, Nathaniel Hawthorne, and an historical con-

sciousness profoundly shaped his art; yet New England produced at least four historians of permanent distinction—
Parkman, William H. Prescott, John Lothrop Motley, and
Henry Adams. Clearly, the New England intellect distrusted
the rational abstractions of political theory and the relaxing
temptations and fabrications of the novel. It preferred the
solid instruction, the concrete down-to-earth verities, of
history. The voice of the Puritan still echoed through the
advice that Edwin Gay, a prominent twentieth-century historian, received as a youth from his father, a lumber magnate
of New England descent:

> 'Reading is part of the training for life. . . . Now while
> you are training you should read only what will give you
> strength; and story books, at least some of them, are cake
> and pie to you mentally, and take strength from you
> instead of adding it. You ought not to read them. [Instead,]
> read histories and travels and lives of great men. Learn to
> consider what quality of mind or heart made them great
> or brave or good, and then cultivate those qualities your-
> self. See where they made mistakes.'[1]

The quality of historical writing improved enormously,
however, when it no longer had to meet the prescriptions of
Puritan theology. In the rationalistic atmosphere of the
eighteenth century the desire to fathom the will of God
ceased to control the scrutiny of human affairs. Historiography became relatively independent of religious sponsorship, socially as well as intellectually; for a new basis appeared
with the accumulation of wealth and leisure in the hands of
individuals. Historical scholarship is a laborious, time-con-
suming enterprise, and a highly cultivated one, not to be
expected without access to many books, and opportunity for
sustained reflection. Fortunately, in raw, bustling America, a
few eighteenth-century gentlemen had good private libraries

---

[1] Herbert Heaton, *A Scholar in Action: Edwin F. Gay* (Harvard
University Press, 1952), p. 16.

and some time to spare from an active life to use them. By the middle of the nineteenth century a few men were giving, for long periods, substantially all of their time to history.

The patrician historian had, through pride of ancestry, a sense of personal connection with the past. He responded sympathetically to great occasions and to acts of virtuous individuals. He gave much attention to wars, to the forming of governments, and to the etiquette of public transactions. In appraising the actions of men, he enjoyed a relatively independent stance. Indebted to no one, he felt capable of exercising an unconstrained judgment with entire impartiality. He usually enjoyed playing a judicial role, weighing the evidence, ascribing motives, and pronouncing the magisterial verdict of history. Familiar with the great classical historians, he followed their practice of holding up to posterity examples of errors, failings, and laudable deeds.

Although the patrician historian felt a patriotic pride in free institutions, he generally took the conservative side on most social issues. Typically, he idolized George Washington, disliked Thomas Jefferson, and despised Andrew Jackson. The principal historians writing before and during the American Revolution became loyalists. Later generations inclined first to Federalism, then to Whiggery, and always to the politics of respectability. Accordingly, in the mid-nineteenth century, most historians disapproved of contemporary reform movements, and in the late nineteenth century they firmly opposed the rising economic unrest.

Yet their philosophy of history changed considerably during their long period of dominance. Men of wide culture, the patrician historians kept abreast of European historiography, adopting its advancing methods and changing forms. In the eighteenth century they began to utilize documentary evidence in the careful, critical way exemplified by the Bollandist fathers in the Netherlands. They began to make the temperate judgments congenial to an age of reason. They took a new interest in the history of political institutions in the manner of David Hume. One American, the Rev. Samuel

Miller, undertook a history of modern culture on a scale as broad as Voltaire's and in a more critical spirit.[1]

The best of the eighteenth-century historians was Thomas Hutchinson, who wrote a *History of the Colony and Province of Massachusetts-Bay* in three volumes during the decade preceding the American Revolution. In his splendid Boston mansion Hutchinson had gathered an outstanding collection of early manuscript sources. He served as Chief Justice of Massachusetts while writing the first two volumes, and he took special interest in the constitutional and legal history of the province. After an ill-fated interval as royal governor during the deepening revolutionary crisis, he completed his work in unhappy exile. Yet his mind on the whole was unusually irenic and judicious. He appreciated the relativity of customs and standards. He had a shrewd understanding of the arts of political management. He could justly say at one point: 'I am not sensible of having omitted any material fact, nor have I designedly given a varnish to the actions of one party, or high coloring to those of the other . . . I profess to give a true relation of facts.'

In the nineteenth century historians were not content simply to give a true relation of facts, with accompanying conclusions. They became exponents of the concept of development, seeking to exhibit in a coherent, integrated narrative the unfolding continuity of human experience. Now history must reveal not a mere chronological sequence but rather the realization, through connected events, of some underlying principle. Historians therefore organized their books around one or more of the great principles of nineteenth-century bourgeois culture: liberty, nationality, and progress.

History cast in a dramatic pattern of development lent itself to the purposes of art; the patrician historian in the nineteenth century regarded himself distinctly as a man of letters. Under the influence of the romantic movement, which

[1] *A Brief Retrospect of the Eighteenth Century* (2 vols., 1803). Miller wrote this remarkable book while associating with a cultivated literary circle in New York City. Later he moved to the Princeton Theological Seminary and renounced such secular pursuits.

greatly heightened appreciation of the past and vitalized its description, good history reached a very large audience. American publishers, pirating cheap editions of Macaulay's history, sold four times as many copies as were distributed in Great Britain, and Prescott's sumptuous *Conquest of Mexico* (1843) enjoyed a comparable success. These writers managed, as no one had before, to re-create with visual immediacy striking scenes and heroic characters.

The romantic approach proved notably congenial to the patrician mind, with its taste for grandeur and its literary inclinations. The only major American historian in the mid-nineteenth century who rejected romanticism was an 'outsider', socially unaccepted and intellectually unorthodox. His work was coolly received, and he had to abandon it for lack of support. Richard Hildreth was a pungent anti-slavery and temperance pamphleteer, devoted to Benthamite utilitarianism. His coldly analytical *History of the United States* (6 vols., 1849–52), the first scholarly account extending as far as 1821, was remarkable for its realistic interpretations. Hildreth presented American worthies—as he himself said—'unbedaubed with patriotic rouge, wrapped up in no finespun cloaks of excuses and apology, without stilts, buskins, tinsel, or bedizenment, in their own proper persons'. He produced the work during an eight-year period when his pretty young wife supported him by painting portraits. Thereafter, to earn a living, he had to return to partisan journalism.

In contrast to Hildreth, another man of modest clerical origins and unorthodox opinions, George Bancroft, gained immense success by adapting himself to the cultural milieu. As a young man ambitious to cut a figure in the world, Bancroft braved the disapproval of Boston society by becoming a professional Democratic politician and writing history with a vague but loud democratic accent. But Bancroft's history glowed with romantic nationalism, and in time its author became a proper gentleman. With the aid of a fortune acquired through marriage and shrewd investments, he withdrew from active politics and from controversy, devoting the rest of a long, distinguished life to his famous *History of the*

United States from the Discovery of the American Continent (12 vols., 1834–82).

The last of the romantic historians, Francis Parkman, brought to near-perfection the narrative techniques of that school. His seven-volume *France and England in North America* (1865–92) arrayed French absolutism against Anglo-Saxon liberty in a struggle for control of the American wilderness. Wherever possible, an intrepid individual—La Salle, Frontenac, Montcalm—supplied a focus for the forest drama. No one surpassed Parkman's painstaking research and factual accuracy; no one equalled his feeling for scene and place, or his vivid arrangement of action. Unfortunately, a sheltered life and an excessive fixation on martial exploits limited the range of experience in which he could imaginatively participate.

By the 1870's the romantic presuppositions on which Parkman operated were giving way to a positivistic suspicion of such conscious art. Patrician historians still held to the idea of history as narrative, still played the role of men of letters; but they reverted in good measure to Hutchinson's ideal of telling unvarnished facts. Under the spell of scientific thought, historians came to distrust the studied patterns of romantic history, its emphasis on great men, and its pictorial quality. In selecting data, they sought to be more inclusive, in organizing a narrative more open-ended, lest the 'real' past be artificially curtailed. In presenting situations, they endeavoured to stand apart, observing them from the outside. An array of long, solid histories, produced in the 'eighties and 'nineties by James Schouler, Justin Winsor, John Bach McMaster, and James Ford Rhodes, reflected these changes.

But the new positivistic standards had not yet quite supplanted the older romantic aims. When the tension between the two was acute and sustained, a man might create a masterpiece. Henry Adams had the instincts of an artist together with the philosophy and the analytic intelligence of a scientist. His *History of the United States of America during the Jefferson and Madison Administrations* (9 vols., 1889–91) enacted a moral drama of individual character against a majestic background of impersonal power. In conception deterministic, in execution full of ambiguity, the work has more than lived up to Adams's boast: 'I am writing for a continent of a hundred million people fifty years hence.'[1]

From the life of a literary gentleman in Washington, Adams departed for a few years in the 1870's, when he taught the first historical seminar in an American university. Thus he bridged the social transition from patrician to professional history, just as he straddled the intellectual divide between romanticism and science. The modern American university grew up during Adams's lifetime, and Americans who studied in Germany transplanted to it the canons of professional history. Restrictions that Adams could tolerate only briefly became the terms on which historical scholarship underwent a great transformation.

The immediate consequence of professionalization was a more radical and decisive thrust in the direction in which the patrician historians were moving. While patrician history retained a discursive, narrative form, the professionals disclaimed all literary pretensions. They conceived of themselves as scientists. 'The old union between history and literature is now broken in all the growing colleges,' Carl Becker was told in 1896, when he was selecting his graduate studies at the University of Wisconsin. To achieve a thoroughly positivistic history, the professionals put great emphasis on critical examination of original texts, on checking evidence, and on bibliographical apparatus. To penetrate as deeply as possible into past events, they welcomed specialization and wrote monographs on carefully limited subjects. To cleanse scholarship of the subjective coloration of the historian's own personality, the professionals endeavored to banish the function—so dear to patrician hearts—of passing moral judgments on men and movements.

This whole program heightened uniformity in historical writing at the cost of individuality. The other side of specialization was co-operation. Professional historians sought to

---

[1] Modern scholarship has, however, corrected Adams's findings at some points. See especially vols. IV–VI of Irving Brant's *James Madison* (1953–1961), and Bradford Perkins, *Prologue to War* (1962).

integrate their activities through such devices as the seminar, the learned society, the scholarly journal, and the Dewey decimal system for libraries. To synthesize monographic research and to handle subjects beyond the reach of any single specialist, they began to publish collaborative works. Thus, the coming of age of professional history was signalled by the publication of the *American Nation* series (1904–7), in which twenty-four authors contributed separate volumes to a single history of the United States.[1]

In addition to its scientific emphasis, professional history had another consequence, not so quickly apparent but in the long run equally important. In time, the new conditions facilitated a great democratization of historical scholarship. Institutionalized in a vast educational system, research became a possible and attractive career for men of many sorts and conditions. It ceased to be a near monopoly of a patrician class. Students who came to history from diverse backgrounds brought with them a sympathetic interest in aspects of the past beyond the patrician's range of vision.

The full impact of this wider interest was not felt until after 1910, because the first generation of professional historians pursued the narrowly institutional studies they had learned to cultivate in Germany. The second generation, trained in American graduate schools, turned attention toward popular movements, social processes, and economic conflicts. Even George Bancroft, in tone the most democratic of the nineteenth-century historians, had merely celebrated democracy as an abstract principle while actually writing about a ruling élite. From 1910 to 1945, however, many professional historians took as their theme the functioning of a democratic society. They did so with an egalitarian commitment to protest and reform, and to that extent compromised the ethical neutrality desired by the scientific school.

[1] Among the authors of this series were several who are important in the following chapters: Charles M. Andrews contributed *Colonial Self-Government, 1652–1689*, Frederick Jackson Turner *The Rise of the New West, 1819–1829*, William A. Dunning *Reconstruction, Political and Economic, 1865–1877*, and John H. Latané *America as a World Power, 1897–1907*.

This change occurred under the favoring influence of the Progressive movement, which shaped the mind and politics of the early twentieth century, survived the 1920's, and enjoyed a renaissance (in an altered form, as Professor Mann shows in Chapter 9) during Franklin D. Roosevelt's New Deal. The democratic emphasis in historiography during those years flourished under the leadership of two great historians: first, Frederick Jackson Turner; later, Charles A. Beard. Both were middle-class Middle Westerners. Although Turner concentrated on the sectional opposition of West to East and Beard on the conflict of classes, both found the main theme of American history in the struggle between under- and over-privileged groups. Neither had much sympathy for the moneyed and patrician groups of the East. Many chapters of the present book reveal the impact of their interpretations on virtually every phase of American history.

Since World War II, a third generation of professional historians has come to the fore. The writers of this book belong to that generation. Like the present incumbent in the White House, all were born in the twentieth century. Their average age is forty-three. The work of this third generation is still unfinished, but the following chapters give some report of what it has accomplished to date.

Let it be clear at the outset that the authors of this book do not constitute a school in any conscious sense. Doubtless certain affinities conditioned our common willingness to participate in this undertaking. But no partisan preconceptions controlled the choice of authors. I sought collaborators whose critical intelligence I valued, and whose views about a chosen field of research had not yet been broadly stated. In studying a particular area of American history, each scholar had reached a point where he might suitably venture a mature appraisal. But no injunctions prescribed the approach he should adopt or the conclusions he should seek. Each contributor was encouraged to give his essay a personal stamp. Although each has striven to be fair in treatment and reasonably representative in coverage, none has had an obligation to encompass any more of his subject than he could conveniently handle within the limits of a short essay. Some fascinating and important aspects of American history are quite untouched in the following pages.

Nevertheless, these essays give a substantial impression of how American history looks today. Also they enable us to make a tentative estimate of how far the third generation of professional historians has moved from the posture of the second. Without attempting a close or exhaustive analysis, one may find evidence here of several notable changes.

1. *No great leaders.* In contrast to the second generation, ours does not seem to have produced a decisive leadership. We have no Turner, no Beard, to rally round. Our generation is overhauling the interpretive structure that Turner and Beard built; new hypotheses are replacing parts of their work. But we have not yet constructed another framework for American history as impressive and substantial as theirs once seemed. Many of the following chapters reflect the suppleness, the critical awareness, and the search for new formulations so characteristic of contemporary scholarship; but whatever agreement this book reveals comes largely from the recognition of common problems and the sharing of common moods, not from a unifying principle of explanation.

2. *Attraction of intellectual history.* Instead of following paths blazed by a recognizable leadership, the third generation has explored a relatively unfamiliar aspect of the American past: the history of ideas. Long neglected by professional historians, intellectual history has become in recent years a major interest. Its influence—visible in many of the following chapters— stands out especially in the efforts to re-define the meaning of Puritanism (Chapter 2), Jacksonian democracy (Chapter 5), and modern American reform (Chapter 9).

Actually, the organized study of American intellectual history began in the 1920's and 1930's, during the heyday of the second generation. The classic formulation came from a professor of literature, Vernon L. Parrington, in a three-volume work, *Main Currents in American Thought* (1927–30). For the historians of his day, however, and even in a sense for Parrington himself, ideas had a distinctly subordinate status in historical reality. Tangible, external things, like economic interest and environmental conditions, seemed more important. The third generation of professional historians has largely given up its predecessor's belief in the preponderance of material forces in history. We have no alternative theory of causation; but much of our energy has gone into discovering the subjective meaning that events had for participants.

3. *Decline of economic interpretation.* The swing toward intellectual history is one of the factors that have diverted scholars from economic interpretations of American history. Another reason, undoubtedly more basic, is the hugely satisfying performance of the American economy in the last two decades. Historians interpret the past most readily in the light of the concerns uppermost in their present. Today, questions about national values, about the individual's place in a mass society, or about international responsibilities seem more urgent than difficulties in the production and distribution of income. Accordingly, as the following chapters suggest, the emphasis that many historians a generation ago put on economic motives for the Puritan migration to New England, the outbreak of the American Revolution, the writing of the Constitution, the Civil War, imperialism, and American entrance into World War I, has been superseded. In fact, historians now distrust all impersonal, deterministic explanations. They try to take account of economic influences, not as sovereign forces with a preordained outcome, but as part of the complex and unstable make-up of particular human beings.

4. *Beyond 'scientific' history.* The narrowly scientific outlook that the first generation of professional historians adopted has undergone a slow but relentless revision. Some of the leaders of the second generation, notably Beard and Carl Becker, questioned the feasibility and the conservative implications of the ideal of rigid objectivity. In their later years they tried to re-establish the old nineteenth-century connection of history with philosophy and literature. Many in the third generation have gone farther in this direction, without necessarily sharing Beard's spirit of protest and reform. Instead of trying to stand entirely outside of the subject under investigation, contem-

porary American historians commonly attempt to see events through the eyes of participants. Historians are also more willing than formerly to venture unprovable speculations. Professor Ernest May, discussing recent American foreign policy in Chapter 10, reasserts Leopold von Ranke's austere ideal of finding out what actually happened; but other contributors are just as much interested in what may have happened, and in the moral overtones of what did. Indeed, this book could not have been written without a lively professional concern about the interplay of perspectives, interpretations, and the like.

5. *The ambiguity of American experience.* If no single interpretation of American history stands out today, have we arrived at least at a comprehensive image of our past? Do the following pages have a characteristic and recurrent theme? The most influential historians of the second generation described an America divided between the democratic many and the privileged few. Has the third generation fixed upon another design? Certainly there has been since World War II a strongly conservative movement to minimize the magnitude of social conflict in American history, and to depict a relatively homogeneous society. Most of the following chapters deal—at least implicitly, often explicitly—with this revolt against the great progressive historians. On the other hand, many chapters suggest that the theme of conflict is far from exhausted, that the spirit of Turner and Beard is far from dead. Thus Professor Rowland Berthoff, while writing from a somewhat conservative point of view, argues that historians have not yet done justice to the distinctive role of a working class in American history; and Mr William Miller, in the next chapter, reaffirms certain truths in the progressive indictment of the American tycoons. We can not conclude that an image of consensus has decisively replaced the old image of conflict.

Perhaps a better keynote to contemporary historiography may be found in the frequent attempt to combine such antithetical principles as consensus and conflict without entirely negating either alternative. Like modern literary critics and theologians, many present-day historians seem to say that life

Is ambiguous. America, therefore, becomes a realm of paradox: a nation born of a revolt that was moderate, yet genuinely revolutionary; a society that is liberal in its ideals, yet conservative in its behavior; united in its divisions, and divided in its unity. Professor David Potter's concluding essay on national character works toward a coherent image of American experience by exploring contradictions.

An historian may find life ambiguous, but he is seldom content to leave it that way. So long as contradictions frame our understanding of the American past, it presents an exciting challenge to the rational intellect. To judge from the evidence of the following pages, the reconstruction of American history is vigorously under way.

© John Higham 1962

2

THE PURITAN STRAIN

BY RICHARD SCHLATTER

THE most famous ship in American history, the *Mayflower*, anchored off what is now Plymouth, Massachusetts, in November 1620. A vessel of about 180 tons, bearing an undistinguished name common to other ships of the period, the *Mayflower* had made the voyage from Southampton in about sixty-four days. (The *Queen Elizabeth*, 86,673 tons, crosses in four and a half days, but is a less famous ship.) One hundred and two English passengers came ashore and founded the first permanent settlement in New England. The Plymouth Colony, founded by the Pilgrim Fathers, maintained its separate existence until 1691 when it merged with its more powerful neighbor, the Massachusetts Bay Colony.

The *Arbella*, a ship of 350 tons, less famous but perhaps more important than the *Mayflower*, led a flotilla to Boston Bay in 1630 to found the Bay Colony. Two thousand English people had settled in the Bay Colony by the end of that year. During the Great Migration, 1630–40, the population of New England grew to about 20,000. A small colony was founded at Providence, Rhode Island, in 1636, and at New Haven, Connecticut, in 1638. New England had 50,000 inhabitants in 1675, and about 100,000 in 1700. Boston, the largest town in seventeenth-century America, had about 1,200 inhabitants in 1640; 2,400 in 1660; 3,200 in 1680; and 6,700 in 1700. Rarely have so few been so famous and so much studied by historians.

The founders of New England were Puritans. Just what percentage of even the earliest settlers were in whole-hearted sympathy with the religious views of the leaders is hotly debated by present-day historians. But all scholars agree that it was the Puritan leaders who shaped the culture of New England, whatever the rank and file may have wanted. Government, religion, Church-State relations, education and learning, literature and the arts, family life, customs, morality, and the philosophical assumptions of the whole culture, bore the Puritan hallmark.

Consequently, historians of New England must begin their studies by trying to define Puritanism. No one definition can permanently satisfy. Drawing on the immense labors of modern historical scholarship in Europe and England, American scholars have put together an image of the Puritans as Protestants, English Protestants, Congregationalists; the heirs of Augustine, Calvin, Ramus, Cartwright, and Perkins; the Christian revolutionists whose slogans were predestination, justification by faith, and the Bible an all-sufficient guide; one branch of the English religious party, which formed in the days of Elizabeth, cut off the head of Charles I, suffered under Charles II, and petered out soon after 1688.

The founders of New England were Puritans, but they were also seventeenth-century Englishmen. Their Puritanism gave a distinctive hue to their culture and for its sake they were ready to leave England, which they loved, and settle in a wilderness which had for them no romantic attractions. Nevertheless, perhaps 90 per cent of their ideas, manners, prejudices, and beliefs were those of all seventeenth-century Englishmen. Historians, consequently, must try to see the Puritanism of New England in perspective, against the common background of seventeenth-century English and Western culture. The exact discrimination of these various strands is one of the major tasks of modern Puritan historiography.

The impulse to study the Puritans intensively is easily understood. Their history is an important chapter—one of the opening chapters—in the story of the United States. For nearly 100 years Puritans dominated New England; and New England was the most populous and richest area in America. Puritanism, as a living religious tradition, died out in the course of the eighteenth century, but elements of the tradition lived on. Descendants of the original Puritan families—Cabots, Saltonstalls, Conants, Bradfords, Coolidges, Winthrops, Hoars, Chaunceys—are still leading citizens. New Englanders settled the Ohio Valley and the Middle West. Until far into the nineteenth century American literature was mostly New England literature written by Puritans and their descendants; American colleges were mostly New England colleges founded by Puritans or their descendants, and New England still has more colleges than any other section of the country. Most of the modern historians of Puritanism are professors in New England colleges; and Harvard, the oldest and most Puritan of all, is the source of many of the best modern studies of Puritanism. Until quite recently New England dominated American culture and New England was wholly Puritan in origin. Reason enough, then, for studying the Puritans.

The study of the Puritans takes place, not in isolation, but within the characteristic framework of American historical studies. American scholars have seen their total culture as originating in waves of European influence washing up on the American continent. The waves were christened in Europe before they journeyed to America—Romantic, Industrial, Conservative, Protestant, Catholic, Feudal, Monarchic, Republican, Egalitarian, Imperial, Constitutional, Federal, Utilitarian, Mercantile, Rational, Transcendental, Natural, Real, Social, Capital, Liberal, each with 'ism' added to make it substantive, are the more familiar. And 'Puritanism' is the first. Having identified the European 'isms' 'flying from the depravations of Europe to the American strand', as Cotton Mather put it, the next task of the American historian has been to discover how these 'isms' were modified by the American environment. This leads him to try to define the environment: the Great Plains, the Mississippi Valley, the Appalachians and the Rockies, Tidewater and Piedmont, and the like, are all familiar words in American historical studies. They are all included in the grand idea 'frontier' which Frederick Jackson Turner made a central concept in American historiography at the turn of the last century. Ever since, much of American history, including the history of Puritanism, has been the story of how the 'isms', the European inheritance, were modified by the 'frontier', the characteristic American environment. Much of the best writing, many of the most interesting controversies, have been attempts to define the terms exactly, and get the relationships straight.

In so far as the historians are able to do all this, they are helping to solve the great American riddle—what is an American, what is the American character, what is the American tradition? The compulsive desire to solve this riddle is a function of the shortness of the American past, the diversity of the national origins, and the derivative nature of American culture. Americans do not know who they are and are always trying to find out. An Englishman does not ask himself, 'What does it mean to be an Englishman?'; a Frenchman does not ask himself, 'How can I write a French novel?'; a German does not ask himself, 'Is there such a thing as the German language?'; nor are there Un-English, Un-French, or Un-German Activities Committees officially charged with keeping the national tradition pure. Only American historians would try to define the peculiar national characteristics of their own scholarship.

Here, then, are the principal assumptions and motives which direct American studies of New England Puritanism. One of the most eminent of the historians of New England has written:

> 'Puritanism may be described empirically as that point of view, code of values, carried to New England by the first settlers. These were English Protestants, and in their fundamental convictions were at one with the Protestants, or at least the Calvinistic Protestants, of all Europe. But the peculiar isolation of the New England colonies—the homogeneous people, the sparse soil, the climate, the economic struggle—quickly made these Protestants a peculiar people. Because their societies were tightly organized, and above all because they were a highly

articulate people, the New Englanders established Puritanism—for better or worse—as one of the continuous factors
in American life and thought. It has played so dominant a
role because descendants of the Puritans have carried
traits of the Puritan mind into a variety of pursuits and all
the way across the continent. Many of these qualities have
persisted even though the original creed is lost. Without
some understanding of Puritanism, and that at its source,
there is no understanding of America.'[1]

This is an accepted view today. Nevertheless, until the
1920's the best historians of the colonial period were less
interested in Puritan culture than in other aspects of early
New England history. The monumental volumes of Herbert L.
Osgood and Charles McLean Andrews belong to that era of
American historiography which focussed on imperial history—
the relations of colonies and mother country. Osgood and
Andrews studied imperial constitutional history in an attempt
to understand the Revolution. They were not much interested
in Puritan culture and ideas, although Andrews's rich work
touches on every phase of colonial life.

Those historians before 1920 who were interested in
Puritan culture were mostly pious New England antiquarians.
The books of Henry M. Dexter, John G. Palfrey, and Williston
Walker are still consulted by specialists collecting facts. But
the important books on the Puritans have been written by men
who are still at work: Samuel Eliot Morison, Kenneth B.
Murdock, and Perry Miller, to name the three most eminent,
in whose work Harvard piety and provincial pride are
incidental.

After the First World War, in an atmosphere of isolationism and disillusionment with the politics and culture of
Europe, American critics lost interest in the older history
which had tried to see colonial America in its imperial setting
as an offshoot of British culture. They now sought for the
unique in American history, the peculiar American character,

[1] Perry Miller, *The American Puritans* (Doubleday Anchor Books,
1956), p. ix.

the separate American tradition. In doing this they took a new look at Puritanism.

One group came to the straightforward conclusion that Puritanism was un-American and no part of the true American heritage. The most effective satirist of the 1920's, H. L. Mencken, identified Puritanism with canting hypocrisy, inhibitions, joylessness, witch-hunting, and tyranny masquerading as moral earnestness. Prohibition, Blue Laws, Fundamentalism, the narrow-minded censoring of books and plays and pictures, public and legal interference with private behaviour, together with a sniggering licentiousness behind the scenes—this has been the popular meaning of Puritanism since the 1920's as it was once before in Restoration England.[1]

More sophisticated and scholarly versions of the anti-Puritanism of the 1920's are *The Founding of New England* (1921) by James Truslow Adams and V. L. Parrington's *Colonial Mind* (1927). Adams's book is still the best one-volume synthesis of New England history in the seventeenth century (an up-to-date re-doing would be useful), but it is especially weak on Puritan culture and religion. An exponent of the economic interpretation of history which dominated American historiography in the 1920's, Adams read Puritan theology and philosophy as an ideology constructed to further the ambitions of an economic class: Puritanism is 'the reasoned expression of the middle-class state of mind'. As an admirer of eighteenth-century liberalism, he was repelled by 'repression and conformity, the two key-notes of Puritan New England, [which] were to continue to mould the life of her people throughout the long "glacial age" of her early history'. Bigotry, intolerance, and censorship 'nullified, to a great extent, the benefits which might have been derived from her "educational" system. . . . In the other colonies, men may

[1] The serious scholar feels that his profession is contemptuously scorned when the Regius Professor of History at Oxford, writing for an American Sunday newspaper audience brought up in the tradition of the 1920's, purveys the old caricatures as if all the historians of Puritanism, English and American, from Thomas Carlyle to the present, had never written. H. R. Trevor-Roper, 'Puritans—from Calvin to Castro', *New York Times Magazine*, 20 March 1960.

have been more ignorant of books, but they were healthy-minded.' Finally, an admirer of the 'Greek picture of the perfect life as the fullest development of the entire man, body and soul', Adams was impatient with a Calvinism which proposed 'the utter surrender of one's own will to the divine will as expressed in minuteness of detail . . . even to the style of hats for a minister's wife, in the old Semitic writings' and which stripped 'God of every shred of what we consider moral character'.[1]

V. L. Parrington's *Colonial Mind* is the first volume of his great work, *Main Currents in American Thought*. A Westerner, a supporter of the Progressive Movement, Parrington had originally meant his work to be called *A History of American Liberal Thought*. And he described Puritanism as the enemy of that liberalism which was, or which he wanted to make, the heart of the American tradition. Of their 'reactionary theology', he wrote:

'To the formalist who demanded an exact system, and to the timid who feared free speculation, the logical consistency of Calvinism made irresistible appeal . . . academic thinkers and schoolmen, men whom the free spaces of thought frightened and who felt safe only behind secure fences, theologians like John Cotton and his fellows, made a virtue of necessity and fell to declaiming on the excellence of those chains wherewith they were bound. How narrow and cold was their prison they seem never to have realized.'

To Parrington, theology was essentially political ideology: 'That Calvinism in its primary assumptions was a composite of oriental despotism and sixteenth-century monarchism, modified by the medieval conception of the city-state, is clear enough today to anyone who will take the trouble to translate dogma into political terms.' Anti-democratic, opposed to religious toleration, orthodox Puritanism was foreign to the progressive American tradition: 'Later critics of Puritanism

[1] *The Founding of New England* (Atlantic Monthly Press, 1921), pp. 78, 82–3, 85, 111, 370–2.

discover in the theocratic experiment of Massachusetts Bay a preposterous attempt to turn back the pages of history.' Parrington's true Americans were the rebels and heretics— Roger Williams, Anne Hutchinson, and their like: 'In banishing the Antinomians and Separatists and Quakers, the Massachusetts magistrates cast out the spirit of liberalism from the household of the Saints.' Finally, Parrington's judgment of Puritanism is summed up in his paragraph on the imprecatory sermons of Jonathan Edwards, the last and greatest of Puritans:

> 'Unfortunate as those sermons were in darkening the fame of an acute thinker . . . we cannot regret that Edwards devoted his logic to an assiduous stoking of the fires of hell. The theology of Calvin lay like a heavy weight upon the soul of New England, and there could be no surer way to bring it in to disrepute, than to thrust into naked relief the brutal grotesqueries of those dogmas. . . . Once the horrors that lay in the background of Calvinism were disclosed to common view, the system was doomed. . . . In this necessary work of freeing the spirit of New England, no other thinker played so large or so unconscious a part as Jonathan Edwards.'

The accounts of Adams and Parrington do not satisfy recent students of Puritanism. To judge the Puritans by the yardstick of nineteenth-century liberalism is old-fashioned and unhistorical. Worse, the historians' firm conviction that the Puritans were a repulsive crew made it difficult for them to read Puritan works with scholarly care and patience. Adams and Parrington found New England sermons—the principal literary crop of the region—as hard going as most of us find *Mein Kampf*. Samuel Eliot Morison's judgment is just: '*The Colonial Mind* . . . is a brilliant synthesis of history and literature, but the writer shows little evidence of having read carefully the works of the authors he writes about.'[1]

[1] Parrington, *The Colonial Mind* (Harcourt Brace, 1927), pp. 12, 13, 15, 22, 159–60; Morison, *Builders of the Bay Colony* (Oxford University Press, 1930), p. 347.

The writers of the 1920's who saw Puritanism as un-American revived interest in the subject. But the men who initiated the new study lacked the sympathetic open mindedness and the patience for painstaking scholarship which precedes full understanding and just judgment. They made the study of Puritan culture a battleground of ideas and touched off a most remarkable outburst of scholarship. Historians became interested, for the first time, in New England intellectual history and made the study of that history one of the great successes of modern American historiography.

Three years before Parrington published his *Colonial Mind*, the first important work in the new historiography of Puritanism had already appeared.

Kenneth B. Murdock's *Increase Mather* (1925) is a full-length study of Puritanism in the modern style of scholarship. Increase Mather, the second in the powerful ministerial dynasty that dominated the intellectual, religious, and political life of seventeenth-century Boston, a prominent figure in the witchcraft scandals, a Puritan of Puritans, was not a sympathetic figure in the America of the 1920's. Parrington referred to the book as 'a somewhat meticulous defense . . . an extraordinarily painstaking document, that has added to our knowledge of Increase Mather's life and work, but it was unhappily conceived in the dark of the moon, a season congenial to strange quirks of fancy'. Of Harvard studies of the Puritans, Parrington wrote: '[They] are excellent in their way, but a consciousness of dealing with Harvard worthies would seem to have laid the writers under certain inhibitions. Exposition too easily slides into apologetics.'[1]

Parrington's criticisms are just, but they miss the point. *Increase Mather* has all the faults of a Ph.D. thesis which tries to overturn custom-hardened stereotypes by proving too much, claiming too much, and giving the hero the benefit of all doubts. Nevertheless, *Increase Mather* is a work of disciplined scholarship—Murdock has read the sources. And his sympathy with Mather and Puritan culture, which is sometimes

[1] *Colonial Mind*, p. 88.

strained and does sometimes slip into apologetics, is nevertheless the very quality which made it possible for him to read the documents with imaginative understanding. This is the stance of modern historical writing about the Puritans. Historians disagree about the meaning of particular facts; they differ as to what the essence of Puritan culture was; they admire or dislike this or that Puritan leader and their differences of judgment are often personal differences of taste. But all agree that exact scholarship and a willing suspension of disbelief sufficient to give the historical imagination scope are both essential. Since 1925 Murdock has gone on adding to our knowledge and understanding of Puritan culture.

The reconstruction of the Puritan story began with a biography and the next important work was also biographical. In 1930 Samuel Eliot Morison published *The Builders of the Bay Colony*. The preface to that volume is the manifesto of that modern Puritan historiography which grew to maturity in the 1930's and which still flourishes:

'Most of the people described in this book would have led obscure lives but for a dynamic force called puritanism which drove them to start life anew in a wilderness. The common-wealth which they helped to create was not a large one in their time. . . . The total population was something between fourteen and sixteen thousand persons in 1640. . . . Search the modern world, where will you find another community of like extent and age, containing so many outstanding, pungent individuals as those described herein? . . . It is not easy to describe these people truthfully, yet with meaning to moderns. For the men of learning and women of gentle nurture who led a few thousand plain folk to plant a new England on ungrateful soil were moved by purposes utterly foreign to the present America. Their object was not to establish prosperity or prohibition, liberty or democracy, or indeed anything of currently recognized value. Their ideals were comprehended vaguely in the term puritanism, which nowadays has acquired various secondary and degenerate meanings. These ideals, real and imaginary, of early Massachusetts, were attacked by historians of Massachusetts long before 'debunking' became an accepted biographical mode; for it is always easier to condemn an alien way of life than to understand it. My attitude toward seventeenth-century puritanism has passed through scorn and boredom to a warm interest and respect. The ways of the puritans are not my ways, and their faith is not my faith; nevertheless they appear to me a courageous, humane, brave, and significant people.'

The Builders of the Bay Colony, Morison's *Puritan Pronaos* (1936), and his three fat volumes on the history of Harvard (the founding, 1935, the seventeenth century, 2 vols., 1936) are learned and attractively written accounts of real men and women. To replace the comic-book caricatures of the Puritans manufactured by Menckenesque journalists of the 1920's with believable people has been one of the major achievements of American historical scholarship in the twentieth century, and the honor is Morison's. From him we have learned to think of John Winthrop as a 'Puritan Squire' and a wise man of practical affairs, of John Hull, the goldsmith, as an artist and shrewd man of business, and of John Winthrop, Jr., as an industrial pioneer; from him we have learned that the private libraries and bookshops of seventeenth-century Boston were better, relatively, than those of any American city in later centuries, and that New England produced a remarkable number of Fellows of the Royal Society. Morison's Puritans are not only believable humans who loved good beer and gay clothing: they are admirable men and women who preserved in the midst of the wilderness a passion for learning and education unique in modern history.

What that learning was, what place it held in Puritan culture, we now know. Perry Miller's two volumes on *The New England Mind* (1939, 1953) are works unsurpassed in the whole corpus of American historical scholarship. They are not easy, and the second is more graceful and mature than the first; but together they are models of what learned intellectual history should be.

The first volume is an 'anatomy of the Puritan mind' in which Miller is 'concerned with defining and classifying the principal concepts of the Puritan mind in New England, of accounting for the origins, inter-relations, and significances of the ideas', on the assumption that 'Puritanism was one of the major expressions of the Western intellect, that it achieved an organized synthesis of concepts which are fundamental to our culture, and that therefore it calls for the most serious examination'. Miller has elucidated Non-Separating Congregationalism, the Federal Theology, and the Half-way Covenant; he has traced the origins of Puritan thought and showed how large a place reason held in the theology; he has given us a detailed picture of Puritan cosmology, anthropology, and sociology.

The second volume is the story of how that synthesis of concepts changed in the concrete setting of New England from 1620 to 1720. 'It is a case history of the accommodation to the American landscape of an important and highly articulate system of ideas.' Here we see in detail the original Puritan philosophy slowly metamorphosing into the philosophy of the Enlightenment—'somehow, in a century of American experience, the greatness of man's dependency had unaccountably become a euphemism for the greatness of man'. By accounting for that change, Miller's work is much more than an intensive study of a small group which happened, in the lottery of history, to become the founders of America; it is a splendid study of an important era in the intellectual history of Western man.

However, even twentieth-century Harvard historians are sometimes provincial. Morison's apologetics sometimes make the Puritans too human: 'One gets the impression of a healthy and hearty community, untroubled by the inhibitions and prohibitions that have made latter-day Puritanism so unpopular. . . . They were a free and happy people.'[1] After all, some Puritans, some of the time, were ascetics with a prurient

[1] *Founding of Harvard College* (Harvard University Press, 1935), pp. 155–6.

interest in obscenity and a pathological fear of witchcraft,[1] and no Puritan would have subscribed to the statement that any earthly city could be free and happy. And Morison sees J. T. Adams's strictures on the Puritans, not merely as exaggerations, which they are, but as treasonable attacks on the honor of the builders of the Bay Colony.

In addition, the outsider suspects that Plymouth, Rhode Island, and Connecticut have received less attention than they deserve from the scholars of the Massachusetts Bay Colony. In Cambridge and Boston, but not in the rest of America, the *Arbella* is a more notable ship than the *Mayflower*. Perry Miller too easily rejects the old theory that the aristocratic intellectuals of Massachusetts Bay derived part of their church government from the Plymouth Pilgrims—'a small and earnest band of simple souls', 'home-spun, hardworking farmers', 'a relatively insignificant community, completely overshadowed by Massachusetts Bay' (but a community which produced in Bradford's *History* the best work of early New England literature). The issue is important since the Puritan theory of church government had an influence on later American theories of democracy. To argue that if the leaders of the Bay Colony took their theories from Plymouth, 'How can we have much respect for the intellectual development of these people?' is unconvincing.[2]

In emphasizing the literature, learning, and ideas of the Puritans, the Harvard historians may also connect them too closely with Renaissance humanism. One gets the impression that the founders of New England were intellectuals, followers of Erasmus and Ramus, whose piety and religion were secondary concerns. But 'the essence of Puritanism', Alan Simpson reminds us, 'is an experience of conversion which

---

[1] See Murdock's review of *The Puritan Pronaos* in *New England Quarterly*, IX (1936), pp. 510–19; and Miller's remarks on Morison's defence of Cotton Mather, 'the most nauseous human being' of his period, *The New England Mind: From Colony to Province*, p. 204.

[2] *Orthodoxy in Massachusetts* (Harvard University Press, 1939), Foreward. A note of petulant arrogance on the same subject occurs in the Preface to the 1959 edition.

separates the Puritan from the mass of mankind and endows him with the privileges and the duties of the elect. The root of the matter is always a new birth, which brings with it a conviction of salvation and a dedication of warfare against sin.'[1]

All criticisms aside, historians of New England Puritanism have succeeded dramatically and admirably in rewriting the first chapter of New England history. But what have we learned about its relation to the rest of the story? What residues of Puritan experience have survived into our own time? After a generation of work, the question still cannot be answered precisely.

Kenneth Murdock has stated the problem with characteristic moderation:

'It is pretty generally admitted that somewhere in America's total cultural heritage and the complex of qualities which make up the "American character" there are traces of Puritanism. It is very difficult, however, to be sure just what these traces are, partly because the continuing influence in intellectual history of any past "state of mind" is always hard to assess, and partly because the special "state of mind" of the New England colonists has often been misunderstood. . . . The fertilizing tradition is a matter of spirit and idea; the fruitful heritage of the past comes from ways of thought and feeling, fundamental intellectual and emotional points of view, which have the power to stimulate new attempts to map the changing current of life. Such things are hard to categorize; their nature defies precise definition. . . . The evidence is rarely conclusive enough to support dogmatic assertions, but there are bases for reasonable conjectures. Even guesses have value, since they bear upon a strain in American intellectual history the existence of which few historians

[1] *Puritanism in Old and New England* (University of Chicago Press, 1955), p. 2. Simpson's book is an excellent critique of American scholarship by a student of English Puritanism.

would doubt even though its exact nature may be
impossible to define.'[1]

The discussion of the Puritan tradition in America has
centered around five or six major topics which are themselves
summaries of what the modern historian sees as the essence of
Puritanism.

1. *Morality and religion.* We have now a juster understanding of the original Puritan moral code and we no longer blame
the Puritans of the seventeenth century for the canting, genteel
piety, and the stuffy respectability which Mencken attacked
in the twentieth century. But we do recognize that the moral
and religious tone of much British and American criticism—
economic, political, artistic, etc.—is partly Puritan in origin.

Fundamentalism, revivalism, and sectarian splintering in
American religious history are all connected in complex ways
with what happened in early New England. But again, our
perspective has changed. Puritan Fundamentalism was intellectually respectable; it dovetailed with the best learning and
science of the day. Seventeenth-century Puritans were not
ignorant, superstitious bigots who had to reject biology,
physics, geology, and historical criticism, in order to maintain
their dogma. In fact, the religion of the Puritans was a highly
intellectual religion and it is used by contemporary critics as
a stick to beat the sentimental, tender-minded, anti-intellec-
tual and genteel religiosity of the twentieth century. The
recent neo-Calvinist movement in theology has tried to revive
some parts of the Puritan's religious philosophy.

2. *Education and literature.* The Puritan respect for learning
has come to be the quality which modern historians find most
admirable. Certainly no other colonists in the history of the
world have set up a university six years after settling in the
wilderness. The foundation of Harvard College in 1636 is a
unique and awe-inspiring achievement. 'After God had
carried us safe to *New England,* and we had builded our houses,
provided necessaries for our livelihood, reared convenient

[1] *Literature and Theology in Colonial New England* (Harvard University
Press, 1949), pp. 173–5, 191–2.

places for God's worship, and settled the civil government: One of the things we looked for, and looked after was to advance *Learning* and perpetuate it to Posterity; dreading to leave an illiterate Ministry to the Churches, when our present Ministers shall lie in the dust.' These words from *New England's First Fruits* (1643), reprinted more than once by recent historians, have become a part of the American heritage. The history of Puritan colleges, elementary and grammar schools, and of Puritan libraries has been zealously studied, and no one doubts that the tradition of learning and education is continuous from the seventeenth century to the present.

In literature, perhaps, the line of descent from the Puritans is clearest. The 'plain style', biography and autobiography which reveal the inner life of the subject, historical writing, and a continuous tradition of symbol and allegory running through Hawthorne, Melville, Emerson, Thoreau, and James have all been traced back to their seventeenth-century origins.[1]

3. *The Puritan ethic in business life.* The major studies of the relation between the Puritan ethic and the spirit of capitalism were made by Weber and Tawney and other European scholars. But American historians have asked the same questions of the American record and there is general agreement that some connection can be traced between Puritanism and a later American business ethic—business as a 'calling', the moral significance of profits and thrift, the moral dignity of work, a distrust of aristocratic leisure and dilettantism, the suspicion that the poor are ungodly and hence shiftless, the conviction that Andrew Carnegie and John D. Rockefeller are numbered with the Elect because God has prospered them —all these are somehow and complexly related to the attitudes of seventeenth-century New England.

4. *Democracy and limited government.* English historiography about the Civil Wars and Commonwealth, perhaps because the political thought and activities of English Puritans is so

[1] See Murdock, *Literature and Theology*, and F. O. Matthiessen, *American Renaissance* (1941).

rich and varied and well documented, is precise and definite on the subject of Puritanism and politics. The American historian works with relatively meager materials. Certainly the Puritan strands in American political thought and practice are exceedingly difficult to unravel. Here, perhaps, the simple-minded liberal interpretations of Puritanism have been at their weakest: nothing is accomplished by a rapid scanning of the sources and a separating of the apparently 'democratic' statements of the seventeenth century from the apparently 'theocratic'. Out of context, John Winthrop's speech on liberty (3 July 1645) sounds pretty much like an example of what Isaiah Berlin has called the totalitarian concept of 'positive' liberty; in its setting, as Edmund S. Morgan's recent biography of Winthrop makes clear, it appears much less sinister.

The founders of New England were not democrats; but there was an irrepressible democratic dynamic in Puritan theology which could not be stifled. The congregational idea of voluntary churches bound together by covenant eventually, in the American environment, passed over into politics: the Mayflower Compact—the first formal social contract in modern history, the Fundamental Orders of Connecticut, the writings of John Wise, and much else, are part of the democratic tradition in America.

As seventeenth-century English opponents of Stuart absolutism, the Puritans naturally supported constitutionalism and limited government, although John Winthrop was tempted in the early days of the Bay Colony to claim unbounded authority for himself and his fellow magistrates. Here, too, the 'Puritan conscience' plays its ambiguous role. The Protestant doctrine that the conscience of the individual is the ultimate judge of right becomes, in politics, the subversive doctrine that a man must refuse to obey a law, however legitimately promulgated, which violates his own sense of right. When Ralph Waldo Emerson said of the Fugitive Slave Law, enacted by Congress, signed by the President, and declared constitutional by the Supreme Court, 'I will not obey it, by God' his Puritan conscience was at work. Whatever leanings the magistrates of the Bay Colony had toward absolutism were bound to be defeated by this built-in principle of nonconformity:

> 'Boston never wanted a good principle of rebellion in it, from the planting until now; there is always a minority unconvinced . . . some protester against the cruelty of magistrates to the Quakers . . . some defender of the slave against the politician and the merchant; some champion of the first principles of humanity against the rich and luxurious . . . some noble protestant, who will not stoop to infamy when all are gone mad, but will stand for liberty and justice, if alone, until all come back to him.'[1]

5. *Frustrated Utopianism.* The most-quoted phrases of Puritan literature are those of John Winthrop, written aboard the *Arbella* in 1630: 'Men shall say of succeeding plantations: the lord make it like that of New England: for we shall be as a City set upon a Hill, the eyes of all people are upon us.' The sense that they are a peculiar people, designed by Providence to live in a more perfect community than any known in the Old World, the sense that it is America's mission to set an example to other nations, is part of America's Puritan inheritance. It echoes through the *Battle Hymn of the Republic*, the Gettysburg Address, and the crusade to make the world safe for democracy. At its worst it becomes the vulgar, naive, chauvinistic idealism of the innocent abroad and the *Quiet American*.

Finally, the Puritans who sought to build a holy community ended in frustration and disillusionment. Their failures were the more bitter since their hopes had been so high. One of the recurring themes in American culture is the bitterness of failure, the frustration of never achieving the ideal. Americans see themselves as the standard-bearers of freedom and democracy, and Little Rock is the town in the headlines of every newspaper in the world. America has rejected the

[1] R. W. Emerson, quoted by Murdock, *Literature and Theology*, p. 200.

militarism and imperialism of the Old World, but Hiroshima
and 'Yanks Go Home' are familiar phrases.

But an exact description of the Puritan contribution to
American culture is not easy. Professor Murdock has outlined
some of the difficulties in the passage already quoted, and
there are others. How can we distinguish that which has been
a continuous element from the seventeenth century to the
present from that which was forgotten and then revivied by a
later generation as an analogy, a paradigm, or a metaphor?
When Perry Miller says his 'mission of expounding' American
history came to him as a 'sudden epiphany' on the banks of
the Congo, he is translating Gibbon's 'musing amid the ruins
of the Capitol' into Puritanese: this is obviously a conscious
metaphorical revival, not an unbroken tradition of language
and idea. But in the large picture of American culture as a
whole the distinctions are not so easy. We will not be able to
identify with precision the elements of the Puritan tradition
in modern America until we have patiently and carefully
studied the whole record. Until we do know the story in detail,
talk about the Puritan tradition in America will be mostly
speculation.

To thumb hastily through the record looking for the good
and bad which Puritanism has contributed to the modern
American character is a Puritan way of writing history and it
ends in propaganda. The result is either unhistorical apologetics or the vilification which disfigures, for example, the
work of J. T. Adams and V. L. Parrington. The result was
implicit when they began by asking what was truly American
in the Puritan tradition instead of asking what Puritanism
was, in its own terms.

Perry Miller asks the question rhetorically in his prefaces,
but writes like a historian in his texts, and gives no bald, dogmatic answers. He still speaks of 'the uniqueness of the
American experience' (how can it be more unique than any
other historical experience?), but he actually tells the 'massive
story of the movement of European culture into the vacant
wilderness of America', and gives us profound case-studies of
the relation of ideas to communal experience. *The second*

volume of *The New England Mind*—the best single book on American Puritanism and a classic of modern historiography— attempts no formal answers to questions about the uniqueness of the American tradition and experience; yet its rich narrative, immensely learned and powerfully imagined, tells us what the first century of New England experience was, and answers the questions by implication.[1]

Compared with the historiography of English Puritanism, the historiography of American Puritanism appears to be almost exclusively the history of ideas. English historians, following R. H. Tawney, have produced rich studies of the social and economic aspects of Puritanism and since the 1930's, influenced by Marxist and English socialist ideas, have studied intensively the class structure and the political character of Puritanism. But in America the Harvard historians reacted strongly against the economic and social interpretations of the 1920's, especially Parrington and J. T. Adams, and concentrated on the history of ideas. In doing so they sometimes left out of account the circumstances, the concrete times and places and social networks in which the thinkers lived. But this is the American part of the story— the wilderness which produced the American modifications in the transplanted European intellectual system. The Puritan contribution to American culture can be described only by looking at all aspects of Puritanism and all aspects of American culture. Puritan historiography in America has been too exclusively intellectual.

But now the force of the reaction appears to be spent. Miller's second volume is a history of Puritan ideas in action in seventeenth-century New England. A new generation of historians of New England, for whom the debates of the 1920's are historiographical rather than personal, are widening the

---

[1] In the same way, Miller's careful reconstruction of the actual ideas and events in 'Thomas Hooker and the Democracy of Connecticut', *Errand into the Wilderness* (1956), tells us more about Puritanism and democracy than the usual exegeses of Puritan texts lifted out of their historical setting and glossed with the insights of modern social sciences.

angle of vision to include all aspects of colonial life: among the most notable recent books are Edmund S. Morgan's *Puritan Dilemma: The Story of John Winthrop* (1958), Bernard Bailyn, *The New England Merchants in the Seventeenth Century* (1955), and Anthony N. B. Garvan, *Architecture and Town Planning in Colonial Connecticut* (1951).

The work of the historian is never, of course, done. Every new generation of historians of Puritanism will discover hiatuses, blind spots, limited perspectives, and errors in the work of its predecessors; but contemporary scholarship devoted to seventeenth-century New England has achieved the level of learning and objectivity, grace and sophistication, of the best historical writing of the twentieth century.

3

THE REVOLUTIONARY ERA

BY WESLEY FRANK CRAVEN

IN ORDER to understand the controversies which today enliven the field of Revolutionary studies in the United States, it is necessary to begin, surprisingly, with some attention to a nineteenth-century historian—George Bancroft, first among his countrymen to attempt a comprehensive reading of the American experience on a grand scale. He published the initial volume of his *History of the United States* in 1834, when Andrew Jackson was serving his second term in the White House. It dealt with the earliest English settlers in America, and struck the great theme of his entire work by identifying their migration to America with a quest for freedom. Partly because of repeated commitments to the public service, Bancroft did not publish his final volumes, on *The Formation of the Constitution*, until 1882, almost half a century after the first volume had appeared and shortly before the centennial of the constitutional convention that was celebrated in Philadelphia in 1887. Bancroft's history was the moving story of a free people who in 1776 had refused to surrender their freedom, even at the cost of sacrificing a long-cherished connection with England, and who had discovered the true basis of their constitutional union in the struggle to preserve that freedom.

Given the history of nineteenth-century America, marked as it was by bitter political strife and even by bloody conflict, one can wonder at the popularity so obviously enjoyed by such a pretty picture of the nation's origins. But the explanation is not difficult to find. At a time of conflict and division, Bancroft consistently reminded the American people of the many beliefs they held in common. In other words, his history met a need, and one that was especially acute in the period immediately following the Civil War. The work had the virtue, moreover, of a heavy concentration on the Revolution. Indeed, his discussion of the colonial period can be described as a relatively brief introduction to the history of the Revolution, and it is perhaps not too much to say that his concluding two volumes on the Constitution formed something of an epilogue to his stirring account of the struggle for American independence. In the history of that struggle all Americans, however else divided, shared a great pride.

The term epilogue may be misleading, for Bancroft's handling of the problem of the Constitution is of first-rate importance. It had ever been a controversial document, and never more so than during the very years in which Bancroft wrote the main part of his history. He was fortunate in that the Revolution kept him busy until after the Civil War. By then linking the Constitution with the Revolution, making it even the culminating phase of the Revolution itself, he at once expressed the new attitude toward the Constitution that was developing after the war and significantly contributed to the veneration with which the document was generally viewed by the opening years of the twentieth century. Faithful to the end, in his lifelong mission as an apostle of nationalism, Bancroft lent the sanction of the Revolution to a union that was finally given permanence only by the force of arms.

However acceptable and useful to the American people may have been Bancroft's history at the time of its completion, it could not serve the country long. Its high moral tone, and occasional florid passages, were better suited to the taste of the nineteenth century than to the mood of twentieth-century America. Its nationalism was easily interpreted, with not a little justification, as but another expression of the parochial pride which often limited the value of a growing body of literature devoted to state and local history. More important, it became increasingly difficult to fit Bancroft's grand theme of a nation united by the common devotion of its people to the principles of a free society into any acceptable interpretation of the country's later history. Bancroft's *History of the United States*, it must be remembered, had reached its climactic end with the establishment of the federal union. Unless one was prepared to accept an interpretation of the national period of American history that was posited upon an assumption of serious decline, both in the ability of the American people to agree on their common objectives and in the quality of their leadership, there was need for a different view of the nation's origins. By the 1920's, though Bancroft's history was still to be found on the shelf in any gentleman's library, and though patriotic societies still echoed his views, few Americans bothered to read him and those who did were often offended by what they read.

By the 1920's it was also becoming evident that the effort to rewrite Bancroft's history was marked by two contrasting, even conflicting, tendencies. On the one hand the so-called imperial school, under the leadership of George Louis Beer and Charles M. Andrews, had proposed nothing less than to take the discussion of national origins completely out of the context of national history. On the other, a growing response to the views expressed by Charles A. Beard in *An Economic Interpretation of the Constitution*, published in 1913, promised to pull the discussion of the Revolutionary era into the full context of a national history that was indisputably marked by conflict and controversy.

First attention belongs to Beer and Andrews, because they at first held the lead among the revisionists. As they saw it, the need was to begin anew with the original settlement of the colonies, where Bancroft had begun, and to follow the story down to the Revolution in the broad context of Britain's overseas expansion. Not even the Revolution, it was suggested, could be safely interpreted as a problem of national history. In a series of important essays on *The Colonial Background of the American Revolution*, Andrews in 1924 declared: 'The years from 1607 to 1783 were colonial before they were American or national, and our Revolution is a colonial and not an American problem.' The same point had been made by Beer, somewhat less explicitly but none the less emphatically, in an extraordinarily significant study of *British Colonial Policy, 1754–1765*, published in 1907. There he disclaimed any purpose of commenting directly on the American Revolution. Instead, he described himself as a student of the British Empire, and to that attitude he consistently held in his later works: *The Origins of the British Colonial System, 1578–1660*, published in 1908, and *The Old Colonial System* which appeared in 1912 as his final contribution to the subject.

Andrews assumed no such pose as did Beer. Indeed, his essays of 1924 strongly suggest that he viewed the full effort of an unusually fruitful career as a commentary on the American Revolution. He had won a reputation well before the First World War for contributions to the early history of the colonies that were distinguished by the author's breadth of view and by his exploitation of fresh materials drawn from British archives. He had begun, also, to train at Yale the large number of Ph.D.s who over the years would greatly expand the literature and the influence of the imperial school.[1] Andrews himself was destined to fulfil a scholarly ideal by having the time and the energy to write his own *magnum opus* after retirement from teaching, in four impressive volumes entitled *The Colonial Period of American History* (1934–8). Of these, three volumes were devoted to the period of original settlement. The fourth provided an unusually well-informed study of *England's Commercial and Colonial Policy* before 1765.

Speaking broadly, and without regard for the extraordinary success achieved by the imperial school in rewriting the story of seventeenth-century English settlement in North America, one can suggest that the chief contribution of Beer and Andrews was to bring discussion of the Revolution into a new and broader framework. More particularly, they made it difficult to attribute the Revolution to the restrictive influences of mercantilist policy, in part by the clarification they gave to the character of the old colonial system, and in part

[1] The most productive of Andrews's students has been Lawrence H. Gipson, whose monumental *The British Empire before the Revolution* (1936–   ) has now reached a total of nine volumes.

by the fresh attention they directed to new problems of empire confronted by Britain as a result of the changing character of the empire itself and the great victory won over France. Both men, for Beer fortunately ignored his disclaimers of an intent to comment on the Revolution, rejected any fundamentally economic interpretation of that development and strongly favored the view that the quarrel with England had been basically constitutional in character. The old empire, Beer affirmed in 1907, had 'shattered itself' on a problem of defense, because 'of the inherent difficulty of creating an efficient and equitable system of defence in a decentralized empire'. For Andrews, the history of the empire, from the earliest days of settlement down to 1783, was to be read in the terms fixed by two fundamental and conflicting tendencies: on the part of the colonies toward 'intensive self-government', and on the part of the mother country 'toward empire'. When the final clash occurred, moreover, the contest opposed one to the other two radically different societies.

This last point was implicit in much that Andrews wrote, but it was chiefly developed in his essays of 1924 and in his presidential address of 1925 to the American Historical Association on the subject of 'The American Revolution'. Here he talked of the long, 'silent and peaceful revolution' which had preceded the final break with Britain, and in which the colonists, as they adjusted to the demands and opportunities of a new soil, were casting aside the outworn notions of the old world to lay the foundations for a distinctively new social order. Those who may have assumed, as many Americans have, that the imperial school was consistently guided by a pro-British bias will want to note Andrews's summation. 'On one side was the immutable, stereotyped system of the mother country, based on precedent and tradition and designed to keep things comfortably as they were,' he insisted, and 'on the other, a vital dynamic organism, containing the seed of a great nation, its forces untried, still to be proved.' However much George Louis Beer may have deplored the disunion of the 'Anglo-Saxon race' resulting from the Revolution, to Andrews it was unthinkable that such a connection as he had described could have long endured.

Andrews delivered his presidential address very close to the end of the period in which the imperial school had its greatest influence on Revolutionary studies in the United States. The findings of Beer and Andrews, to which the latter had much yet to add, would continue to discipline in an important degree every discussion of the coming of the Revolution. Their interpretation of its origins, moreover, continued to be the most acceptable one for many historians, and especially those whose chief interest was the constitutional history of the United States. But there can be no doubt that a growing preference was shown after 1925 for an economic interpretation of the Revolution, one that drew its chief inspiration from Charles A. Beard. Andrews himself virtually conceded his defeat in a lengthy, and somewhat ill-humored, footnote on the economic interpretation of history he appended to the fourth and final volume of his great work in 1938.

Many years earlier, George Louis Beer had drawn an interesting distinction between the positive and negative conclusions he presented at the end of his first major study of colonial policy. He claimed there to have established positively only that the old empire had 'shattered itself' on a problem of defense. His other conclusions regarding the Revolution were described as negative, in the sense that they had not been demonstrated positively by the evidence of his own investigations. Perhaps the distinction will be helpful on the question of Andrews's influence. However well argued may have been his essays on the Revolution, and however substantial his contribution to an understanding of its background, it was, after all, the background of the Revolution, rather than the Revolution itself, which his studies, and those of his students, principally illuminated. The point may be carried a step further by noting that most of Andrews's work dealt with the period of the seventeenth century, and there very largely with the initial stages of English settlement in the several provinces. Only when dealing with imperial policy and administration, Beer's special field of interest, did he get well forward into the eighteenth century. Thus the whole era of the Revolution, and to a considerable extent the colonial period itself, remained an area of investigation into which others could move more or less freely in their search for an interpretation effectively linking the period to the later history of the country.

Although Charles A. Beard's *An Economic Interpretation of the Constitution* shocked some Americans at the time of its publication, and though it has been subjected to severe criticism from that time to the present, it was destined to give him an influence on the interpretation of American history comparable only to that held formerly by George Bancroft, and in Beard's own day, by Frederick Jackson Turner.

Beard later denied the charge that his famous book was a Progressive political tract. The charge, nevertheless, has not a little justification. The work was written against the background of the agrarian protests of the late nineteenth century and at the height of the Progressive reform movement of the early twentieth, in which Beard had an active interest. At a time when popular veneration for the Constitution strengthened the hands of conservatively minded legislators and judges, his insistence upon a more realistic view of the history of the document undoubtedly aided the cause of reform. But it must also be said that his book faithfully reflected the current trends in American historical scholarship. He shared, and especially significantly, in the common effort to rewrite Bancroft's history. His tendency toward economic determinism brought him into sharp conflict with the opinions held by many of his contemporaries, but to establish the growing popularity of a deterministic view of history at the time it is necessary only to recall the great vogue enjoyed by Frederick Jackson Turner's frontier thesis. Even Beer and Andrews talked much of the underlying forces which shaped the course of history. They refused only to narrow the focus to a single dominant factor.

Although Beard was careful to state his proposition as an hypothesis requiring fuller proof than he had been able to provide, he presented the arguments for its acceptance with great vigour. By drawing attention to the property held by members of the constitutional convention of 1787, and more especially to their holdings in the more fluid forms of capital investment, those chiefly identified with commerce, finance, and other speculative ventures, he found support for an argument that members of the convention in significant numbers had been bound together by a community of economic interest transcending state or other local considerations, and so encouraging them to seek a stronger central government. Economic nationalism, in other words, led toward political nationalism, and the founding fathers became something more, or less, than a disinterested band of far-sighted patriots. For this view, he found further support in the contest over ratification, by popularly elected conventions meeting in each of the states. In general, Beard held that the eastern seaboard in its advocacy of the new constitution had been opposed by the frontier, the great planter and the great merchant by the small farmer, the creditor by the debtor, and so on. He concluded that a majority of the people probably had been opposed to the new constitution. The ability of the nationalists to prevail was explained by the special advantages they enjoyed—of superior educational attainment, greater political experience, and a more effective organization.

Such a view naturally implied that the work of the constitutional convention could be interpreted as counterrevolutionary in character. In fact, Beard made the point somewhat explicit by suggesting that what occurred at Philadelphia in 1787, when the delegates had no mandate to draft a new constitution but only to revise an older one, would be described quite simply in other countries as a *coup d'état*. The point became more explicit when he published, with his wife, in 1927 the two first volumes of *The Rise of American Civilization*, a powerful reading of the full history of the American people. (A supplementary third volume was added in 1939 and a fourth in 1942.) In writing of the colonial period, Beard emphasized especially the growing wealth, power, and maturity of the colonies as they approached the break with Britain. He interpreted the crisis leading to the final break as a clash of economic interest between metropolis and colony, George Louis Beer to the contrary notwithstanding. He pictured the Revolution as a victory for the more popular forces in American society, they being primarily agrarian in character and often in conflict with representatives of a nascent capitalism as well as with an older political leadership. The constitution, in turn, marked the ultimate triumph, within the limits of the Revolutionary era, for a conservative resistance to the populist tendencies of the Revolution. In short, for Bancroft's grand theme of unity Beard had substituted a theme of economic and social conflict.

Beard's interpretation suffered no loss of appeal from the publication, also in 1927, of the first volume of Vernon Parrington's *Main Currents of American Thought*. The work significantly marks a growing interest among American scholars in intellectual history, but Parrington agreed with Beard that economic interest governed the political ideas employed by men. Parrington emphasized the conflict at the time of the Revolution between the high hopes of agrarian America and the ambitions of a rising mercantile class, freed now not only from the restraints of London but also in a significant degree from the restraining influence of an older colonial élite. Every circumstance in the life of the colonies before 1765 had favored decentralization of political authority, and the Revolution had been fought in defense of the rights identified with that trend. But the Revolution also had given birth to a new central authority established in the interest of finance capitalism, and so it had shaped the great political issues to be confronted by every generation of Americans living thereafter.

Other scholars had helped prepare the way for acceptance of Beard's interpretation, though not necessarily because they were in full agreement with his view of history. His dependence upon Turner's inclination to identify democracy with an agrarian frontier is obvious. Carl Becker, Turner's most brilliant student, had used a phrase in his Ph.D. dissertation of 1909,[1] which came in time to be so frequently repeated as

[1] *A History of Political Parties in the Province of New York.*

to suggest that it is the single most influential statement ever made by this very talented historian. The Revolution, he remarked, was more than a struggle for home rule, for there was also the question of who would rule at home. Arthur M. Schlesinger's study of *The Colonial Merchants and the American Revolution,* in 1918, not only gave strong impetus to a renewed interest in social history but encouraged a belief that the division on the eastern seaboard at the time of the break with England bore an important relationship to considerations of wealth and social status. J. Franklin Jameson's *The American Revolution Considered as a Social Movement,* published in 1926, persuasively argued, with the special authority belonging to a dean among American historians, that the Revolution had brought significant changes in American society. Though as small in size as it was broad in compass, Jameson's book had an influence over the next several years almost comparable to that enjoyed by the works of Beard and Parrington.

In evidence of the growing popularity of Beard's interpretation many citations could be given, but the most general reference to any successful college textbook on the history of the United States that was in use at the beginning of World War II will be enough. In other words, by that time Beard's views had very largely shaped the standard interpretation of the Revolutionary era.[1] If additional proof be needed, it is surely found in the vigorous attack on Beard that has followed the Second World War. No other American historian, except George Bancroft, has had his views brought under a comparably severe assault following his own death. The parallel can be carried even further, for once again the revisionist effort is marked by two significantly contrasting trends.

First mention belongs to a group of somewhat senior scholars, men who grew to their maturity in the very period

[1] In Curtis Nettels's *The Roots of American Civilization,* an influential text on the colonial period published in 1938, one found a promise even that the theme of economic and social conflict might soon be the standard interpretation of a period long the conceded special province of the imperial school.

of Beard's greatest influence, and who may be conveniently and not misleadingly described as the biographers. No one can look over the bibliography of recent works on the Revolutionary era without recognizing that the weight of it, whether viewed quantitatively or qualitatively, falls in the general category of biography. It is necessary only to list Douglas Freeman's *Washington* (1948–57), Irving Brant's *Madison* (1941–61), Dumas Malone's *Jefferson* (1948–), and Broadus Mitchell's *Hamilton* (1957–), all multi-volume biographies and the latter two still to be completed. But the list could be impressively lengthened by attention to less ambitious studies, and the point is heavily underscored by the extraordinarily ambitious projects for the comprehensive publication of the papers of Jefferson, Adams, Franklin, Madison, and Hamilton, among others, that have been launched in recent years. Washington's papers had been made available to scholars in more than thirty volumes at the time of the celebration of the centennial of his birth in 1932. The leadership in this more recent development belongs to Julian P. Boyd of Princeton University, who in 1950 published the first volume of *The Papers of Thomas Jefferson*, now complete for the Revolutionary era in fifteen volumes. Thirty-seven more have been promised. Other projects have been planned on a comparable scale.

This turn to biography has in itself very great significance. It is a form of historical study long favored among Americans, and especially for this period of their history. But the biographical approach had been discouraged by the leading scholars of Beard's generation, and the most famous of the Revolutionary biographies published after World War I had been Rupert Hughes's 'debunking' biography of George Washington (1926–30). Carl Van Doren's appreciative study of *Benjamin Franklin*, 1938, will serve well enough to mark the turn. Irving Brant's monumental biography of James Madison, father of the Constitution, can be used to suggest the new direction that has been given by the biographers to interpretation of the Revolutionary era. Mr Brant argues that Madison's nationalism was born of the Revolution, and more

particularly of his strong devotion to the enlightened principles introduced into American life by the Revolution. He
has no great quarrel with Beard's *An Economic Interpretation of
the Constitution*, which depended for a significant part of its
documentation upon Madison's own writings, but Brant also
insists that no 'greater error can be made than to say that the
Constitution was written either in a spirit of blind self-interest
or of hostility to democracy'. Such is the depth to which the
biographers have carried their investigations, and such the
variation from one career to another, that no general summation can be safely attempted. Even so, one observation seems
to be very much in order. Beard's antithesis between the
Revolution and the Constitution has been very largely dismissed, and this has been done without depriving the country
of a long-cherished belief that it possesses a great revolutionary
tradition.

One finds all the more interest, therefore, in the very
recent development of another and more aggressive revisionist movement. It is led by younger men, scholars who have
achieved maturity during the years which have followed the
Second World War, and who have been conveniently desig-
nated as the conservative or neo-conservative school. The
frequently repeated charge by some of their critics that they
represent nothing better than a 'back-to-Bancroft' movement
does less than justice to the sophistication with which their
case is argued, but the charge nevertheless has some foundation. For Beard's theme of economic and social conflict the
conservatives, or at the least most of them, would substitute
the idea that a general consensus, in some degree or other
uniting all Americans, actually exerted the controlling influence on the development of events. The concept is by no
means limited in its application to the Revolutionary era, but
for obvious reasons the impact on studies in that period has
been especially sharp.

No better evidence of this could be asked than is found in
the unusual vehemence with which *An Economic Interpretation
of the Constitution* has been attacked in recent years. Since
1956 no less than three analytical critiques of the book have

been published between hardback covers.[1] The most constructive of these, Forrest McDonald's *We the People* (1958), acquires more than momentary significance through its reexamination of the evidence pertaining to the economic interests which could have affected the decision for or against a stronger central government. The study calls into question especially Beard's central contention: the overriding importance of economic interests persumably transcending local and other such special considerations. The latest of the three critiques, found in Lee Benson's essays on *Turner and Beard* (1960), combines a critique of the master with a critique of the master's critics. One can hope that this points toward an early end to the whole discussion of Beard's methodology. That hope, let it be also said, finds some reinforcement in Mr Benson's sensible suggestion that too much of the discussion has turned on an assumption that there is some one-to-one relationship between economic interest and political opinion. Restated in broad social terms, as Benson would have it done, an economic interpretation undoubtedly has much to contribute to an understanding of this chapter in history, as of others.

This sharp focus on Beard's most famous work can be misleading, because the critical problem for the conservatives is posed by the Revolution, not the Constitution. Although there are differences of approach and emphasis, the heart of the conservative argument can be stated quite simply. The colonists, it is maintained, enjoyed before the break with England so many of the advantages they might otherwise have sought through their Revolution that it had little compulsion to undertake extensive and fundamental change. Thus, Edmund S. Morgan, in his brief summary of *The Birth of the Republic* (1956), argues that the Americans, from 1765 to 1787, were consistently guided by principles adequately and appropriately expressing the needs of a self-governing community in which property already was widely distributed. Louis Hartz, in his very suggestive discussion of *The Liberal*

[1] The earliest was Robert E. Brown's *Charles Beard and the Constitution* (1956).

Tradition in America (1955), depends upon a contrast with contemporary Europe. Almost in the act of migration, it is contended, the colonists had escaped the 'feudalism' of the old world, and they had built in America before the Revolution a distinctively new and modern type of society. The American Revolution thus had no need to spend itself in the destruction of an *ancien régime*.

The implications of the new interpretation are far reaching, but it is necessary here to state only some of the more obvious. The Revolution, if it can be called a revolution at all, takes on a very conservative coloring, but what it conserves is liberal. The most acceptable explanation for the rebellion of the colonists becomes a refusal, as Bancroft argued, to surrender the freedom they already enjoyed. Such changes as accompanied the Revolution can be viewed as little more than an accentuation of deep-rooted trends in American life, or developments incidental to the rejection of British authority. With the Revolution thus discounted, there remains little if any cause for talk of a counter-revolution. The emphasis properly falls, rather, on the underlying continuity of the American experience.

The principal difficulty is that the whole structure presently rests on a very uncertain foundation. There is help enough to be had from the works of the imperial school for the conservatives' rejection of an economic interpretation of the coming of the Revolution. Moreover, no one doubts the existence of significant contrasts between colonial society and the standard set by Europe, even by England. Despite an obvious inclination to follow the conventional customs of the homeland, the colonists had managed to reproduce here no more than a pale reflection of the original. But the 'silent and peaceful revolution', to quote Andrews again, which presumably preceded *the* Revolution, lacks as yet anything approaching full documentation. Clinton Rossiter's *Seedtime of the Republic* (1953) or Daniel Boorstin's *The Colonial Experience* (1958), however suggestive, can provide no substitute for the required monographic study. We know all too little even of the history of the legislative assemblies during the great period of their development, from 1689 to 1765. Morgan's *The Stamp Act Crisis* (1953) establishes a strong presumption as to what that history may have been, but the history itself is still to be written.

For the years after the Stamp Act the record is much clearer, and very helpful to the conservative point of view. It now seems to be evident enough that no general proposition identifying the Revolution primarily with a frontier type of agrarianism can stand the test of examination. Nor does there appear to be reason for believing that considerations of economic and social status generally governed the sharp divisions brought to the American people by the Revolution. Leadership at the close of the era belonged substantially to the same segment of the society as it did at the beginning. If the test of a revolution be the extent to which social conflict shapes its course, or the degree of change within the community in its political leadership, surely the American Revolution is not a very impressive revolution.

Was it then only a War for Independence, necessarily bringing a significant reorganization of the community's life but nothing justifiably viewed as revolutionary? The answer depends very much on the attitude one takes toward the influence that was exerted in the course of this reorganization by the principles, the doctrine, from which the Revolution drew its justification. And this poses a difficult issue. Not only is there the old question of the influence ideas exert in the practical affairs of man, but the American Revolution is easily interpreted as a bundle of hard-headed compromises, among which a compromise with the principles it proclaimed, as in the case of slavery, is the most evident of all. In recent literature several choices are offered the reader. He can follow Boorstin in his belief that talk of the eighteenth-century Enlightenment in connection with the American Revolution is fundamentally misleading, because the American has ever been a pragmatist inclined to avoid visionary schemes. One can take Morgan's view that the Revolutionary leaders were definitely men of principle, but that they had a firm grasp on the principles which guided them through the Revolution well before it came. One can turn to Brant's *Madison* or Malone's *Jefferson* for consideration again of the evidence that American life gained some new sense of the direction its development should follow from the Revolution, and more particularly from the enlightened principles it planted in the very foundations of a new nation.

The difficulty in resolving the broad issue of the Revolution will help to explain a growing interest in the political practices of the American people before and after the Revolution. Following many years of neglect, the subject of the voting franchise suddenly has become very much alive. Investigations so far made indicate that a remarkably high percentage, by contemporary standards, of the adult free males in the colonies were qualified to vote, and frequently did so. Chilton Williamson's study of *American Suffrage . . . 1760–1860* (1960) estimates that the percentage of those qualifying under the freehold requirement may have ranged between 50 and 75 per cent. That the colonists had made substantial progress toward democracy has been one of the chief arguments for the conservative view of the Revolution.[1] But Professor Williamson also credits the Revolution with the most significant reform of suffrage requirements in the entire history of the country. For it was then, he tells us, that the American people, speaking generally and without regard for notable exceptions, abandoned the traditional English freehold standard for more easily met property qualifications, thereby leaving the opponents of a fully democratic suffrage no opportunity except to fight a delaying action. The democratic franchise, long identified with the age of Jackson, thus becomes Jeffersonian—the gift, that is, of the Revolution.

Important as is the test provided by the franchise, there may be a still more significant test. For whom did the democratic electorate cast its vote? Charles S. Sydnor's judicious *Gentlemen Freeholders; Political Practices in Washington's Virginia* (1952) leaves no room for doubt that, in the largest and most important of the colonies, the vote was consistently cast for

[1] As in Robert E. Brown's *Middle-Class Democracy in Massachusetts and the Revolution* (1955).

members of the ruling élite. There is little reason for believing that the social conventions governing the choice for office in other colonies were significantly different. Even in New England, where democratic procedures long had been a common practice at all levels of government, the upper classes ruled. It is also evident that the social conventions governing the employment of the colonial franchise survived the Revolution without serious impairment. Did the Revolution, then, make no difference except to enlarge the number of people who were entitled to choose among their betters?

One difference, and one of very great significance, is suggested by Robert J. Taylor's study of *Western Massachusetts in the Revolution* (1954). The inhabitants of the western counties formerly had lagged lamentably behind the eastern part of the province in their readiness to defend American rights, but with the coming of the Revolution they bought the whole doctrine of Thomas Jefferson's Declaration of Independence. They became henceforth, as in the procedures they demanded for the adoption of the state's constitution, somewhat literal minded in their interpretation of philosophical propositions other men had been content to accept as the basis only for a working political compromise. Men who stood for public office might still depend upon an ancient tradition determining those who were qualified to hold public office. But they had to answer to an electorate newly insistent that the ultimate power lay with the people—a people who might discriminate among candidates according to the evidence they gave of accepting a new doctrine of popular sovereignty. Once that discrimination came to be made, the opponents of full democracy had no opportunity, if we may borrow from Professor Williamson again, but to fight a delaying action.

The suggestion lends additional interest to a firm warning to his colleagues in the field of American history that has been issued recently by R. R. Palmer, a distinguished American authority on the French Revolution. In his comprehensive volume on *The Age of the Democratic Revolution* (1959), Professor Palmer finds—in the bitter division of the American people, in the techniques of the committee system employed, in the substitution of the doctrine of popular sovereignty for the traditional sanctions upon which government theretofore had depended, and in the development of the constitutional scheme of government—ample evidence that the American Revolution was truly a revolution. He views it, moreover, as one which set the pattern for a revolutionary movement that would soon shake and reshape the Western world.

As one looks back over half a century of historical study in the broad field of the American Revolution one observation seems to be called for above all others. A very large part of the literature has been revisionist in its inspiration. The revisionist has, of course, a vital function to perform, but the very character of the function encourages overstatement, which in turn can invite new revisionist efforts. What is most needed today perhaps is a little more tolerance by revisionists for other revisionists, past and present, and a little more awareness of the contribution each group has made, and can make, to the clarification of a problem that is as complex as it is significant for the history of the nation.

© Wesley Frank Craven 1962

4

THE CHANGING WEST

BY EARL POMEROY

ACCORDING to whom one asks, the history of the West is either one of the most or one of the least significant fields of American history, one of the most or one of the least controversial. The Western field has overshadowed most others in volume of output published; at some graduate schools dissertations on Western topics have exceeded those in all other fields combined; and at some colleges there are advanced courses in no other American field. Yet Western historians have done both some of the most forward-looking and some of the most backward-looking work. In no other field has there been such diversity of interpretation and reputation.

The popularity and proportions of Western studies seem to follow in large part on the influence of one historian, Frederick Jackson Turner (1861–1932). Most of the elder statesmen in the field have acknowledged themselves his disciples or felt obliged to explain why they were not; and although he retired from teaching two generations ago, the author of a recent textbook offered it as essentially an expansion of the syllabus that Turner prepared. Before Turner Western history did not even appear in the colleges' curricula, although nine-tenths or more of the area of continental United States has been the West or still is. He virtually introduced into the standard subject-matter the story of the movement of early traders and settlers over the Appalachians into the Ohio Valley in the eighteenth century; the organization of territories and new states; the disposition of the public lands; conflicts with Indians and Europeans; the advance of pioneer settlement over the Mississippi Valley into Texas and the trans-Mississippi West;

the fur trade in Southwest and Northwest; the Mexican War and the definition of national boundaries; the Far-Western gold rushes; the development of transportation from riverboat and stagecoach to railroad; the rise of the range-cattle industry; Western agrarian discontent and the Populist movement. In the general histories since Turner these topics have been fairly fixed: one might not suppose that there were different schools of thought about them as there are about the American Revolution, the Civil War, the progressives. Yet even those who look to the master have differed sharply in how they define the field, in the use they make of the basic framework, and in what they add to it.

The various shapes of Western historiography correspond to different elements of Turner's own work and thought, and in turn to different conditions that prepared his contemporaries for him. Perhaps his most enduring achievement was in method: he superseded the German-trained scientific school, demonstrating that human affairs were so complex that inductive processes alone could not significantly unravel them; and moreover he so mastered technique and detail, showing so fruitfully the possibilities of geographical and statistical approaches to data that traditionalist historians had passed by, that they acclaimed him without fully realizing that he had destroyed them. He was so much aware of the flux of historical interpretations, of the light and shadow that present and past cast on each other, that twentieth-century instrumentalists and economic determinists and historical sociologists could legitimately look to him as their progenitor, though no one had striven more scrupulously after objective historical reality or brought more poetry to his science. As a social scientist, he looked to the West for the record of social processes, not for tales of frontier adventure; simple narrative history never much interested him. He liked to refer to the frontier as a 'social laboratory' and to the historian as the counterpart of the geologist, dealing with data so complex that he had to resort to multiple rather than single hypothesis.

The West offered Turner not only new data and room to synthesize them in but a new interpretation of the distinctive course of national development. The local historians had assembled data without trying to construct a pattern; the national historians had constructed a pattern too exclusively from European and Eastern materials. Turner accordingly set forth, in the paper that he read on 'The Significance of the Frontier in American History' (1893), 'a programme, and in some degree a protest against eastern neglect . . . of [the] institutional study of the West, and against [the] antiquarian spirit [of Westerners] in dealing with their own history'. Trying to see American processes 'as a whole', he distinguished himself from 'those who thought in terms of North and South, as well as from those who approached the west as fighting ground, or ground for exploration history'.[1]

More specifically, Turner suggested that the process of occupying new lands on the Western frontier had significantly affected national life by fostering a more democratic spirit and condition than had prevailed in Europe. 'The existence of an area of free land, its continuous recession, and the advance of American settlement westward, explain American development.' This thesis tended to focus the study of Western history on the westward movement into unoccupied land, rather than on the region that at any one time was filling up with settlers.

The almost universal acclaim that Turner received testifies only in part to the power of his analysis or even to the engaging personality that he revealed to his friends and students. That public and profession capitulated to him so readily suggests that his was not entirely an intellectual and a personal victory, or theirs an intellectual and a personal surrender. For Americans of the late nineteenth and early twentieth centuries, the rural West had deep emotional connotations. It had been their national childhood. In the generation after the Civil War they were moving into another life, urbanized and industrialized as never before, and eventually they paused for the pleasant pangs of nostalgia. 'As America grows older,'

[1] 'Turner's Autobiographic Letter', Turner to C. L. Skinner, 15 March 1922, in *Wisconsin Magazine of History*, XIX (September 1935), pp. 96, 101. The essay itself is in Turner's *The Frontier in American History* (1920).

said Turner in 1913, 'more and more it exhibits a tendency to turn back to the heroic age of its explorers and pioneers.' So did his readers, and so did Turner himself. Even while he protested against romantic, antiquarian approaches and in his monographic work set an example of a new analytical method, he served the popular taste in two ways: by gaining for Western history as a whole (including the older styles as well as the new) a new academic respectability and by expressing a romanticism of his own, as in his paper on 'The Significance of the Frontier'. The public and many of his academic colleagues remembered best the rhetorical passages of this most analytical of historians: they sensed that he responded not merely to the challenge of analyzing the consequences of frontier life in national history but to the atavistic pulse of the frontier itself.

Turner argued the case for frontier as against foreign influences, for environmental as against inherited factors, for the Western-agrarian origins of American democracy, at a time when national pride, biological and social Darwinism, anxiety over imported ideas and racial strains, and the spectacle of the Populist revolt in the rural West and South prepared both the public and himself for his arguments. His readers did not wait for his research, though they were glad to cite it as proof; they were prepared to accept his hypotheses simply after seeing the newspapers. When he wrote in 1891 that '*Each age writes the history of the past anew with reference to the conditions uppermost in its own time*', he might as well have referred to the reception of ideas as to their genesis. He wrote so much in the general climate of opinion that it is futile to try to demonstrate his specific influence outside historiography.

Thus Turner had many allies in raising the status of Western history, if not necessarily in giving it the direction that he favoured. They included many who were already reading and writing histories. In the 1880's Hubert Howe Bancroft (1832–1918) had sold a million dollars' worth of sets of his histories of the Far-Western states and territories and of Mexico and Central America. These were compilations of notes more than literature: Lord Bryce wondered whether their popularity represented penance for what the Californians had done to the Mexicans and Indians whose land they occupied. The Western state historical societies prospered in the same years and issued their collections, mingling reminiscence, documents, and necrology, while the commercial publishers found markets for works as different as Theodore Roosevelt's stirring *Winning of the West* (4 vols., 1889–96) and Justin Winsor's ponderous cartographical and bibliographical volumes.[1] Both Turner and some of the amateur antiquarians knew that he and they were not kindred spirits; he had to choose his words carefully when he eulogized Reuben Gold Thwaites of the Wisconsin State Historical Society in 1913, remarking that 'The history of institutions, of industrial development [,] of laws and governments, appealed to him less than the history of individual achievement. The narrative of action and the documents on which it was based gained his most loving care.' But Turner and his students had been tenants and debtors of the Society in the enormous building that it erected at the edge of the state university campus in 1900; and the Bancroft Library, which the University of California bought in 1905 upon Thwaites's recommendation, was to become the main resource of a school of Far-Western historians.

By the time Turner retired at Harvard in 1924, Western history seemed both flourishing and respectable. Turner had trained a remarkable group of disciples, including several future presidents of the American Historical Association. Although the history of the West was still primarily the history of the Ohio Valley, his students had established outposts at California, Stanford, Oregon, Washington, and Oklahoma. At Wisconsin Frederic L. Paxson, who succeeded Turner in 1910, published in 1924 the first synthesis of Western history, *The History of the American Frontier*. Still in his forties, Paxson had seen the Westerners working first in almost pioneer conditions, academically speaking, without bibliographies or professional status, then creating graduate courses, scholarly

[1] *Narrative and Critical History of America* (8 vols., 1884–9) and *The Westward Movement* (1897).

organizations, and an excellent journal, *The Mississippi Valley Historical Review* (1914–).

The Westerners moreover had published solid series of documents. Thwaites established a new standard for historical-society publications from the sixteenth volume of the Wisconsin *Collections* (1902), devoting them thereafter exclusively to documents and ordinarily to coherent subjects or periods. When he edited his *Early Western Travels* (32 vols., 1904–7) and other series, he deferred still to non-professional taste, selecting documents by the criterion of popular interest and presenting them in translation and without full scholarly annotation. But Clarence W. Alvord brought the field abreast of the best continental traditions with his *Cahokia Records* (1907) and subsequent volumes on the early Illinois country.

As in these enterprises, Western history in the 1920's continued to emphasize beginnings: exploration, diplomacy, the founding of settlements. Although nationalism fostered interest in the West, and the documentary series recording the Western past resembled the vast projects in medieval scholarship that had come out of European nationalism, many of the major monographic studies concerned British and French colonial policy and expansion rather than the development of American society and character. Thus Alvord's great work was *The Mississippi Valley in British Politics* . . . (2 vols., 1917); and Louise Phelps Kellogg, who had studied with Turner and assisted Thwaites, wrote on *The French Régime in Wisconsin and the Northwest* (1925).

On the west coast Herbert E. Bolton (1870–1953) went much further in emphasizing imperial themes. Moving from Wisconsin to Texas and then to California, Bolton inherited the resources of the Bancroft Library at Berkeley, but he and his students concerned themselves less with Anglo-America and more with Latin America than H. H. Bancroft had done. In their hands the study of the borderlands, which Bolton described as the site of the interaction of several cultures and empires, became essentially the history of Spanish penetration into areas near those which Americans much later settled. Thus if Turner concentrated on the West to correct overemphasis on the East in national history, Bolton concentrated on Latin America to correct overemphasis on the American home-steader in Western history. To him *frontier* was not so much region or process as outpost and salient; frontiersmen were not mere settlers but agents of empire. Bolton occupied himself increasingly with the careers of Spanish explorers; his major work was the life of Eusebio Kino, the seventeenth-century Jesuit missionary who discovered that Lower California was not an island.

In Eastern universities diplomatic historians addressed themselves more to the advancing Anglo-American frontier in its international framework. One of Turner's students, Arthur P. Whitaker, in two books on *The Spanish-American Frontier, 1783–1795* (1927) and *The Mississippi Question, 1795–1803* (1934), succeeded probably more than anyone else in treating the economic and social development of the border-lands in a perspective significant for American history. Both Whitaker and Julius W. Pratt, who wrote on the *Expansionists of 1812* (1925), were interested in the tendency of sections to oppose each other on international issues, as Turner had been in his work on Franco-American and Spanish-American relations of the 1790's.

Such active concern with international frontiers in the 1920's contrasted with a striking dearth of substantial analytical works along the lines of Turner's interest in frontier democracy and Western traits and social institutions generally. Large parts of Western social and economic history lay fallow for twenty years or more. Few historians questioned Turnerian doctrine, but orthodoxy was yielding some very dull history, superior to the antiquarianism of the previous century in technical form rather than in idea or style. The chronological framework that Turner sketched out became an end in itself: narrative excluded analysis. It was as if some of Turner's auditors had accepted his plea too soon, without stopping to hear all of it, and rushed away with new sense of justification to resume as academicians 'that noble dream' of piling monograph on monograph.

In fact the approach of many Westerners was neither in-

ductive in the sense of the nineteenth-century scientific school
nor Turnerian, since they tended to convert hypothesis into
definition of the field: moving from Turner's suggestion that
American democracy found a new vitality at the raw edge of
civilization, where settlers had at least to rearrange their cultural inheritance, they sometimes arbitrarily ignored as non-
Western all those elements of Western life that were not clearly
democratic and atavistic. Fixation on pioneer experiences and
on the early stages of rural settlement stultified particularly
the study of the Middle West. Since Turner had based his
principal generalizations on its early history, it became
almost the closed preserve of his disciples. Thus some of the
liveliest Western history of the 1920's and early 1930's concerned the West beyond, as Texas, Wyoming, and Montana,
which apparently had so resisted becoming like the East that
the historian could more easily consider all phases of their
history without wondering whether his material was too
urban, intellectual, industrial, or national to qualify as
Western. At the Wisconsin State Historical Society, one of
Turner's students, Joseph Schafer, had announced in 1920
the ambitious project of a 'Wisconsin Domesday Book'. But
only five small volumes of Schafer's Domesday series had
appeared when the depression cut off support in 1937, and
none of them significantly followed Turner's suggestion of
trying to correlate 'party votes, by precincts, wards, etc., soils,
nationalities and state-origins of the voter, assessment rolls,
denominational groups, illiteracy, etc.' While Turner himself
continued to work laboriously on the sectionalism of the 1830's
and 1840's, the general theme of sectional conflict arising from
competing economic interests appeared less clearly in most
other Western studies than in Eastern-oriented works of
Charles A. Beard and his followers.

The West became less interesting in those years both because of what its historians were writing, or failing to write,
and because as a section it seemed to offer less to the nation
than it once had, to look backward where it once had led.
Middle-Western progressivism had declined, yielding to
isolationism and nativism. Novelists such as Sinclair Lewis

(*Main Street*, 192(, and *Babbitt*, 1922) made the Middle West represent small-town provincialism. In an urban and industrial age the rural West seemed out of touch with the main currents of national life. 'What contributions have serfs, landlords, freeholders, peasants, and land toilers as such ever made to letters, arts, and sciences?' asked Beard (1928), going on to suggest that many conservatives had always cherished rural society as a check to the revolutionary mobs of great cities. 'However valid may be the agrarian thesis in respect of the past that lay behind 1900 . . . , there can hardly be any question about the course of affairs since that date.'

The irrelevance of Western backgrounds and of Western history itself seemed all the clearer in the economic depression of the 1930's. The historians' preoccupation with local, rural, atavistic and military themes had at least served popular nostalgia in time of prosperity; but in the domestic crisis of the 'thirties Americans felt that they could afford neither localism nor militarism. Progressives of the early years of the century had looked back to the frontier as the source of national virility; but New Dealers relying on big government instinctively distrusted the legend of frontier individualism and the idea (which Turner's successors had elaborated) that the frontier had served as a 'safety valve' to release Eastern discontent and urban threats to democracy. Some New Dealers ingeniously adapted the idea of the 'safety valve' to new conditions, arguing (as Turner himself had suggested) that the exhaustion of free land required that government substitute for nature; but many liberal scholars wondered if the safety valve ever had worked. Thus they took their cues for studying the past from the present as directly as Turner had taken his. Some of them, being urbanites at a time when most of America had been so long urban as to forget when it had been mostly rural, simply ignored the rural West.

Coinciding roughly with the trough of the depression and with the skepticism about the West and Western history that the depression brought to focus, Turner's death in 1932 was the occasion for more than the warm and affectionate tributes that he might have commanded a decade or so earlier. His followers' praise of him was more defensive than is conventional at such times. When they turned from eulogy to reply to his critics, they fell back chiefly on his sweeping generalizations instead of carrying on the vigorous analysis and marshalling of evidence that Turner had also practiced. The opposing parties in the ensuing academic skirmishes over the 'Turner thesis' sometimes seemed, in fact, to have mixed their banners. While innocently regarding themselves as disciples rather than as antagonists, some of Turner's followers had helped to repel from the field those students with the analytical and synthetic powers that it demands, by a kind of academic Gresham's law. Turner had failed not merely in that his critics were able to argue persuasively that democracy had not come from the forest—that is, that the facts did not sustain his most striking hypotheses—but in that many of his defenders had been unaccustomed to analyzing data relevant to the 'Turner thesis' or any thesis. Meanwhile some other historians who were more Turnerian in method, in that they advanced new hypotheses that may help us to understand the West, and tested them by sifting the local evidence, appeared as antagonists because they rejected some of Turner's speculations and conclusions or denied that they applied to all of the West.

Some of the sharpest of the critics of orthodox Western history in the 1930's thought so little of the field as to confine themselves to brief papers whose principal effect may have been to suggest that better opportunities for research lay elsewhere. But others wrote substantially, particularly with respect to economic and social structure. One of Turner's students, Thomas P. Abernethy, detailed the triumph of privilege, opportunism, and speculation over democracy in the old Southwest of the eighteenth and early nineteenth centuries. In careful studies of corporate and public records, Paul W. Gates revealed the triumph of insiders and monopolists in the early Northwest as well; his books more clearly recalled Turner's passion for cartographical analysis than any other work in the field except that of some of his own students. Gates and Fred A. Shannon went on to find the Homestead Act of 1862 a sham, its promise of free land to the settler outdated before it took effect.[1] Shannon's emphatic and factual exposition of the misfortunes of wheat farmers in the western Mississippi Valley, where he himself taught during the depression, recalled the bitterness of the Kansas Populists of the 1890's. Economic historians denied that there had been a Western safety valve, political scientists that there had been significant Western origins of American democracy.

It seemed for a while in the 1930's and 1940's that revisionist scholars had succeeded not merely in correcting excesses among the Westerners but in diverting serious students elsewhere by minimizing dynamic elements in Western society. Shannon had all but proved that there had been no westward movement except of those drawn west by false expectations. Abernethy had turned Andrew Jackson into a conservative; Arthur Schlesinger, Jr., went on to convert him into a spokesman for Eastern radicals and disposed of rival theories of his Westernness largely by ignoring the Westerners.[2] Especially in the older Middle West, where it had once been most attractive, Western history declined relative to other fields. Turner's old course temporarily dropped from the curriculum even at Wisconsin and California; it was becoming fashionable to organize history more by periods than by themes or areas, perhaps in deference to the centripetal trend of the times. The *Mississippi Valley Historical Review* proclaimed itself *A Journal of American History* (1938) and gave no more attention to Western or Mississippi-Valley themes than to any other phases of American history. At the same time, at many colleges there were enough students who had to take courses in state history to meet requirements for teaching in the public schools, or who chose to write graduate dissertations in Western history because it seemed to be easy, so that members of college faculties might still teach Western or state

[1] Thomas P. Abernethy, *From Frontier to Plantation in Tennessee* (1932); Paul W. Gates, 'The Homestead Law in an Incongruous Land System', *American Historical Review*, XLI (July 1936), pp. 652–81; Fred A. Shannon, 'The Homestead Act and the Labor Surplus', *ibid.*, XLI (July 1936), pp. 637–51; and *The Farmer's Last Frontier: Agriculture, 1860–1897* (1945).

[2] Schlesinger, *The Age of Jackson* (1945).

history exclusively and thus live apart intellectually from the new currents of scholarship in other fields.

Alongside those who began in the 1930's to deny that the Western environment had offered economic opportunity and inspired democratic institutions, other historians suggested new environmental interpretations. Deeply aware of the differences between his native Texas and the Mississippi-Valley background of most of the early Western historians, Walter P. Webb had not even read Turner when he wrote *The Great Plains* (1931), a study of man's accommodation to the arid Southwest; but his geographical determinism far exceeded Turner's. Turner merely tended to determinism, for he acknowledged more than one force in history and emphasized environmental stimuli more than environmental limits. As he developed his argument in later essays, Webb not only accepted none of the substitutes for geography that Turner had suggested (such as governmental intervention) but explained the main forces in all modern history by the one principle. Whereas Turner gave great comfort to American nativists and isolationists by seeming to agree that the noblest American traits were home-grown, Webb went further to contend flatly that the prosperity, dynamism, and freedom of the European world of the last 400 years were drafts on the bank account of America, which was now approaching exhaustion. The implications were as bleak as those in the work of the sharpest anti-environmentalists.

Physical environment suggested an entirely different approach to another Southwesterner, James C. Malin. While Webb tended to project the experience of west Texas over not merely the whole West but the whole world, Malin insisted that his state of Kansas and everyone in it were unique. Arguing as staunchly as Pieter Geyl that history is the guardian of the particular, he emphasized the virtues of local history as a corrective to overly broad national or sectional (including Turnerian) interpretations.[1] Paradoxically, both Webb and

[1] James C. Malin, 'On the Nature of Local History', *Wisconsin Magazine of History*, XL (summer 1957), pp. 227–30; *Winter Wheat in the Golden Belt of Kansas* (1944); *Essays on Historiography* (1946).

Malin denied that they were social scientists, though the one stated laws that left man little essential choice, while the other brought the specific findings of natural science to bear upon historical problems. Malin, Shannon, and Webb all emerged with different definitions of history as well as with different solutions for the exhaustion of free land, the end of the old frontier: the way out for each part of the West was different from every other, or it led to the city, or it led nowhere.

Despite all the obituaries that both Easterners and Westerners published for them, Western studies survived the unfriendly atmosphere of the depression. By the 1950's, questioning Turner's specific propositions seldom aroused deep emotion. The best of Western history became more Turnerian after the Second World War than it had been after the First, in the sense of working toward higher levels of generalization about American history as a whole by applying the keenest tools of analysis to data that bore on new and suggestive hypotheses. It had advanced in part because the revisionists had jarred Turner's defenders into testing their assumptions, in part because historians were importing into Western studies techniques and hypotheses that proved to be as fruitful as those that Turner had inspired in various fields of both American and European history. Turner's prestige was still so great in 1946 that a general appraisal of American historical scholarship credited him with 'nearly all the ideas more recent American historians have pushed further',[1] but some of the more original Westerners were drawing freely on other branches of history and on other disciplines.

The concern of the revisionists of the 1930's with economic and social structure extended into that of Turner's defenders and of younger scholars who worked without the older generation's sense of personal involvement. Merle Curti, one of Turner's later students, undertook to analyze social institutions in a Wisconsin county in what amounted to a long-

---

[1] John H. Randall, Jr., and George Haines, IV, 'Controlling Assumptions in the Practice of American Historians', *Theory and Practice in Historical Study*, Social Science Research Council, Bulletin 54, Report of the Committee on Historiography (1946), p. 50.

deferred addition to the Wisconsin Domesday series, using punch-card techniques to establish correlations. Both he and Allan and Margaret Bogue, who studied the ownership of land in Middle-Western counties, drew effectively on the methods of modern sociological research; their findings suggested, for the areas they studied, trends somewhat closer to Turner's hypotheses than to those of his opponents, though more complex than either.[1] On the other hand, Henry Nash Smith, who brought to Western history the methods of literary criticism, accepted in the main the arguments of Shannon and others that historians and Americans generally had overrated Western opportunity and asked how and why they had overrated it. In *Virgin Land: The American West as Symbol and Myth* (1950) Smith wrote not so much about the West as about how others thought about the West in the context of their times. Thus he helped historians to free themselves from the rigidity of formulas popularly attributed to Turner and to look again at the West as freely as Turner did, and he influenced them specifically on topics as varied as attitudes toward the Indian, Western architecture, travel, outdoor recreation, radicalism, and even exploration. After him the words 'image', 'legend', and 'myth' became common currency.

Much of the freshness of the new Western history seemed to follow on a strengthening of those contacts between Western and national themes that Turner himself had maintained when he included in the syllabus of his course on the history of the West at Harvard such topics as Combinations and the Development of the West, Conservation and the West, the Progressives, and the West in the World War and Reconstruction. Although most of the textbook writers confined themselves still to traditional themes, other historians broke through orthodoxy to concern themselves also with the parts of the West that extended beyond first settlements and that included the city as well as the countryside. Whereas Shannon

[1] Curti *et al.*, *The Making of an American Community; a Case Study of Democracy in a Frontier County* (1959), Allan G. Bogue, *Money at Interest* (1955); Margaret B. Bogue, *Patterns from the Sod: Land Use and Tenure in the Grand Prairie, 1850–1900* (1959).

and other economic historians had belittled Western history, in effect, because the city was the most dynamic part of American society, the new reply was that the West included the city. As literary historian of San Francisco, Franklin Walker opened a new dimension of Far-Western cultural history;[1] later Richard Wade described *The Urban Frontier* (1959) of the Ohio Valley.

Broader dimensions were especially evident in the development of Western religious history, which had received little attention in the 1920's and which in most general accounts had served chiefly to illustrate conventional generalizations about Western democracy and Western crudity. By the late 1930's there were substantial signs of change among both secular and clerical historians, corresponding to changes in religious history in the colonial and national frameworks. By the 1950's even historians of frontier evangelism were taking it seriously and concentrating on its social and theological significance rather than on its occasionally eccentric forms. The most striking changes of all were in the historiography of the Mormons (Latter-day Saints) of Utah, which only recently had seemed divided between the unsympathetic and sometimes malicious accounts of outsiders and the inexorably dull, painfully defensive annals of the Saints themselves. The new generation of Mormon historians related religion to economic institutions, politics, and immigration, all with remarkable objectivity.[2]

Some of the liveliest work since the 1930's pertained to the Far West and the recent West, although some historians still protested that the great themes of Western history had exhausted themselves when Turner called attention to the end of the conventional line of advancing settlement in the census of 1890, that what happened thereafter was anticlimax, or at least the business of the national historian or the

---

[1] *San Francisco's Literary Frontier* (1939). See also Walker's *Literary History of Southern California* (1950).

[2] Leonard J. Arrington, *The Great Basin Kingdom: An Economic History of the Mormon People* (1958); Thomas F. O'Dea, *The Mormons* (1957).

social scientist rather than of the Westerner. The newer Wests invited more attention in part simply because they were growing so spectacularly after 1945. California's population, for instance, increasing from 6,907,387 in 1940 to 10,586,223 in 1950 and 15,506,974 in 1960, and promising to pass New York's before 1970. And the states that grew fastest, in the Southwest, were those whose terrain and parts of whose economies recalled pioneer beginnings, or whose tourist industries propagated legends of the unique and picturesque; the inundation of new population easily supported a new curiosity about the past that was disappearing under automobile freeways.

Yet Western history did not confine itself to antiquarian and picaresque themes even in those states where pioneer survivals seemed prominent. With growth came confidence: Westerners were no longer so uncertain about the status and future of their section that they had to insist that it was different. Precious and overcolored versions of the past persisted more as entertainment than as serious scholarship or deep emotional release; trips into the mountains were quests for scenery, fresh air, and exercise rather than pilgrimages to the sites of ancestral experience. Research libraries that once had refused to collect anything more recent or more revealing of frontier society than gold-rush diaries now tried to repair lost opportunities.

Instead of seeming to be anticlimax, the post-frontier West had come to be to twentieth-century America what nineteenth-century America had been to Europe in Tocqueville's day. America is the oldest country in the world, Gertrude Stein told her French friends, because it was the first to enter the twentieth century; and in various respects—in patterns of urban culture, in transportation, in politics—the West matured before the East did. 'The real peculiarity of our present Pacific civilization,' a young historian, a friend of Turner, had written as early as 1883, when the coast still imported most of the seeds of innovation from older sections, 'is that it is, perhaps, the most completely realized embodiment of the purely commercial civilization on the face of the earth.' California 'has gone so much further on the same path, that the achievements therein of New York must still be ranked as "tendency", the full blossoming of which may be seen here'. Perhaps this was premature at that time, but much of the West had been so even then, when sentimental nostalgia for the Spanish and Mexican past was just beginning to compete with the ordinary Western tendency to follow Eastern models. Most of the West had become so since then, preparing itself as 'a launching platform for the future', as a contemporary Western historian recently said,[1] and promised to explain America's present and future as the colonial East once explained America's past. The rest of the nation, which seemed to be going west to live, according to the postwar censuses of population, was also writing its fears and aspirations on the modern Western scene. Accordingly, modern Western historians were shifting away from localism. Books such as George Mowry's *The California Progressives* (1951) emphasized the national developments that were coming to focus in the West.

The range of Western historical scholarship since the 1940's was as broad as it had ever been. Much of it was as traditional as if nothing had happened in the field since Turner or Bancroft; Pulitzer prizes went to works in Western history that were completely conventional in interpretation. Some historians were still content to elaborate the old framework of the westward movement with new data and without responding to its dramatic possibilities. But the public also welcomed sound and well-written histories of discovery and exploration, of which Bernard De Voto's were the first and most widely read and Dale L. Morgan's probably the most scholarly, while no less artistic. Both De Voto and Wallace Stegner, who re-created the adventures of John Wesley Powell in canyons that modern dam-builders proposed to obliterate, were ardent conservationists and as romantic in their way as the pre-Turnerians in theirs, while far removed from antiquarianism.

[1] Charles H. Shinn in *Overland Monthly*, 2nd series, II (December 1883), p. 657; Wallace Stegner, 'West Coast: Region with a View', *Saturday Review*, XLII (2 May 1959), p. 41.

And new studies of Western political parties and institutions, such as those by Robert W. Johannsen and Howard R. Lamar,[1] resembled the best work on the regional backgrounds of Eastern and national political figures.

In academic circles Western history in the most literal and limited sense may have lost ground relative to its condition of a generation or two earlier. Scholars in other fields sometimes remembered the aspersions of the 1930's more than Westerners did. It was hard to abandon quickly the assumption that weak graduate students belonged in Western seminars. Still, most indications in the early 1960's were that the field was prospering, that it had gained much more than it might lose by re-entering the main stream of American studies, and that there was room for all approaches—Turnerian, pre-Turnerian, post-Turnerian, neo-Turnerian, the history of the West as process, as pioneer background, and as distinctive region.

© Earl Pomeroy 1962

---

[1] De Voto, *The Course of Empire* (1952), *Across the Wide Missouri* (1947), and *Year of Decision* (1943); Morgan, *Jedediah Smith and the Opening of the West* (1953); Stegner, *Beyond the Hundredth Meridian* (1954); Johannsen, *Frontier Politics and the Sectional Conflict* (1955); Lamar, *Dakota Territory, 1861–1889* (1956).

5

THE AGE OF THE COMMON MAN

BY JOHN WILLIAM WARD

To speak of an age, or a man, as 'common' is, one might quickly think, to speak with a certain contempt. Yet, in the United States, the concept of the worth of the common man has been so intimately bound up in our thought with the value of democracy that the term has always carried an emotionally positive connotation with it. Because an American's inherited attitude toward the nature of society presumes the potential worth of the average man, he cannot say with Plato, 'How little does the common herd know of the nature of right and truth'. Even when dismayed by some of the consequences of the common man's rise to power in American society, the American historian has never been able to reject him with Plato's flat contempt.

The matter can be put succinctly by a look at the first work by an American historian to use the phrase, 'common man', in its title, Carl Russell Fish's *The Rise of the Common Man, 1830–1850* (1927). For Mr Fish as for other American historians, although not all use his precise dates, the age of the common man in American history is the period of the early nineteenth century, somewhere between Jefferson and the Civil War, roughly coincident with Andrew Jackson's coming to power and the formation of the Democratic party.

For the epigraph to his book, Mr Fish used the words of a contemporary of the period:

'Ours is a country,' wrote Calvin Colton in 1844, 'where men start from an humble origin . . . and where they can attain to the most elevated positions, or acquire

82

a large amount of wealth, according to the pursuits they elect for themselves. No exclusive privileges of birth, no entailment of estates, no civil or political disqualifications, stand in their path; but one has as good a chance as another, according to his talents, prudence or personal exertions. This is a country of self-made men, than which nothing better could be said of any state of society.'

But along with this praise of a society open to every man, Mr Fish chose also to put as a frontispiece to his book a reproduction of a political cartoon of the election of 1844, the very year of Colton's words. It shows a riot before 'Jefferson House', with a rudely dressed orator addressing his 'feller citizens' and a corrupt politician in the background dumping the contents of a ballot box out the window while a mob struggles back and forth in front of the polling place. In the left foreground of the cartoon, a top-hatted, frock-coated gentleman with a walking-stick complains, 'I have been a voter in this ward thirty years but since rowdyism rules the day . . . I must relinquish my privilege of Citizenship.'

Mr Fish's volume was part of the series, *A History of American Life*, edited by Arthur M. Schlesinger and Dixon Ryan Fox. In a foreword these two general editors made explicit the ambivalence toward the rise of the common man implicit in the juxtaposition of Mr Fish's epigraph and cartoon. 'Many readers,' wrote Schlesinger and Fox, 'will leave this volume with mixed feelings . . . it is clear that the older view, which saw in these years only . a lowering of standards, must be offset by the picture . . . of a society which in many vital and enduring respects was leveling up as well as down.' Americans, including their historians, have had from Jackson's time to the present 'mixed feelings' about democracy and the common man it exalts. Was the rise of the common man the rise to power of a rude, unenlightened majority and the populistic rejection of intellect and the virtues of a social élite? Or was the rise of the common man a vindication of the worth of everyman and the rejection of the artificial distinctions of class and social status? The values that each American historian has brought to his analysis of the early nineteenth century have determined, quite as much as the facts of what happened, his judgment of the age of the common man.

This is not to say that the facts did not offer themselves for evaluation. One could stress the moving simplicity of Jackson's unattended march on the day of his inauguration from his hotel to the steps of the Capitol and applaud the instincts of democracy; or, one could recoil from the rude crowd who trampled through the White House afterward, crowding the reception rooms and breaking glass until punch bowls were placed on the lawn to draw them out. Jackson's political philosophy lent itself to the same double interpretation. Before his election, presidents had risen through cabinet service to the presidency. Although he had prior political experience, Jackson was the first 'outsider' to become president, just as he was the first president close enough to the people to be known by a nickname. In his first annual message to the Congress, Jackson carefully rejected the notion that training and experience were primary requisites for election to high office. Long tenure led to the corrupt notion of considering office 'a species of property, and government rather as a means of promoting individual interests than as an instrument created solely for the service of the people'. So Jackson argued for 'that rotation [in office] which constitutes a leading principle in the republican creed', thus firmly establishing the spoils system in American national politics. Those who value experience and training in public life have used this declaration to point to the incompetent leadership which is a consequence of naive democratic theory. Although Jackson's action had the practical goal of providing financial support for the organization of a national political party, his rationale for his action was more subtle. His view of political power was largely negative; he believed that legislation should not obstruct the normal channels of individual enterprise and that, therefore, 'the duties of all public officers are, or at least admit of being made, so plain and simple that men of intelligence may readily qualify themselves for their performance'.

His attack on training for office and long experience in governmental affairs was that *they* led to corruption; the spoils system was offered as a species of reform. It was possible to say so only on the assumption of the competence of the common man and in the context of a society which saw little need for government anyway.

What the Jacksonian party in politics and Andrew Jackson in his own person dramatized, as I have tried to show in *Andrew Jackson: Symbol for an Age* (1955), was the widespread belief in early nineteenth-century America in the untutored wisdom of the common man whose uninhibited action would, guided by Providence, create the good society. What was acted out in politics and symbolized by Andrew Jackson found its historical voice almost immediately in the writings of George Bancroft, himself a Democratic partisan and Jacksonian politician. Bancroft wove all through his *History of the United States*, which he began in 1834, the bright thread of the Jacksonian belief that 'the many are more sagacious, more disinterested, more courageous than the few'. For Bancroft, the common people were the reservoir from which statesmen and poets and religious leaders drew their strength and truth. 'The spirit of the colonies,' he wrote in his general preface, 'demanded freedom from the beginning . . . Virginia first asserted the doctrine of popular sovereignty; . . . the people of Maryland constituted their own government; [the New England colonies] rested their legislation on the popular will.' Whatever distortion this did to American colonial history, it triumphantly vindicated popular democracy. Bancroft rejected the sceptical notion that 'the fortunes of a nation are . . . under the control of a blind destiny' and declared that the object of his *History* was 'to follow the steps by which a favoring Providence, calling our institutions into being, has conducted the country to its present happiness and glory'. God Himself, working through the course of history, was behind the common people.

Since Bancroft, American historians have been somewhat less ready to see the finger of God in the American past. They have offered more secular reasons for the rise of the common

man to social and political power: the influence of a conti
nental environment, the absence of an articulated social
structure, the economic openness of the society, or sheer
political necessity. But they have all generally agreed that
Andrew Jackson represented the aspirations of the average
man of his time. Where they have differed is in deciding who
this average man was. If the early nineteenth century is the
age of the common man, what did Americans then have in
common?

The writing of American history in the twentieth century
has offered three different answers to this question. Although
all three still have a continuing share in the historical debate
on the meaning of our early national life, their major spokes-
men can be arranged in rough chronological order. The first
was Frederick Jackson Turner, who named the westward
movement of the American people as their unique and
characteristic historical experience and identified the common
man of the early nineteenth century as the Western pioneer.
Partially in reaction to Turner and partially in response to
the conditions of modern American life, there emerged a
second reading of the Jacksonian period as one whose ideology
was provided by emergent labor groups and Eastern, urban
reformers. The chief voice in this revisionary reading was
Arthur Schlesinger, Jr., in *The Age of Jackson* (1945). Mr
Schlesinger's book stimulated a host of new studies of the
Jacksonian period which suggested that the common man of
the early nineteenth century was neither a backwoodsman
nor a disgruntled lower-class democrat, but an enterprising
capitalist on the make. This third group is not so clearly
marked by a single voice but its best statement is to be had
in Richard Hofstadter's essay on Andrew Jackson in *The
American Political Tradition and the Men Who Made It* (1948).

Frederick Jackson Turner wrote his now famous essay,
'The Significance of the Frontier in American History', in
1893. From then until his death Turner argued his 'thesis'
which, put bluntly at first, was that 'the existence of an area
of free land, its continuous recession, and the advance of
American settlement westward, explain American develop-

ment'. Arguing a kind of ecological determinism, Turner asserted that:

> 'American development has exhibited not merely advance along a single line, but a return to primitive conditions on a continually advancing frontier line, and a new development for that area. American development has been continually beginning over again on the frontier. This perennial rebirth, this fluidity of American life, this expansion westward with its new opportunities, its continuous touch with the simplicity of primitive society, furnish the forces dominating American character. The true point of view in the history of this nation is not the Atlantic Coast, it is the Great West.'

It is important to remember the period in which Turner wrote. History had, so to speak, caught up with the frontier. The American landscape now displayed factories and machines, great cities, recent immigrants who had never shared the shaping experience of pioneer life. 'Today,' Turner wrote in 1914, 'we are looking with a shock upon a changed world.' When he collected his major essays in *The Frontier in American History* (1921) it remained a question for Turner, as he put it in his preface, 'how large a part of the historic American ideals are to be carried over into that new age which is replacing the era of free lands and of measurable isolation by consolidated and complex industrial development and by increasing resemblances and connections between the New World and the Old'.

In Turner's dramatization of history, the Old World fell easily into the role of the evil and corrupt villain. The hero was, of course, the new man created by a new environment. 'The men of the "Western World",' said Turner in 'Contributions of the West to American Democracy' in 1903, 'turned their backs upon the Atlantic Ocean, and with a grim energy and self-reliance began to build up a society free from the dominance of ancient forms.' The result of their building was social and political democracy.

'Among the pioneers,' wrote Turner in an essay on 'Pioneer Ideals', 'one man was as good as his neighbor. He had the same chance; conditions were simple and free. Economic equality fostered political equality. An optimistic and buoyant belief in the worth of the plain people, a devout faith in man prevailed in the West. Democracy became almost the religion of the pioneer. He held with passionate devotion the idea that he was building under freedom a new society, based on self government, and for the welfare of the average man.'

Since Turner felt that the 'advance of the frontier has meant a steady movement away from the influence of Europe' and that 'to study this advance is . . . to study the really American part of our history', he was forced into a curious dilemma. If the 'really' American part of our national experience was negative, that is, a movement away from civilized society to a wilderness landscape, then what social meaning did the hero of that action have? 'Other nations,' answered Turner, 'have been rich and prosperous and powerful. But the United States has believed that it had an original contribution to make to the history of society by the production of a self-determining, self-restrained, intelligent democracy.' The contribution of the frontier experience to the history of society was the self-willed, self-propelled American Democrat. 'In a word,' said Turner, using fourteen, 'the unchecked development of the individual was the significant product of this frontier democracy.' Andrew Jackson was its 'very personification'. Because the meaning of America was west, and because the meaning of America was democracy (which, when Turner paused to define it, largely meant freedom from restraint,) there was, obviously enough, only one place to look for the American Democrat. 'Here [in the Mississippi Valley], by the thirties,' wrote Turner, 'Jacksonian democracy flourished, strong in the faith of the intrinsic excellence of the common man, in his right to make his own place in the world, and in his capacity to share in government.'

But, as I have already suggested, Turner wrote at a

moment in American history when 'the unchecked development of the individual' seemed more a threat than a guarantee
to the success of American society. Freedom from restraint had
not established an ideal bucolic democracy, but rather increasing concentration of wealth and the demand for positive
action by government on behalf of the common man of the
Progressive period to maintain what Herbert Croly called the
'promise' of American life. 'Democracy and capitalistic development,' remarked Turner, 'did not seem antagonistic' in
the earlier period, but they did seem so at the turn of the
century. And all through Turner's celebration of the pioneer
democrat there sounds a submerged note of disapproval. As
well as the 'simplicity of primitive conditions', the frontier
meant 'savagery' and the disintegration of civilization; if the
frontier developed 'stalwart and rugged qualities', it also gave
rise to 'all the manifest evils that follow from the lack of a
highly developed civic spirit'; if the frontiersman was assertive
and optimistic, he was also 'naive'. But although he saw all
the weaknesses of the ideal type he had constructed, Turner
could never believe that it would be anything but a terrible
mistake if Americans deserted the ideals of the common man
of frontier America and turned 'to some Old World discipline
of socialism or plutocracy, or despotic rule, whether by class
or dictator'.

Turner could never decide if the twin American ideals of
social equality and individual freedom could survive the
passing of the frontier; if, in a more complex age, one might
not have to give way to the other. Nor did he know if the
frontier experience had not shaped a basic antipathy in the
American character to the training and excellence which a
new age demanded. But he never doubted that the American
Democrat had, like some mythic Antaeus, found his strength
in contact with the earth and that what Americans had
historically in common was this brief escape from the complexity of civilization to the rude good fellowship of the frontier.
Writing when escape was no longer possible, he put both his
nostalgia and his fear in two sentences: 'It is in the Middle
West that society has formed on lines least like those of Europe.

It is here, if anywhere, that American democracy will make its stand against the tendency to adjust to a European type.'

Turner's attempt to find in the frontier experience some unique element which differentiated America from Europe led him, later historians thought, to neglect forces which were basic to the development of American society. During the depths of the depression, in an article in the liberal *Nation* magazine, the historian, Louis M. Hacker, flatly asserted that 'only by a study of the origins and growth of American capitalism and imperialism can we obtain insight into the nature and the complexity of the problems confronting us today'. Hacker felt that Turner had turned America's eyes inward 'at exactly the time when all trained eyes should have been on events going on' in the international world and named Turner and his followers as 'the fabricators of a tradition which is not only fictitious but also to a very large extent positively harmful'.[1]

Clearly, Turner's reading of the American experience offered little help to an industrial and capitalistic society in a moment of crisis. If the past reveals itself from the perspective of the present, then it is understandable that a new reading of the age of the common man should have emerged in response to a heightened awareness of what the United States had become. So it was that Arthur Schlesinger, Jr., began his prize-winning and immensely popular *The Age of Jackson* with the words: 'The world crisis has given new urgency to the question of the "meaning" of democracy. If democracy is indeed to be the hope of the future, we know now that we must have its lineaments clearly in mind.' Quoting Franklin D. Roosevelt to establish the relevance of the 'Arcadian simplicity' of Jackson's time to the problems of the present, Arthur Schlesinger, Jr., suggested that Jacksonian democracy was 'not so pat a case' as some have thought of Western influence in American government and put at the front of his book the words of George Bancroft that 'the feud between the capitalist and the laborer, the house of Have and the house of Want, is as old as social union'.

The Age of Jackson insisted that 'the East remained the

[1] *Nation*, CXXXVII (26 July 1933), p. 108.

source of the effective expression of Jacksonian radicalism' because 'the East simply had the consistent and bitter experience which alone could serve as the crucible of radicalism'. In arguing that 'the demand for economic equality is generally born out of conditions of social inequality', Arthur Schlesinger, Jr., emphasized the importance of Eastern intellectuals and labor reformers in providing an ideology which gave coherence to the democratic impulses of the common man of the early nineteenth century.

The central thesis of *The Age of Jackson* had been suggested many years before by the author's father, Arthur Schlesinger, Sr., in an essay on 'The Significance of Jacksonian Democracy', in *New Viewpoints in American History* (1922). Although the first section of his essay was largely a summary of the Turnerian view of Jacksonian Democracy, in the second section the elder Schlesinger drew attention to the fact that 'while democracy was working out its destiny in the forests of the Mississippi Valley, the men left behind in the eastern cities were engaging in a struggle to establish conditions of equality and social well-being adapted to their special circumstances'. Himself a historian of the rise of the city in American life, Arthur Schlesinger, Sr., felt that for a full understanding of the Jacksonian democratic movement 'it is necessary to consider the changed circumstances of life of the common man in the new industrial centers of the East since the opening years of the nineteenth century'. Turner himself, of course, had not been blind to the facts of labor unrest and the criticisms of urban intellectuals in the early nineteenth century, but with his predisposition to associate democracy with the West he generally wrote as if the East were responding to breezes blowing off the broad and open prairies.

In the elder Schlesinger's essay, the common man of the Mississippi Valley and the common man of eastern industrialism stood uneasily side by side. But in the younger Schlesinger's book the common man turned out to be nearly everyone who was not a business man. 'The irrepressible conflict of capitalism,' he wrote, has been 'the struggle on the part of the business community to dominate the state, and on the part of the rest of society, under the leadership of "liberals", to check the political ambitions of business.' The leadership of the liberals was quite as important as the rest of society and it was, therefore, much easier for Arthur Schlesinger, Jr., to find a place in the army of the common man for the intellectual, even if at the head of the march, than it was for Turner for whom feelings of equality and individual worth were more the promptings of the heart than the reasons of the head.

Although *The Age of Jackson* concluded with a damning indictment of the political incapacity of the American business community and although 'capitalism' and 'class' echoed through its pages, Arthur Schlesinger, Jr., was careful to keep the Jacksonians—and Americans—free from any leanings toward socialism. If, as to some critics it often seemed, *The Age of Jackson* was an historical mandate for the age of Roosevelt, what it asserted as common to American democratic experience was a resourceful, pragmatic hostility to power in the hands of any class. Further, written during the incumbency of a greatly popular president, it assumed, perhaps too readily, an affinity between the leadership of liberal intellectuals and the emotions of the common man.

One of the great and undeniable virtues of *The Age of Jackson* was the heuristic value it had for other American historians. For a period which had come to be treated in terms of stale clichés, such as, for example, 'the age of the common man', *The Age of Jackson*, written with vigor and an overriding sense of purpose, demanded a new look. It came soon enough. Bray Hammond, a secretary of the Federal Reserve Board, who had long been at work on what was to be a magistral analysis of *Banks and Politics in America from the Revolution to the Civil War* (1957), rejected Schlesinger's thesis that the Jacksonians had any animus toward business. Quite the contrary. The early nineteenth century was not an age of 'triumphant liberalism', asserted Mr Hammond; 'it was as much or more an age of triumphant exploitation'.[1] The common man was really an eager entrepreneur.

[1] 'Jackson, Biddle, and the Bank of the United States', *Journal of Economic History*, VII (May 1947), pp. 1–23.

Bray Hammond was most irritated by the argument of *The Age of Jackson* that the Jacksonian attack on the U.S. Bank was thought out and promoted by reformers and labor groups. He showed that it was as much an attack by the business community, eager for easy credit and restive under the restraints of an institution which performed many of the controls we now associate with a central bank. 'The sober pace of eighteenth-century business,' he wrote, 'was giving way, on the wave of *laisser faire* and the Industrial Revolution, to a democratic passion to get rich quick—an ambition which America seemed designed by Providence to promote.' While Mr Hammond assailed the ideology that Arthur Schlesinger, Jr., had ascribed to the Jacksonian period, other historians looked more closely at the character of the labor groups in the period and found them populated not by incipient proletariats but by skilled craftsmen, many of them masters themselves, and by a liberal sprinkling of professional men. Unskilled laborers and factory operators were rarely involved and the program of these movements was designed more to preserve business opportunity than to attack business itself.

The view of the common man of the early nineteenth century as a nascent entrepreneur had been adumbrated as long ago as Henry Adams's remark in his great history that each man knew that 'every stroke of his axe and hoe made him a capitalist, and gentlemen of his children'. One of the few thorough-going Marxists in American historical writing, Algie M. Simons, had fully developed the thesis in 1911 in *Social Forces in American History*. 'The rampant individualism of young competitive capitalism,' said Simons, 'determined the *Zeitgeist* of the period.' For Simons, the psychology of the 'rising bourgeoisie' dominated both the labor movement and the frontier and he described Jacksonian democracy in one telling phrase, 'the democracy of expectant capitalists'. By 1940, Louis M. Hacker could describe not only the age of Jackson but the main stream of American history as dominated by 'a constantly recurrent petty-bourgeois strain. . . . There is no country in modern times which can come near matching the successes achieved in the United States by the petty-bourgeois political ideas and leadership of Jeffersonianism, Jacksonianism, a part of the original Radical Republicanism, Populism and La Follette Progressivism.'[1]

From the perspective of the twentieth century, American history has seemed to become more and more a conservative affair. Whether viewed by historians of the left who have a certain distaste for the historically necessary petty bourgeois, or by historians of the right who esteem the classic middleclass ideals of equality before the law and protection of property, the Jacksonian period has been affected by this shift in emphasis. 'Democracy' and 'reform' have been more carefully defined in the context of their times. So the major spokesman today for the entrepreneurial thesis, Richard Hofstadter, could conclude that:

'the Jacksonian movement grew out of expanding opportunities and a common desire to enlarge these opportunities still further. . . . It is commonly recognized in American historical folklore that the Jackson movement was a phase in the expansion of democracy, but it is too little recognized that it was also a phase in the expansion of liberated capitalism . . . in the Jacksonian period the democratic upsurge was closely linked to the ambitions of the small capitalist.'[2]

Clearly enough, the common man of the early nineteenth century cannot be at one and the same time a backwoods farmer, an Eastern worker, and an American capitalist. Recently, an American scholar reviewing a book on the Jacksonian period suggested that students of the time are now in the position of the blind men each trying to describe an elephant by touching only one part of the beast. It may be that historians have tried to name an animal which never

[1] *The Triumph of American Capitalism: The Development of Forces in American History to the End of the Nineteenth Century* (Simon and Schuster, 1940), p. 15.
[2] 'Andrew Jackson and the Rise of Liberal Capitalism', *The American Political Tradition and the Men Who Made It* (Alfred A. Knopf, 1949), p. 55.

existed in the garden of America. But two recent books suggest approaches toward order among the conflicting theories we now have. One, Marvin Meyers, *The Jacksonian Persuasion: Politics and Belief* (1957), is a brilliant intellectual portrait of the broad pattern of Jacksonian ideas; the other, Lee Benson, *The Concept of Jacksonian Democracy: New York as a Test Case* (1961), is a painstaking case-study of the social, ethnic, religious, and economic patterns of Jacksonian support in the crucial state of New York. Each, then, attacks the problem from opposite ends; one being a broad study of ideals, the other a carefully documented study of who was who in the movement in one state. Both point to different but related needs: a new general interpretation of the early nineteenth century as well as more particular studies on which valid general theories must rest.

Mr Meyers presents us with a portrait of an age deeply divided, torn between the ideal of the Old Republic of little government and stoic self-sufficiency and the material lures of a new society of acquisitive capitalism. In Mr Meyers's hands, politics becomes a language of moral gesture; the language is public, but the meaning is inner, the realm of 'impalpable motives, feelings, perceptions' which lie beneath the external act. The result is a suggestive probing into the mind of the Jacksonian period. But as one stands back from it, *The Jacksonian Persuasion* presents one large problem. Mr Meyers writes as if the division were general, as if all Americans shared in the ambivalence he attributes to his ideal 'venturous conservative'. Perhaps. No government meant individual self-sufficiency but it also meant freedom to exploit opportunity and the Jacksonian program could serve both interests. The conflict that Mr Meyers discerns may have been social rather than individual; he may be dealing with two groups in society rather than an ambivalence in Americans generally. Having said this, however, one must admit that the public record of the American mind in the Jacksonian period bears out what Mr Meyers says. The common man of the period may at one and the same time have been deeply torn between opposite views of the nature of his experience.

The thrust of Mr Benson's book is forecast in a line from William Blake which he gives us at the beginning: 'He who would do good to another must do it in Minute Particulars.' So Mr Benson proceeds to do good to historians of the Jacksonian period by doing a minute analysis of one crucial state, New York. Summary does little justice to the elaborate analysis of evidence that Mr Benson puts forth, but, broadly, he concludes that the concept of 'Jacksonian Democracy' has little relevance when tested in New York because the sources of leadership, the voting support, and the persuasive metaphors were the same for both major political parties. Mr Benson concludes that in New York the struggle was mainly over who held office and was only secondarily over final goals. 'After 1815, not only in politics but in all spheres of American life, egalitarianism challenged elitism and, in most spheres and places, egalitarianism won.' If we translate Mr Benson's 'ism' back into the language we have been using, then his detailed study confirms the traditional notion that this was the age of the common man. Which only proves that a cliché must have some truth in it to become one.

Mr Benson's book is an argument for the need of a more diligent empiricism. His point is well taken. As one reviews the literature, one is struck by the suspicion that historians have spent their time taking in each other's washing and running it through a different mangle. Despite all the attention paid to aspects of the age of the common man, an astonishing amount still needs to be known. For example, until only recently the notion prevailed that it was a popular democratic expansion of the suffrage that swept Jackson into office; Richard P. McCormick has demonstrated the falsity of this stereotype.[1] Clearly, as Mr Benson insists, we need local studies which use more sophisticated analyses, which look for patterns of multiple causation rather than single factors, whether they be of the frontier, the worker, or the entrepreneur.

But the point of diminishing returns will quickly arrive if historians of the age of the common man in America do not

[1] 'New Perspectives on Jacksonian Politics', *American Historical Review*, LXV (January 1960), pp. 288–301.

also have some broad hypothesis in which their facts will have some meaning. What students of the American past mostly need at present is a self-conscious theory of culture which will enable them to win their way through to a description of the patterns that give coherence to particular events. For example, Americans of the time, as well as foreign visitors, noted again and again the ideological affinity between Jacksonian democracy and the various species of revivalistic religion so prominent in the period. Yet no one has yet worked out the details of that affinity and tested to what degree egalitarianism in religion carried over into social preferences by studying the political and economic behavior of regions most affected by evangelical religion.

At the same time, the rise of literary romanticism with its emphasis upon the individual, the subjectivity of experience, the validity of the emotions and the worth of the lowly and primitive obviously was germane to an emphasis on the intrinsic worth of the common man. But literature and politics exist largely in separate spheres in the writings of American historians. Twenty years ago, F. O. Matthiessen, in the preface to *American Renaissance: Art and Expression in the Age of Emerson and Whitman*, describing the kind of book he was not writing, said that 'another notable book could concentrate on how discerning an interpretation our great authors gave of the economic and social forces of the time. The orientation of such a book would not be with the religious and philosophical ramifications of the transcendental movement so much as with its voicing of fresh aspirations for the rise of the common man.' We do not yet have that book or that kind of cultural history in American scholarship. So what we need most is the imaginative historian who will throw the past into shape and disclose what was the common pattern of the age we have for so long now known simply as common.

6

DISUNION AND REUNION

BY DON E. FEHRENBACHER

OF THE two great rebellions which divide American history into its major periods, the second—the one that failed—has received more attention from recent generations. Americans celebrate their Revolution each year in a perfunctory manner and leave knowledge of its details behind in the schoolroom, but they continue to be fascinated with their Civil War. A stream of books on the latter subject flows endlessly from their presses, feeding a reservoir that now probably contains nearly 100,000 volumes. And the amount of periodical literature is no less immense. Anyone, for example, who set out to read everything written about the Battle of Gettysburg would soon find that he had acquired a lifetime hobby.

Such enthusiasm is excessive, perhaps, but far from groundless; for the conflict that raged between 1861 and 1865 was unquestionably one of awesome magnitude and momentous consequence. A million casualties were counted before the eleven seceding states of the South finally admitted defeat in their efforts to establish an independent republic. Thus, at a terrible cost, the federal union was saved and its indestructibility confirmed. Democratic government had proved itself equal to the gravest kind of internal crisis. At the same time, the pernicious slavery issue was settled once and for all by universal emancipation, while in numerous ways the war speeded the emergence of the urban-industrial order that characterizes modern America.

Yet when the historical importance of the event has been fully demonstrated, its remarkable hold upon scholars and laymen alike is only partly explained. Of course, today's

American finds some of his own experience reflected in the plight of the Civil War generation. He knows what it means to live in a time of persisting crisis and to calculate daily the difference between compromise and appeasement. Furthermore, the place of the Negro in American life remains a burning issue and divides the twentieth-century nation along lines similar to those of 1860. But there is still something more—an epic quality, a textural richness—which has made this sanguinary struggle an enduring theme in American literature and folklore. In retrospect, it seems much larger than life. The swift movement and frequent engagement of massed armies, the picturesqueness of doomed plantation society, the gallantry of a Robert E. Lee and wizardry of a Stonewall Jackson, the tragic destiny of Abraham Lincoln—these are elements of what one writer has named the 'American Iliad'.

A complete history of the Civil War must include not only the four years of actual conflict but also the preliminary period of mounting sectional controversy and the dark, tangled aftermath called 'Reconstruction'. Popular interest has naturally centered upon the war itself, a war that still goes on as countless pens everlastingly prod the opposing armies to life and send them into action, covering every inch of ground, dissecting every battle decision, exploring all that happened and might and should have happened. As a major historical problem, however, the war can be reduced to one simple question: Why was the Confederacy defeated? And in the answers given, despite varying emphases, there has been a considerable amount of agreement. The North was immensely superior in manpower and material resources; Lincoln towered above Jefferson Davis as a national leader; the fetish of state sovereignty weakened the Confederacy, and so did inept diplomacy, short-sighted financial policies, and the pressure of the Federal blockade; the South's stubborn devotion to slavery handcuffed its friends abroad; Southern generalship, although often superb, failed at certain critical moments; and in the later stages of the conflict Southern morale began to disintegrate. These are the determining factors commonly discussed by historians, who for the most part argue over particulars without manifesting any general, fundamental cleavage. The war itself, in other words, has inspired an enormous body of historical writing, including some of admirable quality, but it has not been the subject of a great historiographical debate.[1] The problem of causes, on the other hand, is a major battleground of American scholarship; Reconstruction history likewise crackles with significant controversy; and between the two there are strong interpretative links. This essay therefore circles the mass of war literature to survey what historians have written about the sweep of events toward disunion before 1861, and about the hard road to reunion after 1865.

To seek the origins of the Civil War is to range over much of the nation's early history. One line of investigation traces divergent views of the relationship between states and central government in the federal structure of the republic, with particular attention to the doctrine of state sovereignty and right of secession as enunciated by John C. Calhoun. Another approach to the problem finds deeper meaning in the economic bases of sectionalism, in the challenge of a rising industrial capitalism to agricultural interests and the Jeffersonian image of a happy, rural America. Still another emphasizes the role of political parties and especially the upheaval in the 1850's, which brought death to the Whig organization, disruption to the Democrats, and the emergence of a new sectional power—the Republicans. Again, the ultimate source of civil conflict can be sought in the very character of the American people, with their Revolutionary tradition of appealing from law to moral justice, and their frontier heritage of restless individualism, resistance to authority, and physical violence.

Yet no matter how much weight may be given to other factors, the primary focus of sectional strife was unquestionably the institution of Negro slavery, which by 1845 existed in fifteen Southern states from Delaware to Texas. Not a critical issue in the nation's infancy, when many enlightened Southerners looked forward to its eventual demise, slavery

[1] A brief introduction with some lively differences of view is David Donald, ed., *Why the North Won the Civil War* (1960).

became an explosive subject of controversy in the second quarter of the nineteenth century as a result of several important developments. First a spectacular expansion of cotton culture greatly reinforced the value of slave labor. Then several slave uprisings frightened the South just as a rising spirit of humanitarian reform in the North was spawning its vigorous attack upon the system. Caught between the realities of his situation and the vituperative criticism of abolitionists like William Lloyd Garrison, the Southerner choked back all apologies and began to invoke religion, science, and history in the defense of slavery as a positive good. With this plenary commitment, the boundary separating free from slaveholding states became a deep moral chasm, bridged increasingly by mutual bitterness rather than understanding.

However, since abolition itself was clearly not within the constitutional power of Congress, only certain peripheral aspects of the slavery issue could seriously disturb national politics. Most troublesome by far was the question of whether the 'peculiar institution' should expand westward with the nation; indeed, all the major crises over slavery were bound up with the process of creating new territories and admitting new states to the union. Many moderate Northerners who rejected the extreme views of abolitionism approved the 'free soil' principle of confining slavery to the states where it already existed. Southerners, in return, partly because they were afraid of becoming a helpless political minority, demanded equal access to the virgin lands of the West. In between were the champions of compromise like Stephen A. Douglas, who argued eloquently, but in vain, that the whole problem could best be left to the judgment of nature and the territorial residents themselves. This was the persisting controversy that eventually led to disunion, and through it ran a strange irony. The amount of Federal territory congenial to slavery actually dwindled as the years went by, while sectional feeling on the subject grew steadily more intense, until by 1860 the nation was utterly distraught over an issue that had lost much of its practical significance. For historians seeking to understand the anomaly, there are two main avenues of thought. Either the

American people plunged into civil war for light and transient reasons, or else the spectacular quarrel over slavery in the territories was merely the skirmish line of a larger and more fundamental conflict.

The descent from argument into violence at Fort Sumter followed a sequence of critical decisions reached between November 1860 and April 1861—decisions that summed up an era and embodied the major elements of sectional discord. First came the election of Abraham Lincoln to the presidency by Northern votes alone, then the secession of states in the deep South and the formation of the Confederacy, and finally the Republican leadership's refusal either to offer substantial concessions or to acquiesce in a peaceable separation. Each of these steps toward disaster has been carefully studied by scholars, but the extraordinary action of the South properly commands the most attention. Secession, on its face, was wantonly premature. The victorious Republicans were committed only to the exclusion of slavery from the remaining territories, something that climatic conditions had already partly accomplished, and they were clearly pledged against interference with the institution in the Southern states themselves. Lincoln, considered unusually bold for expressing a hope that slavery might eventually disappear, nevertheless expected it to survive for perhaps another hundred years. In any case, the Republican party controlled neither Congress nor the Supreme Court and was therefore still incapable of achieving even its most limited objectives. Whatever threat to slave society could be read in the verdict at the polls, it was plainly not an immediate one. Yet the Southern states, adding anticipated injuries to those already felt, began leaving the union soon after Lincoln's election, without waiting to see how he would conduct himself as president. Here, truly, was a headlong rush into revolution, and the accumulation of reasoned purposes and unreasoning fears that actuated it will always be the heart of the matter for anyone investigating the causes of the Civil War.

Ultimately, however, the choice between peace and war was made by the North when it decided to keep the United

States intact by force of arms. Again and again, as the mighty struggle progressed, Lincoln asserted that his paramount object was preservation of the union, not the overthrow of slavery. But in the Emancipation Proclamation (1863) he bound these purposes firmly together, and when the South accepted defeat in 1865, it did so knowing that slavery had expired with the Confederacy. Thus the two main consequences of the war were never in themselves subject to question after Appomattox. It was the multitude of problems attending reunion and manumission that delayed reconciliation for so many years and produced scars which are not yet entirely healed. The principle of national unity had indeed triumphed, but on what terms, precisely, and by what methods, was the conquered South to be reincorporated in the system that it had tried to destroy? The Negro had been lifted out of slavery, but how far? What place was he now to occupy in the American social order? These questions, which would have been hard enough to answer *in vacuo*, were hopelessly entangled with each other and with political considerations, economic interests, and the war's abundant legacy of bitterness.

Lincoln wanted the reconstruction of the South to be simple, clement, and under presidential direction. According to his best-known plan, a small minority of citizens, having taken an oath of loyalty and received amnesty, could organize a government in any ex-Confederate state, which would then quietly resume its normal place in the framework of the union. When Andrew Johnson succeeded the murdered Lincoln, he pursued approximately the same policy, so that by the end of 1865 ten states had reconstructed themselves in the prescribed manner and needed only the formal recognition of Congress. But Congress adamantly refused to seat their newly elected representatives and instead developed its own more rigorous program for the liquidation of rebellion.

This peremptory decision sprang from a complex of factors and motives, including the conviction of many congressmen that reconstruction was primarily a legislative rather than an executive responsibility; Republican suspicion of Johnson (a Southerner and a Democrat); a widespread feeling that treason should be sternly punished; a sincere concern for the welfare of the freedmen; certain imprudent actions of the Lincoln-Johnson governments, particularly their enactment of stringent 'black codes' for the control of Negroes; a determination to maintain the political supremacy of the Republican party; and the fear that a resurgent South would challenge the protective tariff, national banking system, and other economic by-products of the war. 'Radical Reconstruction', in short, was an effort to insure the benefits of victory against postwar erosion by erecting governments in the South that were thoroughly purged of the slaveholders' influence and submissive to Republican leadership. Such a transformation could be brought about only if the freed slaves were raised up as a political counterforce to their erstwhile masters; hence Negro suffrage became the keystone of the Radical program.

The Radical-Republican majority in Congress imposed its will upon President Johnson and punished Southern contumacy by instituting a comprehensive system of military rule that lasted a decade in some states. These were the years of Negro-Carpetbagger government under army protection, of lawless reprisals by the dreaded Ku Klux Klan, of wholesale corruption in public life—the dismal closing phase of the sectional conflict. Yet the period was also one of significant beginnings, when the thrust of economic change carried South and North alike into the modern industrial world and tended to make the old hatreds not only obsolescent but unprofitable. Military Reconstruction, although shored up with additional legislation, gradually gave way under the pressure of Southern resistance and Northern disillusionment. In 1877 the last Federal troops were withdrawn from the South, and the last Radical régimes were overthrown, while the Negro, a pawn no longer usable, was callously surrendered to white Southern authority with all the empty promises of equality still ringing in his ears.

Reconstruction presents something less than a classic problem in historical causation; for its events, unlike those of the 1850's, did not converge upon one supreme crisis that exacted total commitments. Instead, the era was essentially anticlimactic, descending from the sharp tragedy of Lincoln's assassination to a blurred ending in weary abandonment. Yet in the very ugliness of the times there is a fascination, and in their unusual complexity there is a severe test of the historian's skill. As the sequel to a great civil war, was Reconstruction shamefully harsh or surprisingly lenient? Was the presidential plan of restoration a sound one? Could Lincoln have succeeded where Johnson failed? Was the latter a miserable bungler or a heroic victim? What were the primary motives of the Radical Republicans? How bad were the Carpetbag governments? How well did the freedman meet his new responsibilities? What part did terrorism play in the ultimate triumph of the Southern 'redeemers'? When did racial segregation harden in its elaborate mold? Such questions continue to be especially worth asking and answering because of the long shadow that Reconstruction cast into the twentieth century.

But there is another, somewhat dimmer shadow that falls the other way; for in written history the influence of an age extends backward as well as forward. The historian's awareness of Reconstruction inevitably affects his interpretation of the Civil War and its origins, just as the four terrible years themselves intrude forcibly upon any study of the preceding decades. And at times the sensitive scholar cannot resist the temptation to confront Americans of 1860 with the impatient question, 'Was it worth the price?'

Over the years Civil War scholarship has become not only more comprehensive and sophisticated, but also more self-conscious; in fact, there is currently a strong disposition to write about what has been written on the subject. These historiographical studies admittedly have characteristic faults mixed with their virtues. In summarizing and classifying a historian's work they necessarily oversimplify it, and by raking out his most unguarded statements they may even reduce him to caricature. Indeed, under sedulous analysis, the rich variety of Civil War historical writing tends to shrivel into formula. Yet with all its hazards the study of interpretative trends can yield valuable results.[1]

The first stage of Civil War historiography was a literary continuation of the hostilities. Bristling with vindication, it fastened the blame for disaster upon individual villains and treated the sectional conflict in narrow constitutional and moralistic terms. But toward the end of the century, with Reconstruction and its animus receding into the past, a second generation of historians began to examine the evidence more dispassionately. They wrote at a time when history was becoming a professional discipline, when the spirit of sectional reconciliation and aggressive nationalism fostered a general acquiescence in the outcome of the war, and when the illusion of Anglo-Saxon superiority was helping to immure the Negro in his dungeon of caste. The outstanding figure among them was a businessman-turned-scholar, James Ford Rhodes.

In his multi-volume *History of the United States from the Compromise of 1850*, which started appearing in 1893, Rhodes presented a Northerner's account of the Civil War, but tempered it with sympathy for the South and a willingness to apportion responsibility between the sections. While concluding that secession was 'wrong and unreasonable', he attributed it primarily to broad, impersonal forces, rather than to the sinister purposes of a few men; and he associated himself, although somewhat equivocally, with those who believed that the conflict was 'irrepressible'. Slavery, according to Rhodes, constituted the 'sole cause of the war'. By this he meant that all other contributing factors were subordinate to the slavery issue and causally insufficient without it. 'If the negro had never been brought to America,' he declared, 'our Civil War could not have occurred.'

Rhodes's views were shared in large measure by a number of his contemporaries, including John W. Burgess, a Columbia

[1] The most comprehensive historiographical study, and one to which I acknowledge much indebtedness, is Thomas J. Pressly, *Americans Interpret Their Civil War* (1954), concerned primarily with the problem of war causation. There is no equivalent work on Reconstruction history.

University professor with roots in Tennessee Unionism. Burgess, to be sure, was more inclined to see the war as a struggle between nationalism and particularism. He placed the theory of state sovereignty alongside slavery as an evil that brought on secession and had to be eliminated in the name of progress. Thus, in one respect, Burgess was more representative than Rhodes of the so-called 'nationalist tradition' in Civil War historiography.

When the two men dealt with the postwar period, however, their sympathies shifted emphatically to the white South and so, in effect, to the principle of local self-rule. Both of them looked upon Radical Reconstruction as an utter calamity. Rhodes said that the program 'pandered to the ignorant negroes, the knavish white natives and the vulturous adventurers who flocked from the North'. Burgess, calling it a 'frightful scourge' and a 'blunder-crime', found the basis of true sectional reconciliation in Northern acceptance of Southern racial attitudes. The two historians openly assumed the hopeless inferiority of the Negro, and it was this racism, thoroughly typical of the age, that controlled their verdict upon Reconstruction.

The Rhodes-Burgess interpretation of the Civil War period, favoring the North up to 1865 and the South thereafter, won enough respect in both sections to approach the status of orthodoxy. Although criticized and revised in the years that followed, it remained fundamentally the standard way of looking at the subject. For one thing, the interpretation had the comfortable effect of ratifying the ultimate results of the conflict, including reunion, emancipation, and the restoration of white supremacy. For another, it was in perfect harmony with the apotheosis of Abraham Lincoln, who had saved the union and freed the slaves, but who presumably would have opposed Radical Reconstruction. Yet the very ambivalence with which it blunted earlier sectional partisanship made the Rhodes-Burgess synthesis to some extent self-impugning. In it, a just and necessary war brought an odious aftermath; the Republicans who were so right in the 1850's became tragically wrong a decade later; and although Nature had designed the Negro for a subservient role, slavery was wholly evil, and its extirpation worth the cost. Such a cluster of contrary tendencies not only invited modification but served as a point of departure for divergent lines of thought.

The influence of Rhodes and Burgess proved to be most durable in Reconstruction history. One reason for this was that their views reinforced those of William A. Dunning, who by the turn of the century was establishing himself as the foremost scholar in the field. Dunning's importance accrued less from his own writings than from the work of numerous graduate students whose research he supervised at Columbia University. The valuable monographs on Reconstruction in individual states which issued from the Dunning group set high standards of scholarly thoroughness and restraint, but they were written by Southerners and in general perpetuated the Rhodes-Burgess interpretation.[1] Dunning himself saw Reconstruction as 'the struggle through which the southern whites, subjugated by adversaries of their own race, thwarted the scheme which threatened permanent subjection to another race'. In the course of time, to be sure, racial bias diminished or at least became less explicit, emphasis shifted more toward economic aspects, and the remarkable complexity of the Reconstruction era was increasingly recognized. But the pro-Southern viewpoint of Burgess, Rhodes, and Dunning continued on the whole to be the orthodox one, reaching its height of popularity with the publication of Claude G. Bowers, *The Tragic Era* (1929), and George Fort Milton, *The Age of Hate* (1930). The Bowers volume, by an ardent Democrat, had all the vehemence of a political tract, while Milton's study completed the rehabilitation of Andrew Johnson, for whom Rhodes had shown little respect. Paul H. Buck's *The Road to Reunion, 1865–1900* (1937), although written in a tone of thoughtful neutrality, seemed to acquiesce in the racial settle-

[1] Representative works of the Dunning school include Dunning's own *Reconstruction, Political and Economic, 1865–1877* (1907); James W. Garner, *Reconstruction in Mississippi* (1901); Walter L. Fleming, *Civil War and Reconstruction in Alabama* (1905); and Charles W. Ramsdell, *Reconstruction in Texas* (1910).

ment that accompanied the close of Reconstruction. Consequently, it did not represent a departure from the Dunning
persuasion.

The continuity so visible in Reconstruction historiography
between the 1890's and the 1930's was not matched in the
literature concerned with the coming of the war. True, one
can see the outline of a 'nationalist tradition' extending from
the Rhodes *History* to Arthur Charles Cole's *The Irrepressible
Conflict, 1850–1865*, published in 1934, but within its vague
limits there was much variety, and toward the end of the
period it came under frontal assault. Moving away from a
narrow concentration upon the slavery issue, historians like
Edward Channing found the sources of civil conflict in the
development of two distinct national cultures, so different in
economic organization and social outlook—as well as in their
labor systems—that they 'could not continue indefinitely to
live side by side within the walls of one government'. Meanwhile, Fredcrick Jackson Turner was pointing to the crucial
role of the West in the sectional controversy and explaining
the Civil War as the product of dynamic national expansion.
These and other scholars broadened the search for causes of
the war to take into account nearly every major factor shaping
American life, but they did so without displacing slavery as
the primary focus of discord. It remained for Charles A. Beard
to push slavery aside and expose a set of compulsive economic
forces at the core of the conflict between North and South.

Beard, who had drawn insights from Marxian thought
without becoming its prisoner, was inclined toward economic
determinism of a non-schematic kind, and at the same time
devoted to the social-reform movements of the Progressive era.
He was neither the first nor the last, but certainly the most
influential historian to interpret the Civil War as a decisive
chapter in the struggle for dominion between an older agricultural order and an emerging industrial one. *The Rise of
American Civilization* (1927), written in collaboration with his
wife, pictured a 'Second American Revolution' in which the
conflict over slavery masked a sweeping transfer of power
from the 'planting aristocracy' to a new combination managed

by Northern capitalists and supported by free farmers. The political agency for this revolution was the Republican party. Lincoln's election in 1860 meant not only civil war but the revival of Federalist-Whig economic policies; and the party's long post-war rule, free of any restraint from the now deci- mated planter class, provided a favorable climate for the triumphant advance of business enterprise. To Beard the his- torian, the collision of rival economies was inevitable. To Beard the reformer, its consequences were repulsive. Looking beyond the casualty lists and material ruin, beyond the ordeal of Reconstruction, he discovered the bitterest fruits of the war in the ruthless exploitation and shoddy social values of the Gilded Age.

A more opportune time for the publication of such views could scarcely have been chosen. Beard's preoccupation with economic factors suited the mood of the depression-ridden 1930's, and his hostility to the business community struck a responsive chord in New Deal liberalism. By disparaging the outcome of the war and the motives of Radical Republican- ism, the Beard thesis tended to merge with the Dunning inter- pretation of Reconstruction. In treating the origins of the conflict, however, the thesis broke sharply with the 'nationalist tradition' fathered by Rhodes. It belittled the significance of the slavery issue, thereby undermining the moral superiority of the Northern cause, and its representation of slave society as a useful curb upon aggressive capitalism followed a course long since charted by Jefferson Davis himself. Thus Beard offered an explanation of the war that more or less incidentally gave much comfort to defenders of the South.

The influence of Beard upon Civil War historiography was more lasting where he did not directly challenge the conven- tional viewpoint—that is, in Reconstruction history. His argu- ment that the causes of the war were almost exclusively economic, though widely accepted for a decade or so, ignored too many salient facts to pass rigorous inspection and eventu- ally lost much of its appeal. From Allan Nevins, in 1950, it received this blunt dismissal: 'Of all the monistic explanations for the drift to war, that posited upon supposed economic causes is the flimsiest.' Yet even if Beard carried his own point only temporarily, he delivered a telling blow to the Rhodes tradition and helped soften it for the attacks that soon followed from an impressive new group of interpreters, the so-called 'revisionists'.

For all their differences, the Beard thesis and the 'nationalist tradition' were alike in one important respect. Both attributed the Civil War to great impersonal forces which swept men and events along toward an irrepressible conflict. To this determinism there had always been some resistance, even from scholars who generally embraced it, but not until the 1930's did the opposition take on the appearance of a major revolt. At that point the center of historiographical interest shifted from the identification of fundamental causes to the question of whether the war had been necessary.

With varying degrees of explicitness the 'revisionists' embraced the concept of a 'needless war'. The phrase has two distinct meanings, however, and this fact is an important clue to the character of 'revisionism'. First, a 'needless war' may be one producing no beneficial results unobtainable by other means. Just such disillusionment with the outcome of the Civil War was nourished by the Dunning school of Reconstruction history and by Beard's mordant judgment upon post-war America. Augmenting it further was the thesis of some scholars that Negro slavery, if left alone, would have given way peaceably before the march of progress.[1] From the conviction that the Civil War had brought much evil and little good it was an easy step to the notion that the conflict had also been 'needless' in the sense of being avoidable. Thus an intense dissatisfaction with the consequences of the war encouraged revolt against the deterministic view of its coming.

'Revisionism' as a general outlook can be found throughout Civil War historiography, from a book by James Buchanan in 1866 to a centennial series of newspaper articles by Bruce

---

[1] Charles W. Ramsdell, 'The Natural Limits of Slavery Expansion', *Mississippi Valley Historical Review*, XVI (1929–30), pp. 151–71.

Catton in 1961. But as a recognizable school of interpretation it emerged during the years between Versailles and Pearl Harbor, a time when the American people, significantly, were experiencing a great revulsion against their participation in the First World War. The pioneer work was *The Peaceable Americans of 1860–1861*, by one of Dunning's students, Mary Scrugham. Published in 1921, this obscure monograph anticipated much of the 'revisionist' argument advanced in the following decade by more prominent scholars like George Fort Milton, James G. Randall, and Avery O. Craven. Milton's chief contribution was a weighty biography of Douglas with its thesis proclaimed in the sub-title, *The Eve of Conflict: Stephen A. Douglas and the Needless War* (1934). Randall and Craven, colleagues for a time at the University of Illinois until the latter moved to the University of Chicago, are generally considered the leading expositors of 'revisionism'. Their views were set forth in numerous articles and books, including the first volume of Randall's *Lincoln the President* (1945) and Craven's *The Repressible Conflict, 1830–1861* (1939) and *The Coming of the Civil War* (1942).

The emotional basis of 'revisionism' was a repugnance for war and to some extent an affection for the South (Miss Scrugham, Milton, and Craven were of Southern background), but the rationale was a historical reconstruction of the antebellum nation stressing its underlying unity and belittling the sources of discord. Craven and Randall were convinced that sectional differences had been exaggerated by historians trying to account for an irrepressible conflict. Neither in slavery nor in any other issue could they find adequate reason for the disruption of the union. All the 'voluminous explanations' of why Americans started killing each other seemed 'unconvincing', said Randall. Yet the war had happened. The problem, therefore, was not to identify and weigh fundamental causes, since they were inadequate, but to determine just how those causes acquired the semblance of adequacy by 1860—or, as Craven put it, 'how events got into such shape that they could not be handled by the democratic process'.

The break finally occurred, the 'revisionists' declared, because ordinary differences had become so emotionalized that the people could no longer think clearly about them. Moral fanatics and blundering politicians, by their unremitting agitation, had magnified a relatively minor issue into an overpowering one. The Civil War was thus an irrational act, fomented rather than compelled, and fought for 'unreal' or 'artificial' causes. This diagnosis had the effect of personalizing responsibility for the conflict once more. It fixed the blame upon extremists of both sections, but especially upon the antislavery radicals as the aggressors in the developing quarrel. At the same time it exalted champions of compromise like Douglas and John J. Crittenden, who were relatively indifferent to the ethical issue of slavery but highly sensitive to the danger of disunion. Naturally, such views did not harmonize well with the Lincoln legend, and Randall, often called the greatest Lincoln scholar, came very close to making Douglas his real hero for the pre-war period.

Provocative and influential, but in some respects exceedingly vulnerable, the 'revisionist' thesis added a new dimension to Civil War historiography and raised questions about the very nature of causal explanation which cannot be explored in a brief essay. The thesis did produce a significant shift of emphasis from objective to subjective factors in the sectional controversy, but its authors were on dubious ground when they treated thoughts and emotions, however intense or misguided, as something apart from reality. Critics also complained that the whole concept of a needless war, being unverifiable by historical methods, was a red herring drawn across the path of scholarship. Yet the 'revisionists' could reply that they were merely freeing themselves from the illusion of inevitability which had led earlier historians astray.

One result, at any rate, was a heightened interest in the dramatic events and decisions that filled the years immediately preceding the conflict. In *The Disruption of American Democracy* (1948), for example, Roy F. Nichols concentrated upon the period of Buchanan's presidency, while the critical winter of 1860–1 was carefully studied in David M. Potter's

Lincoln and His Party in the Secession Crisis (1942) and Kenneth M. Stampp's *And the War Came* (1950). These three works are usually associated with 'revisionism', and in some measure they do incorporate its views. But then almost any close-up of the final crisis will accent contingency, choice, and possible alternatives, rather than irrepressible forces. Even Rhodes, in describing the last efforts at compromise, explicitly refused to pronounce them impracticable and conceded that the war might at least have been postponed. Perhaps every historian of the Civil War has had his 'revisionist' moments.

By the eve of the Second World War a new synthesis of Civil War history seemed to be emerging. Exemplified in Randall's *The Civil War and Reconstruction* (1937), which is still used as a text in many college courses, it combined 'revisionism' with the Dunning view of Reconstruction, though it was generally free of Dunning's frank racism. The synthesis possessed the virtue of consistency, tending throughout to be moderately pro-Southern, or at least anti-Republican, and depicting a conflict that was neither irrepressible nor beneficial. Attuned in several ways to the spirit of the 1920's and 1930's, it enjoyed a brief period of ascendancy, only to be undermined by influences within and without the historical profession.

Even as Randall's book appeared there were signs that Reconstruction history was taking a new direction. Fresh scholarship in the field increasingly reflected the transformation of public attitudes toward race and the Negro which would culminate in the Supreme Court's famous desegregation decisions of 1954. The most explicit call for a re-examination of the whole subject was an essay published in 1939 by the Southern historian Francis B. Simkins, who had already diverged from the Dunning interpretation in earlier writings. Addressing himself primarily to his fellow Southerners Simkins urged them to set aside obsolete prejudices and study the positive side of Reconstruction. The time had come, he said, to stop treating the era as a reign of terror. A similar note was struck the following year by Howard K. Beale in an essay appealing for a more sophisticated analysis of motives

and interests, and for a renunciation of the assumption 'that
carpetbaggers and Southern white Republicans were wicked,
that Negroes were illiterate incompetents, and that the whole
white South owes a debt of gratitude to the restorers of "white
supremacy" '.[1]

Beale, however, while dissenting from the Dunning
tradition with its basis in racism, did not reject the economic
interpretation of Beard. On the contrary, his essay reaffirmed
views already set forth in a book entitled *The Critical Year*
(1930), which was essentially an elaboration of the Beard
thesis that Radical Reconstruction represented the triumph
of a consolidated Northeastern business class over its agrarian
adversaries. Generally speaking, Reconstruction history since
that time has continued to place a heavy stress upon economic
factors. In 1946 T. Harry Williams asserted in an influential
essay that Beale's 'sectional-class' explanation seemed to be
'the most nearly correct analysis of northern motivation'.[2] And
C. Vann Woodward's *Reunion and Reaction* (1951) demonstrated convincingly that the settlement of the Hayes-Tilden
crisis in 1877, nominally the end of Reconstruction, was
primarily an economic arrangement reflecting the ambitions
of railroad promoters. Yet curiously enough, the diligent exploration of economic influences has steadily weakened the
core of the Beard-Beale thesis by dispelling the illusion of
massive, single-minded interest groups. The profit motive may
have been dominant during Reconstruction, but it drove men
in various directions and produced alignments that were complex, unstable, and often anomalous. Woodward, in *Origins
of the New South, 1877–1913* (1951), showed ,Southern 'redeemers' emulating and even joining Northern capitalists in
pursuit of the dollar, while Stanley Coben concluded in a
recent study that 'northeastern businessmen had no unified

---

[1] Simkins, 'New Viewpoints of Southern Reconstruction',
Journal of Southern History, V (1939), pp. 49–61; Beale, 'On Rewriting
Reconstruction History', *American Historical Review*, XLV (1939–40),
pp. 807–27.
   [2] 'An Analysis of Some Reconstruction Attitudes', *Journal of
Southern History*, XII (1946), pp. 469–86.

program to promote [and] opposed each other on almost every significant economic question'.[1]

In other ways modern scholarship has documented the shifting variety and complexity of the Reconstruction period. It is no longer safe to assume that the Radicals were a cohesive group solidly arrayed against Lincoln and Johnson, or that Johnson followed a course carefully planned by his predecessor. Stereotypes of the carpetbaggers and scalawags have likewise been shattered. And close scrutiny has revealed strange complications in the role of the Negro, his relations with the white Southerner, and his ultimate subjugation.[2] Clearly, the long reign of the Dunning interpretation is coming to an end, but as Bernard A. Weisberger points out in the latest survey of Reconstruction literature, it has not been replaced by a new synthesis.[3] The older views persist in many textbooks and in works like E. Merton Coulter's *The South during Reconstruction* (1947). Yet if the promise of the Simkins and Beale essays has been fulfilled only in piecemeal fashion, the day is fast disappearing when historians will treat the restoration of white supremacy as the happy ending of Reconstruction. For they know now that it was neither happy nor the ending.

Meanwhile, the shock of Pearl Harbor was gradually producing a climate of opinion less congenial to 'revisionist' explanations of the coming of the Civil War and by the late 1940's a reaction had set in. Heralded by such diverse critics as Bernard De Voto, Arthur M. Schlesinger, Jr., and the

[1] 'Northeastern Business and Radical Reconstruction: A Reexamination', *Mississippi Valley Historical Review*, XLVI (1959–60), pp. 67–90.

[2] See especially Eric L. McKitrick, *Andrew Johnson and Reconstruction* (1960), which is critical of Johnson much in the manner of Rhodes; David Donald, *Lincoln Reconsidered* (1956), and 'The Scalawag in Mississippi Reconstruction', *Journal of Southern History*, X (1944), pp. 447–60; William B. Hesseltine, *Lincoln's Plan of Reconstruction* (1960); Vernon L. Wharton, *The Negro in Mississippi, 1865–1890* (1947); C. Vann Woodward, *The Strange Career of Jim Crow* (1955).

[3] 'The Dark and Bloody Ground of Reconstruction Historiography', *Journal of Southern History*, XXV (1959), pp. 427–47.

Dutch historian, Pieter Geyl, this reaction in its most emphatic form amounted to a direct attack upon 'revisionism' and a return to the 'nationalist tradition' of Rhodes. That is, the concept of a 'needless war' was either categorically rejected or dismissed as historically unverifiable; the existence of a fierce, fundamental conflict between North and South was reaffirmed; the moral issue of slavery was restored to a position of primacy; and the argument that before long the institution would have passed away quietly was condemned as 'historical sentimentalism'.[1] Once again, in short, the Civil War became a costly step forward instead of a terrible mistake.

More significant, perhaps, than this outburst of dissent from writers not specializing in the field were the changes discernible in the thinking of a leading 'revisionist' like Avery Craven. Without renouncing his essentially tragic view of the war, or his deep sympathy for the South, or his distinction between fundamental causes and the factors which made them operative in 1860, Craven in his later works placed much less stress upon the factitious nature of the sectional controversy and instead emphasized the difficulty of settling great moral questions within the democratic process. In some passages he now seemed to concede the irrepressibility of the slavery issue; in others he approached the Beardian interpretation of the war as a product of the industrial revolution. *Civil War in the Making, 1815–1860*, a volume of lectures published in 1959, may be considered either a retreat from the old 'revisionism', or an advance beyond it, by the scholar who has wrestled most persistently with the problem of why the American nation broke apart a century ago.

The transitional character of recent Civil War historiography is mirrored best of all, however, in Allan Nevins's monumental study of the antebellum period, *Ordeal of the Union* (1947) and *The Emergence of Lincoln* (1950). Magnificently

---

[1] De Voto, 'The Easy Chair', *Harper's Magazine*, vol. 192 (1946), pp. 123–6, 234–7; Schlesinger, 'The Causes of the Civil War: A Note on Historical Sentimentalism', *Partisan Review*, XVI (1949), pp. 968–81; Geyl, 'The American Civil War and the Problem of Inevitability', *New England Quarterly*, XXIV (1951), pp. 147–68.

broad in their narrative scope, the volumes also embraced more than one viewpoint. On the whole, they were substantially in harmony with the 'nationalist tradition', but now and then 'revisionist' sentiments seemed to gain the upper hand. Nevins echoed Rhodes in the assertion that the war was primarily over slavery, and he followed Channing in portraying the North and South as two steadily diverging cultures. His sympathies, although not obtrusive, were plainly with the antislavery movement and hence with Lincoln rather than Douglas. Yet when he turned his eyes to the final crisis Nevins appeared to believe that war could and should have been averted. Like the 'revisionists', he stressed the failure of leadership, the 'unrealities of passion', and the pernicious consequences of the conflict. Because of these ambivalent tendencies in his interpretation, Nevins was subjected to a strange crossfire of criticism. There were Northern reviewers who found him much too tender in his treatment of slavery, while more than a few Southerners marked him down as a 'latter-day abolitionist'.

No one observing the mixed response to the Nevins volumes could doubt that Civil War history was still charged with controversy and emotion in the middle of the twentieth century. Scholarly disagreement abounded, but it had become less sharply defined and often sprang from subtle differences in emphasis. There was a perplexing variety of views, and this, together with the very wealth of factual data, made synthesis increasingly difficult. The present trend, reflecting certain aspects of the contemporary scene, is toward an interpretation less sympathetic to the South than that of a generation ago. But it is obvious that the final word will never be written, for each generation of Americans discovers some new understanding of itself in studying the era of the Civil War.

© Don E. Fehrenbacher

7

THE WORKING CLASS

BY ROWLAND BERTHOFF

IN THE United States, where it is assumed that everyone works, the term 'working class' has never been wholly acceptable. Useful enough in colloquial speech, it is as often rejected, like other economic and social class distinctions. On all levels of society, people 'work', but those for whom work is not manual labor are apt to have little sympathy for the self-proclaimed labor movement. A working-class movement, so it has long been feared, fosters un-American social distinctions in denying that the working man shares a common interest with managers, executives, professional men, and the ubiquitous amateur 'workers' for worthy causes.

The egalitarianism of this country of the common man, or of men who at least in common profess to work, is a peculiarly middle-class doctrine. Already by the early years of the nineteenth century, the age of Jefferson and Jackson, the common man was assumed to be some sort of proprietor—landowning farmer, shopkeeper, professional man, or independent artisan —or to have reasonable prospect of attaining such status. The man who worked for another regarded his position as temporary. The agriculturist without land expected to acquire his share of the public domain; the journeyman would in time become a master; the clerk could hope to set up his own shop. Persons who failed to meet these happy expectations stood out as exceptional and disturbing. They might be ignored for a time, but they could never quite be accepted as part of the normal structure of American society. The historians of the poor and the disadvantaged have, therefore, ordinarily approached them as special cases whose distinctive circumstances required justification or explanation, if not reform.

Accordingly the main stream of American historiography has flowed past these social backwaters, except in so far as they have presented special problems to the middle-class commonalty. Labor—if we limit that term to the wage-earning and servile classes—has long constituted three recognized social and historical problems: first, slavery and indentured servitude; second, immigration of poor foreigners; and of course the labor movement itself. Not until the time of the First World War did any of these long-controverted problems begin to emerge from the distorting shadow of polemics into the light of creditable history. The appearance, within a few years after 1918, of pioneering and definitive works in each of these three fields reflected a certain stabilization of an ancient social problem, a stage of relative quiescence in which at last it was possible to observe slavery or immigration or the labor movement in historical perspective. The historiography of those years laid down the terms of discussion for the next generation.

When Ulrich B. Phillips published his *American Negro Slavery* (1918), the classic work in its field, the last generation of former slaves and slaveholders, and of abolitionist Northern historians, had passed away. Half a century after emancipation a new pattern of relations between white and black seemed well established, and a Southern reinterpretation of slavery promptly appeared. The system of 'white supremacy' which had succeeded slavery was based on the common Southern assumption, shared by Phillips, that the Negro was an innately inferior being. Phillips's generation of Americans, both North and South, was not much troubled by the persistence of racial discrimination. His writings suggested that the problem of containing an 'inferior' race within a democratic society had been handled under slavery about as well as the exceptional circumstances of the case permitted. Phillips could defend slavery as the paternalistic social system of the Old South even while criticizing it as an economic institution. He did not lack sympathy for the Negro as long as the Negro remained in his allotted place.

In those same years, and far more suddenly, the old system of free immigration to America was also reformed, and another national problem seemed to have been stabilized. The Act of Congress of 1924 imposing strict annual quotas on each nationality permanently dammed the flood of newcomers. Although no classic history of immigration comparable to *American Negro Slavery* immediately appeared,[1] historians recognized that the subject was now in their domain. Thus Arthur Meier Schlesinger indicated the elemental role of immigration in his *New Viewpoints in American History* (1922); George M. Stephenson's *History of American Immigration* (1926) was the first survey of the subject not primarily concerned with the 'immigrant problem'; and Marcus Lee Hansen began, in articles later republished in *The Immigrant in American History* (1940), his fundamental restudy of the entire subject. Unlike Phillips, these historians of the immigrant were personally related to the group they were studying; they were sons of immigrant parents. They approached immigration, therefore, as a special prelude to American opportunity, not as a special exception to it.

Sober scholarship likewise entered the long-embattled history of the labor movement with the publication in 1918 of the first two volumes of John R. Commons's co-operative *History of Labor in the United States* (4 vols., 1918–35). Like Phillips on slavery or the new historians of immigration, Commons's study, which appeared during a relatively stable phase of the labor movement, in effect marked the apparent resolution of a major social problem. The national craft unions of the American Federation of Labor had held a line for some thirty years against the threat of technological displacement and its concomitant, the growing majority of unskilled and unorganized laborers. This defensive, 'job-conscious unionism', as Selig Perlman has called it in *A Theory of the Labor Movement* (1928), with its non-political, practical economic aims, seemed

---

[1] The pioneering and still unique sociological study by William I. Thomas and Florian Znaniecki, *The Polish Peasant in Europe and America* (5 vols.), appeared in 1918 but had little effect on historians for another twenty years.

to have proved itself the appropriate kind of labor movement for America. Commons and his associates and followers accordingly limited their labor history to the pragmatic story of progress toward this contemporary pattern.

Such stability as the 1920's enjoyed, whether in race relations, immigration control, or labor relations, of course soon proved to be only a precarious accommodation. As each of these old problems inched forward in the next forty years, American historians' views of the past reflected, in one way or another, their own commitments in the continuing struggle. Labor historians have changed least: most of them have been content to follow the interpretation of Commons and Perlman, just as, in spite of a spectacular shift in the balance of labor relations since 1935, the organized labor movement has not departed essentially from the pattern laid down for it by 1920. American labor history is still mainly trade-union history, with incidental attention to the unions' unsuccessful socialist and anarchist rivals.

Students of the Negro question, on the other hand, have rebelled against their master, Phillips, as a mere apologist for slavery, as his assumptions of Negro inferiority and white supremacy have been shaken by recent anthropology and by the quickening changes in American racial patterns themselves. The most recent major study, Kenneth M. Stampp's *The Peculiar Institution* (1956), though no less scholarly and considerably more detailed within its compass than Phillips, returns to the abolitionist argument 'that innately Negroes *are*, after all, only white men with black skins, nothing more, nothing less'. Yet this too is only a limited shift of interpretation; as Stanley Elkins observes in his essay *Slavery* (1959), Stampp has chosen to disagree with Phillips in a century-old debate, rather than to seek new terms transcending the arguments of either side.

Likewise much of the immigration historiography of the past forty years has run in old channels. As historians among the sons and grandsons of nineteenth-century immigrants have arisen to defend, with more or less subtlety and insight, foreign contributions to American life against the hostile criticisms of the pre-1924 nativists, few of them have sought a new frame of argument. Some have, to be sure; a generation of work on all three aspects of the labor force, for that matter, has inevitably produced history that rises well above its polemical origins. Yet among the old and still-echoing public controversies an integrated history of the various segments of the American working class remains but a remote and dimly conceived goal.

The most satisfactory approach may be found in recent studies of the pre-industrial and early industrial ages of the seventeenth, eighteenth, and early nineteenth centuries, periods in which the lack of an organized labor movement compels the historian to write instead about the laborers themselves. Two contemporaneous works, Abbott E. Smith's *Colonists in Bondage* (1947) and Richard B. Morris's *Government and Labor in Early America* (1946), together provide a definitive account of colonial labor, both indentured and free. Smith, since his chief concern is the transatlantic recruitment of laborers under indenture, also provides the most comprehensive survey of this kind of immigration—that is, of laborers without capital for investment in land or trade or even for their own passage, who comprised most of the white immigrants in the colonial period. According to the varying 'custom of the country' in the different colonies, the indentures held both master and servant to certain obligations: four or five years' service in exchange for proper treatment, instruction, and finally 'freedom dues' of clothing, goods, or money. Morris also explores other aspects of public regulation of labor relations, particularly wages, in that colonial age of mercantilist controls.

Public regulation was essential, not only because these transplanted Englishmen were accustomed to it, but because of the chronic shortage of labor to exploit the resources of the new continent. Except in New England, where the brief but numerous Great Immigration of the 1630's and a high birth rate produced a self-sustaining population, it was continually necessary to attract labor from abroad. With abundant land and commercial opportunity at hand, the indentured immigrant or apprentice was not likely to remain a member of the employed labor force after his term of service was out, but instead became a yeoman farmer, shopkeeper, or independent artisan himself a working proprietor. As Carl Bridenbaugh has pointed out in *The Colonial Craftsman* (1950), the status of journeyman was a transitory one. As the 'leather-apron' man became a 'substantial mechanic', he was no longer regarded as part of an inferior class in society. Colonial society had therefore to be continually replenished at the bottom, mostly by English servants under indenture in the seventeenth century, by Germans, Swiss, and others under the variant 'redemptioner' system in the early eighteenth, and by the beginning, shortly before the Revolution, of a more modern wave of free immigrants, largely British, attracted by the high wages which skilled labor could command in America. When wages were regulated by public authority, in fact, it was maximum rather than minimum rates that were usually prescribed, and these proved so ineffective against the perennial shortage of labor that by 1720 they were generally abandoned. In this working-man's paradise there was virtually no organized labor movement before 1800, though various associations or guilds of artisans—masters and journeymen together—have sometimes been mistaken for early trade unions.

Negro slavery evolved in the seventeenth century in response to the insufficiency of white labor and became fixed on the Southern colonies in the eighteenth. If at the outset the status of Negro and white 'servants' seems to have been indistinguishable, by 1660 a practical and legal distinction was recognized between the involuntary and hence perpetual slavery of the colored man and the temporary servitude of the white. The essential facts of Negro slavery between 1660 and 1860 are not in dispute. By the beginning of the eighteenth century it had become the labor system of the tobacco and rice plantations of the Chesapeake region and the Carolinas; in fact, it was only the perpetual servitude of large numbers of Negroes that gave stability to this large-scale agriculture by freeing the planter from the recurrent search for white laborers. From the point of view of the whites, the Negro was the original American labor-saving device, welcome to the planter who could afford slaves but offensive to the laborer or farmer who could not.

The slave-labor system expanded, declined, and then expanded again as the fortunes of Southern agriculture rose and fell. (It existed in all the Northern colonies as well, but only as an incidental part of the labor force.) The hard times in the tobacco trade in the middle of the eighteenth century led many to expect the eventual extinction of slavery. But new plantation crops—cotton and sugar cane—and land on which to grow them in the new Southwest of Georgia, Alabama, Mississippi, Louisiana, and Texas re-established slavery as the 'peculiar institution' of this greater South in the early nineteenth century, although it was abolished or gradually extinguished elsewhere in the nation. The economic necessity and profitability of slavery as the plantation labor system is still disputed by historians, but the South was not at all disposed to give it up, until emancipation was forced in 1865 as an incident of the Civil War.

Entwined among all the various roots of the War itself was the question of the morality of slavery, still being argued in the present century by such historians as Phillips and Stampp. To say the least, the relegation of Negro laborers to a caste beneath the rest of Southern society was an anomaly among the manifold opportunities which other working men enjoyed of rising rapidly to economic independence and social respectability. Yet it is also true that the original importation and the continuing subjection of the Negroes had been due precisely to the difficulty of maintaining an adequate labor force of whites in the face of such opportunity. Historians are not fully decided whether, in the seventeenth century, it was race prejudice or economic necessity that first forced Negroes into a legally submerged caste.[1] In either case, during the next 200 years the economic, social, and legal considerations were inextricably intertwined with the moral. As Allan Nevins argues in his *Ordeal of the Union* (1947), by the 1850's Southern whites

[1] The two views are argued by Wesley Frank Craven, *The Southern Colonies in the Seventeenth Century* (1949), and Oscar Handlin, *Race and Nationality in American Life* (1957).

of all classes were determined to defend this Negro-caste arrangement as the only stable pattern of social accommodation between the races that they could imagine. Few even of the minority of free Negroes, North or South, were able to cross this barrier of caste prejudice.

By 1865, when the Negro slaves were freed from legal bondage, the white working class of the country had undergone the profound economic and social changes of the Industrial Revolution. The advent of the factory system and of the mines and railways to sustain it involved a revolution not only in the physical conditions of labor but also in the laborer's economic expectations and social standing. White labor tended to sink toward a submerged caste position in industrial society which, as Southern apologists delighted to point out in the 1850's, was hardly preferable to the place of the black slave.

For a time this decline of the working man into a proletarian was held off, in certain industries such as the New England textile mills, by the recruitment of labor from the families of poor but respectable American farmers. The famous mill girls of Lowell in the 1830's were farmers' daughters who gave up none of their respectability or cultural pretensions when they left the farm, to which in any case they expected to return when they had accumulated a nest egg or dowry. Like the colonial journeyman or indentured servant, they thought of their factory work as a step toward independence.

But this was a transitory stage even at Lowell and one which hardly existed in many other industries. Usually the change from handicraft artisan to factory laborer came more abruptly. This revolution is the theme of Norman F. Ware's *The Industrial Worker* (1924). With a breadth and balance that is rare in American labor history, Ware places the incipient labor movement of that time squarely in a context of social and economic conditions, ideas, and popular attitudes. The two decades 1840–60 witnessed the essential impact of industrialization on the status of labor. At the start of this period the artisan shoemaker or weaver was still a person of recognized social standing with at least the hope of economic independence. By the 1850's in most industries the factory laborer had virtually lost hope of independence as he was degraded to a wage-earner subject to his employer's will and unable even to keep up a decent standard of living for his family. In the cotton and woollen mills and shoe factories of eastern New England and Philadelphia, in the iron works and coal mines of Pennsylvania, on the railroads, and in the building trades, a kind of labor force new to America existed, a corps of working men still legally free to become employers or land-owning farmers but practically helpless to do so.

The thoroughness of this change was difficult for the land-owning or middle-class 'common man' of the time to comprehend or accept. Not until recent years, for example, have historians questioned the notion that any depressed factory hand had the practical recourse of going West and taking up a farm. And even though this traditional Western 'safety valve' for discontented city laborers has been flatly disproved, it still survives as a hardy American folk-belief.[1]

The emergence of a modern working class was hastened by an equally modern kind of immigration. The beginning of American industrialization, about 1815, was also the virtual end of indentured immigration. The new economic forces of the nineteenth century—the agrarian and industrial revolutions which swept country after country of Europe in that liberal age—turned peasants and artisans loose from old constraints of many kinds. The millions of them who left for America between 1815 and 1865, and the Europe which they left, are the subjects of Marcus Lee Hansen's comprehensive survey, *The Atlantic Migration* (1941). Poor immigrants now were entirely free of the old legal status of bond servants, but their technical liberty to sell their labor and use their wages as they wished did not hide from them, though it might from

---

[1] Carter Goodrich and Sol Davison, 'The Wage Earner in the Westward Movement', *Political Science Quarterly*, L (June 1935), pp. 161–85, and LI (March 1936), pp. 61–116; Fred A. Shannon, 'A Post Mortem on the Labor-Safety-Valve Theory', *Agricultural History*, XIX (January 1945), pp. 31–7.

others, the rigidity of their new industrial status. Instead of a perennial shortage of labor, America by the 1840's intermittently found itself with far more laborers than its infant commerce and industry could readily absorb. As Brinley Thomas has established in an ingenious study in historical economics, *Migration and Economic Growth* (1954), this European surplus labor force prodigiously stimulated American industrial growth in the middle third of the nineteenth century. As one wave of newcomers found jobs, new waves were in turn drawn from abroad by the industries that had been thus established.

What was stimulating to the American economy, however, was not in all respects so beneficial to the immigrant laborers themselves. Great numbers of them were of nationalities and cultures hitherto little seen in America. The new laborers thus soon came to be doubly different from the old artisans. They were now apt to be Germans, French Canadians, or, most notably, Irish. Like earlier immigrants, most of them were peasants in origin, but unlike their predecessors, whose servitude had often led to land ownership, they were caught in the new urban, industrial proletariat. The economic and social morass in which immigrant laborers could be mired is incisively analyzed by Oscar Handlin in *Boston's Immigrants* (1941), a book which is a landmark in the historical use of sociological concepts. The Irish cottiers who could go no farther than Boston, the closest large American port, were the classic type of poor peasants struggling to come to terms with a crowded labor market, makeshift housing, and a native American population unsympathetic to their culture and hostile to their religion. A minimal relief from their economic plight appeared, largely outside of Boston, in the labor needs of railroad contractors and the textile mills, but their social and cultural discordance with their surroundings continued, partly because of their identification with the new and strange working class.

The organized labor movement of these early industrial years was weak. Norman Ware distinguishes between two phases of its history before 1860. In the first, down to about

1850, the various local trade unions vainly sought to maintain the old community of interest between journeymen and masters and the working conditions of the fast-vanishing handicraft age. These years were also characterized by various movements, some of them political, for labor reform: to make land available to the working man, to provide his children with public education, to establish co-operative workshops and stores. In spite of the radical reputation of the reformers, many of them were actually middle-class persons, and most of their proposals sought the traditional goal of opportunity for the working man to free himself from any fixed status like that of the new proletariat. After 1850 the labor movement, in the hands of working men themselves, adopted more modern aims. 'They had accepted,' Ware says, 'the inevitable loss of status involved in the Industrial Revolution and had organized to demand, in lieu of that status, wages, hours, and conditions of work . . . for their own crafts.' The fact that by then many of them were immigrants with a European attitude toward social class helped reconcile them to this situation, new though it was to America. But their organizations were still weak and their demands unfulfilled.

Among the immigrants of the nineteenth century, to be sure, poor laborers were still a minority. Many European farmers, mostly German, Scandinavian, and British, who brought capital to invest in American farms of their own, never entered the employed labor force or, like many of their colonial predecessors and American contemporaries, joined it only in order to acquire means and experience for undertaking American agriculture. They were part of the westward movement of American farming in the great days of the last frontier. It is true that they, like every group of foreigners, faced some form of the difficulties of the poor Irish laborers in adjusting to American life. The story of the Scandinavians' cultural transition has been particularly well told in Theodore C. Blegen's *Norwegian Migration to America* (2 vols. 1931–40) and George M. Stephenson's *The Religious Aspects of Swedish Immigration* (1932). Strange though prairie life was to these old-world farmers, however, it seems to have afforded them more scope for their own kind of life—to judge from the generally cheerful tone of these histories—than the immigrant members of the industrial working class usually enjoyed.

During the great age of industrialization between the Civil War and the First World War—the age also of mass immigration and of viable labor organizations—the largely immigrant working class fit less and less well the traditional American norm of independent farming and business proprietorship. No full-scale history of immigration since 1865 has yet appeared, but in his short and impressionistic *The Uprooted* (1951), Oscar Handlin sympathetically sketches the dilemma of the deracinated peasant immured in an American city antipathetic to his customary way of life and thought. The problem was perhaps most acute for the millions of Italians, Poles, Russian Jews, and other peoples who came from southern and eastern Europe in the late nineteenth century. This 'new immigration' has not yet been adequately explored by historians; after a spate of contemporary volumes which mixed history with prescriptions for the 'immigrant problem', the only comprehensive study of one of these groups is still Robert F. Foerster's *The Italian Emigration of Our Times* (1919).

Each group of foreigners had to suffer anew all the troubles that the Irish peasant had encountered here—the slum tenements, the unskilled labor at marginal wages, the struggle to maintain some form of the foreign church and community in a country where individualism, even selfishness, was more highly valued. Themselves the impotent tools of the industrial machine which made it possible for them to live at all in America, they were commonly blamed by Americans for all the social evils of the Industrial Revolution. John Higham's *Strangers in the Land* (1955) accounts for this American nativism in terms of reaction to the recurrent economic and social crises, from the depression of the 1870's to the post-war hysteria that produced the restrictive legislation of the 1920's. Although nativism was unfortunately expressed as simple anti-Catholicism, anti-radicalism, or racial superiority, it at least embodied an awareness that the new industrial age entailed novel problems which the mercantile and farming society of the old America had not known. Among these problems was the yet unwelcome idea of a permanent working class.

While southern and eastern Europeans swelled the ranks of unskilled labor, western European immigrants moved up in the industrial hierarchy and in social repute. These skilled immigrants enjoyed American acceptance, or indifference, for their evident ambition as individuals, though they never quite abandoned their European working-class identity. Preeminent in this respect were the English, Scottish, and Welsh craftsmen of my *British Immigrants in Industrial America* (1953). Although they were not subjected to American nativism, and in fact themselves participated in it, they maintained the same kind of immigrant community life, if not with the same desperate intensity, as the less fortunate nationalities. As industrial working men, their group consciousness took the form of trade unionism, for leadership in which their old-country experience had prepared many of them.

During and after the Civil War national unions were established in a number of trades. Several of them have been described in recent historical monographs, usually of indifferent quality. These studies, together with a few biographies of labor leaders, several accounts of major strikes and other violent episodes, and the standard histories of the Knights of Labor and the American Federation of Labor, constitute the bulk of American labor history. Much of this literature falls into a narrow category of institutional annals, too often flat and prosaic—or pragmatic, to use the more charitable description of the Commons school—and evidently inspired by their authors' dedication to labor's side of labor relations. Strikers are 'heroic' and laborers 'embattled', for example, in Almont Lindsey's *The Pullman Strike* (1942), while their opponents are explained only as 'hardheaded businessmen'. Such labor history typically lacks any larger perspective than that of the men and organizations who themselves fought the good fight. An author thus closely identified with his subject is as much a part of the labor movement itself as of the historical profession. Some of this work, in any case, is more social science than history, expressly designed to guide the contemporary labor movement along proper principles rather than to place its history in the larger context of the American past. Outside the Commons tradition, Philip S. Foner's *History of the Labor Movement in the United States* (2 vols. 1947–55) is the most original and detailed of the recent general reassessments of the field, but its Marxist assumptions make it also the most didactic.

David Brody provides a better model for labor history in *Steelworkers in America* (1960). Dealing with the time, in the early years of the twentieth century, when labor unions hardly existed in the steel mills, Brody broadens his scope to comprehend the industrial economy and technology which first undermined the old craft unions and then laid the foundation for the welfare capitalism and industrial unionism of today. Equally understanding of captains of industry and of working men, of the old craftsmen and the unskilled 'new immigrants', this is labor history in the best and broadest sense.

National craft unions were established in the 1860's and 1870's, notably among the shoemakers, iron moulders, machinists, coal miners, and building tradesmen. Their leaders made several abortive attempts to combine in a national federation until, in the hard times of the 'eighties, the Knights of Labor caught the fancy of working men. Less an 'industrial' union (to which it has often been likened) than an indiscriminate collection of national and local craft unions and hitherto unorganized unskilled laborers, the Knights also represented the final attempt of labor to reject the consequences of industrialization and even, through co-operative shops, to restore in some measure the independent artisan of old. For lack of a systematic program or of firm control, the Knights drifted first into the successful railway strikes of 1885 and then into the disastrous movement of 1886 for the eight-hour day. At the same time, however, the less ambitious craft unionism of the new American Federation of Labor, though it did not immediately win labor a larger share of the national income, proved able at least to survive the dark days of the Homestead steel strike of 1892, the Pullman railway strike of 1894, and the virtual destruction of the steel workers' union in the strike of 1901, until a more hopeful era might dawn.

It was an unusual union like the United Mine Workers —founded in 1890 as one of the few 'industrial' unions of all the workers in an industry—that could surmount the complex divisions within the labor force of that time. Differences between skilled craftsmen and common laborers were reinforced by ethnic lines in many industries. The northwestern Europeans who had first secured a foothold in America still held the better jobs, while unskilled Italians and Slavs, like Irish and German peasants before them, had to start at the bottom. Given the central place of the church in the life of immigrant communities, the fact that many of the newcomers were Catholics or Jews intensified the economic and social distinctions, and in politics the readiness of each nationality to rally behind one or the other major party, according to local circumstances, made independent political action by labor virtually impossible.

Even within the Catholic Church there were divisions, again largely on ethnic lines, which for a time threatened the unity of the labor movement. The well-established Irish by then controlled the Church in America, to the annoyance of smaller groups and later arrivals such as the Germans, French Canadians, Poles, and Italians. The practical resolution of this dissension in the 1890's, recounted by Colman J. Barry in *The Catholic Church and German Americans* (1953), was closely related to the success of certain Irish-American prelates in winning, against conservative opposition, papal sanction for the organization of labor. The latter is the subject of Henry J. Browne's *The Catholic Church and the Knights of Labor* (1949). If by the turn of the century the Church played a fairly passive role in the labor movement, at least the religious divisions within the working class had been minimized. The religious peculiarity of a group might, on the other hand, conduce to the strength of the labor movement within it, as Melech Epstein demonstrates in *Jewish Labor in U.S.A.* (2 vols. 1950–3).

One segment of the working class which was not organized,

either in the late nineteenth century or thereafter, was agricultural labor. As Paul W. Gates has demonstrated in a number of articles,[1] a force of agricultural laborers existed, as did a class of tenant farmers, long before the end of the frontier which supposedly assured to all farmers land of their own. With the steady closing of the frontier toward the end of the century, the growth of this class of landless men at last aroused public alarm, though of a different sort from that which the industrial laborers excited. The latter's dependent position was usually held to be their own fault, whereas the agricultural laborer was all too obviously the victim of circumstances beyond his control: the exhaustion, after 300 years of settlement, of the supply of new land.

In the South it was not at all surprising that a class of landless laborers should exist. The end of Negro slavery in 1865 was merely the beginning of the alternative system of share-cropping in the cotton belt. Nominally a tenant on an annual lease, the share-cropper, whether a freedman or a poor white farmer, was hardly more than a peasant laborer, particularly when enmeshed in perennial debt to the planter or storekeeper. Sympathy for the plight of this class, and yet a clear appreciation of the entire economy and society of which it was part, distinguish the definitive history of the South in these years, C. Vann Woodward's *Origins of the New South* (1951), which is unusually effective as a history of labor for being far broader than a 'labor history'.

The newness of the New South was supposed to lie in the introduction of industry—particularly cotton mills and steel mills—into that section, and with it a new industrial labor force. The latter was recruited from the poor white farmers, for whom a new era of opportunity was proclaimed. The opportunity ordinarily consisted of low wages and child labor in a company-dominated town. The surplus agricultural population of the South nevertheless flocked to supply the needs of industry, discouraging, as slavery had formerly done, any considerable immigration of labor from abroad.

[1] Summarized in his essay in *The Frontier in Perspective*, ed. Walker D. Wyman and Clifton B. Kroeber (1957).

In fact, after mass immigration to the United States was cut off by the First World War and the legislation of the 1920's, the South furnished an alternative source of labor for Northern as well as Southern industry. As European immigration dwindled, Southern Negroes and whites, together with Mexicans and Puerto Ricans in some places, became the newest migrant groups in the cities of the Northeast and Middle West. The history of these latest contingents of the labor force is still too recent to have been written in any but general terms.

For the same reason the recent history of the labor movement remains almost wholly in the hands of chroniclers and labor-relations specialists. And yet almost the entire history of effective trade-unionism has occurred in the last quarter-century. Down to 1935, apart from a few minor and mostly temporary gains during the First World War, the labor movement, still under the aegis of the American Federation of Labor, failed to expand or even to maintain organizations in such basic industries as steel and automobiles. Public opinion, still firmly cast in the mold of the middle-class common man, hesitated to accept a class-conscious lower order as a permanent fixture of American society. This attitude the courts turned into public policy by declaring unconstitutional many of such wage and hour statutes as Congress and the state legislatures had been induced to pass. During the depression of the 1930's, however, the federal government shifted the balance of public policy toward a new and sympathetic view of the industrial laborer. Given official support by the New Deal, a new group of labor leaders, dissatisfied with the unambitious craft-unionism of the A.F.L., formed the Congress of Industrial Organizations and within five years brought both skilled and unskilled workers in steel, automobiles, and other basic industries into the ranks of organized labor. As Walter Galenson says in *The C.I.O. Challenge to the A.F. of L.* (1959), this emergence of the industrial labor force at long last into public recognition and organized strength constitutes 'a fundamental, almost revolutionary change in the power relationships of American society'.

The change is still obscured, however, in popular thinking. Through a combination of labor's own effort, governmental support, and the rising productivity of industry, the working-man's wages and standard of living have risen close to a middle-class level. Though frankly accepting his economic role as a member of the working class and accepted as such by others, he finds in his middle-class comforts a modern equivalent for the legendary classlessness of the pre-industrial age. It is still easy to deny the importance and even the existence of economic and social class in America.

Like the larger society of which it is a part, the American working class has always reflected the peculiarly fortunate circumstances of the New World. The American labor movement may puzzle and exasperate Europeans; the American farm hand spurns the name of peasant; even the Negro slave of the Old South was peculiar to his time and place. But neither the comparative affluence of most American working men nor their chance, in an open-class society, of rising to a higher station ought to obscure, at any period in American history, the presence of a working class at the base of society. This is the class, of persons and groups not yet able to share fully in the manifold promise of American life, which has made the dream of upward striving most precious to the middle-class American 'common man'. A coherent history of the working class, however, still awaits a coherent history of the larger American social structure, in which slaves and indentured servants, poor immigrants, and industrial laborers may be seen, for all their evident diversity, to form one of the fundamental strata.

8

THE REALM OF WEALTH

BY WILLIAM MILLER

SHOCKED by the insolvency of many of their respected friends following the financial panic of 1837, a number of leading New York merchants in 1840 drew up a list of the men they knew who continued in business in the City, and for their mutual protection placed beside each name their joint estimate of the man's wealth. No such exacting list had appeared before; and soon the authors were obliged to have numerous copies printed for their convenience and that of other New York business men who willingly added to the pool of financial information.

By 1845 this list, now published by Moses Yale Beach, the proprietor of the New York *Sun*, had grown to some 950 names 'of persons', as the title page said, 'estimated to be worth $100,000 and upwards'. Among these 950 names appeared twenty-one 'millionaires', an American expression that first gained currency in the obituaries of the snuff-maker, Pierre Lorillard, who died in 1843 and left his family valuable parcels of New York land. Off by himself at the head of the list with a fortune placed at $25 million stood another City landholder, John Jacob Astor. By far the richest man in America, he was ranked by contemporaries (whose appetite for such rankings was growing) as the fifth richest man in the world.

Astor was eighty-two years old in 1845 and had but three years to live. Most of the other New York millionaires also were old, retired men or recumbent heirs to estates (largely real estate) of men recently gone to their reward. Cornelius Vanderbilt, eleventh on the list with $1.2 million, was a younker of another sort. A robust fifty one in 1845 and a staunch Whig, during the presidential campaign the year before he had beaten senseless in a street brawl the champion pugilist and Tammany favorite, 'Yankee' Sullivan. Beach's 'Brief Biographical and Genealogical Notice' on Vanderbilt ran:

> 'Of an old Dutch root. Cornelius has evinced more energy and "go aheadativeness" in building and driving steamboats, and other projects, than ever one single dutchman possessed. It takes our American hot suns to clear off the vapors of the "Zuyder Zee" and wake up the *phlegm* of old Holland.'

It has been said on good authority that Beach's estimates, made by conservative merchants and bankers, 'in many cases seem too low'.[1] They proved high enough, however, to serve as marriage guides to mercenary mothers as well as credit guides to moneylenders. They did something more. By singling out 'some of the brightest examples of prosperity in this *touch-stone* land', Beach said, his Catalogues shone 'as beacons for those ambitious of fortune's favors'. Even his own 'brightest examples', Vanderbilt among them, felt the spell of the lights higher up.

Back in his ferrying days on the New York waterfront, 'Cornele the boatman', as he was called, would harangue idle sailors with speeches, well salted from his fine store of profanity, arguing that 'no man ought to be worth more than $20,000'. His pet target was Astor himself. By the time Astor died in 1848, Cornele the boatman had become 'Captain' Vanderbilt, the biggest steamboat operator on Long Island Sound, and his tune had changed. He now 'looked with pained surprise', writes Arthur D. H. Smith, Vanderbilt's most spirited if slightly spurious biographer, 'at the radicals who inveighed against concentration of wealth as hostile to the people's

---

[1] A model modern study of business life before the Civil War is Robert G. Albion, *The Rise of New York Port, 1815–1860* (1939). The opinion on Beach appears on p. 259.

interest. To hear " 'em ye might think a feller didn't have a right to what was his'n".[1]

By the 'fifties, Vanderbilt had outgrown the Sound and the struggle. 'I have a little pride as an American,' he wrote to his friend Hamilton Fish in February 1853, 'to sail over the waters of England and France, up the Baltic and through the Mediterranean, without a reflection of any kind that it is a voyage for gain.'

Ever one to gossip about the ranking of New York's fortunes, Cornele knew then that his own $11 million had made him the most successful man in town, if only the second richest. 'Ain't nobody but [William B.] Astor got more,' Smith has him say with characteristic egotism, 'and his old man left it to him.' Among his associates, the Captain had by now become *Commodore* Vanderbilt. By a parallel process of elevation, 'concentration of wealth' had become more sacred, even, than the private right of a man 'to what was his'n'. Rich men like himself were nothing less than object-lessons to old societies of the opportunities afforded by Democracy. Vanderbilt's object now was to drive this lesson home.

On 20 May 1853 the Commodore did in fact put to sea on a grand holiday cruise in his 'private liner', *North Star*, especially constructed in the most extravagant manner for the edification of benighted Europeans. 'I meant to have the ship in such order on our arrival in a foreign country,' Vanderbilt said, 'as to be a credit to our *Yankee Land*.' The American press readily caught the 'national character' of the voyage, as James Gordon Bennett's New York *Herald* put it. But it was the leading Liberal Party paper in Britain, the London *Daily*

[1] Arthur D. H. Smith, *Commodore Vanderbilt, An Epic of American Achievement* (1927), p. 137. Much the best book on Vanderbilt is Wheaton J. Lane, *Commodore Vanderbilt, An Epic of the Steam Age* (1942). Another illuminating book from which the account below of Vanderbilt's European journey is largely taken, is Wayne Andrews, *The Vanderbilt Legend, The Story of the Vanderbilt Family 1794–1940* (Harcourt, Brace 1941). Smith's biography, like other early ones of business men on whom adequate records seemed scarce, is occasionally fictional. But, as Lane himself says (p. 331), Smith has the estimable 'merit of catching the spirit of the times'.

News, that grasped even more clearly than the American press the full meaning of the Commodore's life and mission. After describing the unbelievably lavish appointments of Vanderbilt's 'monster steamer', the *Daily News* said:

> 'Listening to the details of the grandeur of this new floating palace, it seems natural to think upon the riches of her owner, and to associate him with the Cosimo de' Medicis, the Andrea Fuggers, the Jacques Coeurs and Richard Whittingtons of the past, but this is wrong. . . . Mr Vanderbilt is a legitimate product of his country—the Medicis, Fuggers and others were exceptional cases in theirs. . . . They were not a healthy growth, but a kind of enormous wen on the body politic. It took Florence nearly fifteen centuries to produce one Cosimo, and she never brought forth another. America was not known four centuries ago; yet she turns out her Vanderbilts, small and large, every year.'

The *Daily News* then went on to its principal point:

> 'It is time that the millionaire should cease to be ashamed of having made his own fortune. It is time that *parvenu* should be looked upon as a word of honour. It is time that the middle classes should take the place that is their own in the world they have made. . . . We want the Vanderbilts of England to feel what they are and to show it.'

Three years after Vanderbilt's visit Queen Victoria yielded to the pressure of the Liberal party and for the first time in history named to the precious peerage a British 'millowner' without aristocratic connections. A full thirty years, however, were to pass before (in 1886) a second middle-class British business man would be made a baron. By then Commodore Vanderbilt had been dead nine years, having left an incredible fortune of $105 million in 1877. Even more incredible, in the mere eight years before his own death in 1885 the Commodore's son, William Henry, who had received $95 million from his father, had run his inheritance up to $200 million. There remained no question now as to which name stood at the very summit of the very rich in New York City, in the United States, and probably in the entire world.

The number of American 'Vanderbilts, small and large', in turn, had also soared, as the *Daily News* had foretold. Where Moses Yale Beach, in the 1840's, had found barely a score of New Yorkers worth a million dollars or more, and contemporary researches in other cities may have uncovered, all told, another score, a careful tally by the New York *Tribune* in 1892 disclosed that the number of American millionaires that year had risen above 4,000. Beach's gauge of wealth had been $100,000. But by now, estates in the millions had become much more common than those one-tenth as large only fifty years before.

Whatever may be said of the new 'Vanderbilts of England', moreover, those in America, to paraphrase the Liberal London newspaper, 'felt what they were and showed it'. In 1890 Ward McAllister, high factotum to Society's matrons for a generation, wrote that 'New York's ideas as to values when fortune was named, [had recently] leaped boldly up to ten millions, fifty millions, one hundred millions, and the necessities and luxuries followed suit'. By the turn of the century, such 'ideas as to values' (and as to 'conspicuous consumption' appropriate to values current) would swell to accommodate the $500 million Andrew Carnegie was then said to be worth. A few years later, 'in this *touch-stone* land', there would rise more breathtaking beacons still: not million- but billionaires, a term to measure the share of this world's goods that fell, early in the automobile age, to John D. Rockefeller and Henry Ford.

By the 1890's, no doubt many Americans found the 4,000 millionaires in the New York *Tribune*'s array a far more 'enormous wen on the body politic' than the London *Daily News* in 1853 had found the Medicis and Fuggers. The *Tribune*'s list, indeed, was published explicitly to refute such wild charges as that of the Farmers' Alliance in 1890, that 'there were 31,000 millionaires in the United States, all of them having accumulated their wealth by the "robbery" of the people'. By the early 1900's the number of Americans disenchanted by the spectacle of 'the idle rich' had grown much greater, and their displeasure had deepened. In 1907, for example, John D. Rockefeller lodged this complaint against newspapers that 'regard too lightly' the 'ethical duty they owe to the community':

> 'These stories about my wealth, for instance. They have a bad effect on a class of people with whom it is becoming difficult to deal . . . the stress which is laid in those stories arouses hatred and envy not against the individual only but against organized society. . . . It is the general trend I have in mind, which is arraying the masses against the classes.'[1]

Yet public sanction for the pursuit of private fortune had always been strong in America.[2] The Puritans had brought with them to Massachusetts Bay the belief that great property was the due, as its proper administration was the duty, of the blessed. Franklin's worldly maxims sped many a boy on 'The Way to Wealth'. Washington, the ideal patriot, made a fine example of himself as the richest individual of his day. Urging in 1832 that government policy favor 'enterprising self-made men', Henry Clay coined a phrase that ever since epitomized the Land of Opportunity.

Self-made men showed a dispiriting tendency to become self-serving men. But the principle of private acquisition was sustained, even in the worst of times, by the best of talents.

In 1860, at the very height of his popularity, Ralph Waldo Emerson, the philosopher of individualism, wrote: 'Each man . . . is born to be rich. . . . Poverty demoralizes.' Emerson went on:

[1] Quoted in Sigmund Diamond, *The Reputation of the American Business Man* (Harvard University Press, 1944), p. 107. This is an enlightening study of American attitudes, based on obituaries of the rich from Stephen Girard to Henry Ford.

[2] Excellent on this theme is Irvin G. Wyllie, *The Self-Made Man in America, The Myth of Rags to Riches* (1954).

'The pulpit and the press have many commonplaces denouncing the thirst for wealth, but if men should take these moralists at their word and leave off aiming to be rich, the moralists would rush to rekindle at all hazards this love of power in the people, lest civilization be undone.'

In 1872 Walt Whitman, the poet of Democracy, wrote: 'Democracy looks with suspicious, ill-satisfied eye upon the very poor, the ignorant, and on those out of business.' Whitman acknowledged that 'The depravity of the business classes of our country is not less than has been supposed, but infinitely greater.' Yet, 'for fear of mistake', he said:

'I may as well distinctly specify . . . that the extreme business energy, and this almost maniacal appetite for wealth prevalent in the United States, are parts of amelioration and progress, indispensably needed to prepare the very results I demand. My theory demands riches, and the getting of riches . . .'

In 1869 Charles Eliot Norton, the conscience incarnate of the expatriate élite, wrote: 'Whether our period of economical enterprise, unlimited competition, and unrestrained individualism, is the highest stage of human progress is to me very doubtful.' Some months later, Norton wrote from Italy that 'Rome . . . resists with steady persistency the flood of "American" barbarism and of universal materialism which is desolating Europe.' Yet even Norton, by 1883, had come to find a certain social profit in the acquisitive spirit. That year, for a decade now Professor of Fine Arts at Harvard, he wrote from his native Cambridge, Massachusetts:

'In Europe I could not but feel with pain the ill wrought by the progress of democracy—the destruction of old shrines, the disregard of beauty, the decline in personal distinction, the falling off in manners. Here, as we have less to lose, we have less to regret, and the spread of comfort, the superb and unexampled spectacle of fifty millions of human beings living in peace and plenty, compensates in a certain measure for the absence of high culture, of generous ideals and of imaginative life.'

After some twenty years of teaching Norton remained aware that 'The concern for beauty, as the highest end of work . . . forms no part of our character as a nation. The fact is lamentable,' he insisted, 'for it is in the expression of its ideals by means of the arts which render those ideals in the forms of beauty, that the position of a people in the advance of civilization is ultimately determined.'[1]

Writers more mundane than Norton sometimes joined him in urging expenditures on beautification (if not actually on furthering the ideal of beauty) as 'the highest end of work'. But it was said at Harvard even during his tenure there that 'the methods of Mr Norton were superbly out of date in our specialistic time'. And the sanctions of science, religion, and law leagued with those of philosophy, poetry, and patriotism behind the proposition that, for 'the advance of civilization', the millionaire had best stick to his last.

William Graham Sumner, the sternest of social scientists in the heyday of Darwinism—and an Episcopalian rector and professor of political science—spoke for all three fields when he said in the 'eighties:

'The millionaires are a product of natural selection, acting on the whole body of men to pick out those who can meet the requirements of certain work to be done. . . . They get high wages and live in luxury, but the bargain is a good one for society. There is the intensest competition for their place and occupation. This assures us that all who

[1] Norton's statements are from Sara Norton and M. A. De-Wolfe Howe, *Letters of Charles Eliot Norton* (2 vols., Houghton, Mifflin, 1913). These letters set off the near-Philistinism of Emerson and Whitman. The Emerson quotations are from 'Conduct of Life', as reprinted in *The Complete Essays and other Writings of Ralph Waldo Emerson* (Modern Library, 1950), pp. 695, 697, 699. The Whitman quotations are from 'Democratic Vistas', as reprinted in *Leaves of Grass and Selected Prose* (Modern Library, 1950), pp. 467, 479.

are competent for this function will be employed in it, so that the cost of it will be reduced to the lowest terms.'[1]

A few years earlier, near the end of the unnerving depression of the 'seventies, Sumner admonished those economists 'frightened at liberty especially under the forms of competition. . . . They think it bears harshly on the weak,' he wrote. 'They do not perceive that here "the strong" and "the weak" are terms which admit of no definition unless they are made equivalent to the industrious and the idle, the frugal and the extravagant. They do not perceive, furthermore,' said Sumner with apostolic sweep, 'that if we do not like the survival of the fittest, we have only one possible alternative, and that is the survival of the unfittest. The former is the law of civilization; the latter is the law of anti-civilization.'

'Civilization', conceived in Sumner's terms, must have seemed to Norton and his friends the very dregs of paradox. Sumner himself could not suck a dram of pleasure from his doctrine. But America, as we have seen, was full of men, more sanguine than the Nortons or Sumners, who found Social Darwinism as sweet as it was inescapable. By *annus mirabilis*, 1889, many of them felt, the free play in the United States of 'the incorruptible laws of nature' had carried civilization to its summit.

In June, that wonderful year, Andrew Carnegie published an essay in the *North American Review* on his favorite topic, his and other millionaires' money. In our 'Triumphant Democracy', Carnegie announced, the ancient problem of creating wealth had at last been solved:

'Individualism, [he wrote, in capitals] Private Property, the Law of Accumulation of Wealth, and the Law of Competition . . . are the highest results of human experience, the soil in which society so far has produced the best fruit. . . . Imperfect as . . . these laws . . . appear to the Idealist, they are, nevertheless, like the highest type of

[1] Quoted in Richard Hofstadter, *Social Darwinism in American Thought* (1944), p. 58.

man, the best and most valuable of all that humanity has yet accomplished.'

'The problem of our age,' Carnegie concluded, is 'but the proper administration of wealth,' so that 'the laws of accumulation will be left free; the laws of distribution free; individualism will continue.' The millionaire, as is his nature, must press on his quest for fortune. At the same time—was this his nature too? Carnegie fails to say—he must become 'but a trustee for the poor', administering 'the increased wealth of the community . . . far better than it could or would have done for itself. . . . Such,' Carnegie wrote, 'is the true Gospel concerning Wealth.'

If the 'highest type of man' thus was naturally selected by 1889 to care for those who somehow failed to make the grade, the very *best* of the best had a still loftier task: to see to it that Nature's failures did not hamper the 'highest types' by meddling unnaturally with Nature's Laws. In this work, in the Fifty-first Congress that assembled in Washington in December 1889, none could outdo the new Speaker of the House, the giant Darwinist, Thomas B. Reed. But it was in the Senate of the Fifty-first Congress, known ever since as 'The Millionaires' Club', that, man for man, 'The Preservation of Favoured Races in the Struggle for Life' (Darwin's sub-title for *The Origin of Species*) seemed most splendidly confirmed. The finest specimens of all, perhaps, were California's Senators, Leland Stanford, one of the 'big four' who built the Central Pacific railroad, and the gold-mining millionaire, George Hearst, father of William Randolph. Of Stanford, an enemy once said: 'No she-lion defending her whelps or a bear her cubs, will make a more savage fight than will Mr Stanford in defense of his material interests.' As though to show how such an assault, outside the Senate, must echo like an accolade within, Senator Hearst once told a gathering of his peers at dinner one evening:

'I do not know much about books; I have not read very much; but I have travelled a good deal and observed men and things, and I have made up my mind after all my experience that the members of the Senate are the survival of the fittest.'

And yet murmurings persisted in the millionaires' paradise. The industrious middle class was itself supposed to be the principal beneficiary of 'liberty, especially under the forms of competition'. But the very discovery of the multiplication of great fortunes in recent years, in size as in number, had come more as an incitement than an incentive to those now clearly outdistanced in the race for wealth. And there was more to it than that. By 1907, as we have seen, the murmurings had swelled to such a massive indictment that John D. Rockefeller, the master organizer, believed 'organized society' to be endangered. The 'fittest' personally, their paltry paternalism, their minions, their methods, their whole American millennium, had been marched in review and found wanting.

By 1914, when the indictment was more or less complete, Walter Lippmann could write in *Drift and Mastery*: 'No one, unafflicted by invincible ignorance, desires to preserve our economic system in its existing form.' And as for its sovereign rulers: 'The business man has stepped down from his shrine; he is no longer an oracle whose opinion on religion, science, and education is listened to dumbly as the valuable by-product of a paying business. We have scotched the romance of success.'

By the 1920's Charles A. Beard and Vernon Louis Parrington, the high priests of Progressive history, had inscribed much of the indictment in the Authorized Version.[1] By the 1930's, with certain Marxist glosses accented by the worst business depression in American annals, the appropriate readings and responses had found their way into the litany of the textbooks. And there, to this day, conventionalized, as it were, for country parsonages, the indictment rests. It has been cropped and

[1] Charles A. and Mary R. Beard, *The Rise of American Civilization* (2 vols., 1927); Vernon Louis Parrington, *Main Currents in American Thought* (3 vols., 1927, 1930), especially Vol. III, 'The Beginnings of Critical Realism in America'.

hedged, of course, along lines suggested by more recent scholarship. Yet, with all allowances made for the inevitable exceptions, there has been as yet but one tradition in the general historian's treatment of the so-called 'Robber Barons' in the misnamed 'Gilded Age'.

Let us say that E. L. Godkin, editor of the *Nation*, started it all in 1869, when he put the baronial brand on that paragon of the business breed, the ubiquitous 'Cornele'.

Having turned to railroads in 1862, Vanderbilt was to shock the middle class by quintupling his lifetime steamboat fortune in fifteen lawless years. Midway on this new course, on 10 November 1869, he unveiled atop his new railroad depot in New York City a fifty-ton bronze pediment, 3,125 square feet in area. Across this surface, in low relief, were strewn cogwheels, anchors, and other emblems of his career, 'with a colossal Cornelius Vanderbilt looming up in the midst of the chaos'. On 18 November Godkin wrote:

'In short, there in the glory of brass, are portrayed in a fashion quite good enough, the trophies of a lineal successor of the medieval baron that we read about, who may have been illiterate indeed; and who was not humanitarian; and not finished in his morals; and not, for his manners, the delight of the refined society of his neighbourhood; nor yet beloved by his dependents.'

Thereafter, in occasional newspaper stories, magazine articles, and books, the successive heroes of America's advance each fell under some disenchanted eye. Did the 'landgrabber' blaze the way to the wealth of the ever receding West? Yes, and did he not leave 'A Century of Dishonor' in Indian relations as his legacy? Did the railroad promoter give a stimulus without precedent to the private economy? Yes, and did he not blackmail cities, states, and territories, and otherwise have his hand 'pretty regularly in the public pocket'? Did the industrialist harness science to the factory system and multiply man's productivity and goods? Yes, and did not his agents prowl the very floors of Congress to purchase Protection, and his foremen brutally overwork women and children? Did the financier nurture the country's hard-won capital so that useful enterprises might grow? Yes, and did he not at the same time selfishly manipulate money and credit with his mysterious Midas touch?

Carnegie's 'Law of the Accumulation of Wealth' obviously had elicited some worrisome questions about American life by 1889. Then the terrifying business depression of the 1890's wiped out many fortunes, large and small, and weakened many surviving firms. On a diet of the dead and dying, consolidation quickened. The whole *system* of 'Individualism, Private Property, and the Law of Competition' suddenly stood bared as a Mephistophelean lure. Had America indeed sold her soul to the devil? The questions deepened. And the answers—supplied now by public and private investigators lovingly committed to exposure—offered no reprieve.

With the shocking discovery of overbearing wealth came the even more shocking disclosure of endemic poverty. There were, after all, as Rockefeller said, classes and masses in America. Moreover, as wealth and population grew, the number of the poor seemed to have grown faster. The Great West, in turn, afforded no vent, no 'safety-valve'. Indeed, the 'landgrabbers', it was said, far from opening the West to development, had characteristically kept it closed while they 'waited for the rise'.

Next, the railroad presidents, by discriminatory practices as ingenious as they were illegal, seemed to have repressed certain industries and areas as much as they had stimulated others, to have paralyzed particular enterprises even within favored industries and areas as much as they had galvanized their pets. And what of the lordly railroad men themselves, among whom Sumner had been so sure that competition would churn the cream to the top in a fine 'bargain' for society? Simon Sterne, perhaps the keenest analyst of railroad management in his day, stated in 1894: 'The first explanation' of the insolvency of most of the consolidated trunk lines at the very start of the Panic of 1893, 'lies in the fact that the railways have outgrown the ability of the community to furnish men of the high moral and intellectual order necessary for their proper administration'.

Nor could industrialists and financiers evade the accusing pen. Soon after the turn of the twentieth century, Frederick Winslow Taylor and his 'scientific management' coterie were attacking even 'the best type of management' for abdicating the 'initiative' in production processes to the whim of the individual worker. Thorstein Veblen took the attack a step further when he blandly suggested that abdication here was only to be expected, since, under capitalism, pecuniary not productive processes appropriated the talents of management. G. P. Watkins completed the logic of this phase of the indictment when he declared in 1907 that, were income more evenly distributed, the savings available to industry would be larger not smaller. 'There is a certain weakness,' Watkins concluded, 'in the argument for the importance of the rich as those performing the social function of accumulation.'

By then, much of American large-scale industry, like most of American long-distance transportation, and for similar reasons, had fallen to the care of the 'Money Trust'. Order, not cut-throat competitive growth, appeared to have become the objective of the rulers of the economy. 'But "the great banking houses",' wrote the lawyer, Louis D. Brandeis, in 1913, 'have not merely failed to initiate development; they have definitely arrested development.' He then quoted *The Engineering News*:

'We are today something like five years behind Germany in iron and steel metallurgy. . . . There are plenty of other fields in industry where . . . the real advances in the art are being made by European inventors and manufacturers. . . . With the market closely controlled and profits certain by following standard methods, those who control our trusts do not want the bother of developing anything new.'[1]

Had the Great American Experiment, then, in Moses Beach's 'touch-stone land', been all in vain? Had Emerson's

[1] Louis D. Brandeis, *Other People's Money, and How the Bankers Use It* (1914).

'thirst for wealth' only 'undone' civilization? And Whitman's
'extreme business energy' rudely frustrated 'amelioration and
progress'? In the words of Edward Atkinson, one of the most
articulate business men of the Gilded Age, had 'our whole
democratic organization' worked simply to stultify those fine
middle-class Jacksonian hopes? On 4 July 1826, the fiftieth
anniversary of American independence, the Jacksonian his-
torian-to-be, young George Bancroft, said in a commemora-
tive address:

> 'We hold it best that the laws should favor the diffusion
> of property and its acquisition, not the concentration of it
> in the hands of a few to the impoverishment of the many.
> We give the power to the many in the hope and to the end,
> that they may use it for their own benefit.'

But such 'austere and simple ideals', concludes Bray Hammond,
the eminent modern analyst of Jacksonian economics, 'were
ecologically impossible in a land of wealth and individualism'.

A 'Second American Revolution' (the phrase, of course, is
the Beards'; the idea, Progressive) had indeed taken place in
the United States in the Vanderbiltian decades surrounding
the Civil War. Woodrow Wilson spoke of the withered yield
of this revolution when he told the American Bar Association
in 1910:

> 'Most men are individuals no longer as far as their
> business, its activities, or its moralities is concerned. . . .
> There is more individual power than ever, but those who
> exercise it are few and formidable, and the mass of men are
> mere pawns in the game.'

Still a third American revolution, moreover, one brought
farther along by two world wars and the intervening world-
wide depression of the 1930's, was by then under way. In
certain senses this has been a counter-revolution, a reassertion
of the 'power of the many in the hope . . . that they may use it
for their own benefit'. The details, of course, are beyond the
scope of this essay. But we may note a few 'meddlesome'

headings: graduated direct taxes, strengthened, and strengthened enforcement of, antitrust laws; laws favoring collective bargaining; laws establishing unemployment and old-age insurance; laws furthering the collection of statistics of private enterprise for the use of public administrators newly charged with responsibility for economic wellbeing.

Has public action under such rubrics gained for the nation a new measure of economic growth *and* stability—a combination that eluded the private economy of the past? Certain economists suggest that it has. Has such public action dried up the wells of private energy and incentive? Other economists argue cogently that it has not.[1]

There is, to be sure, another side to the story of the third American revolution, but one all the worse for historians like Allan Nevins, Louis Hacker, and Edward C. Kirkland, who would now rewrite the American past in terms of what Nevins has called 'the heroes of our material growth—the Rockefellers, Carnegies, Hills, and Morgans'.[2]

In 1951, in a widely quoted address that confirmed the hardiness of the Progressive tradition, Nevins called upon American historians to right the great injustice done by that tradition to 'our business history and our industrial leaders'. These leaders, he said, should be allowed to 'stand forth in their true proportions as builders of an indispensable might', without which 'we might have lost the First World War'. As though he were talking favorably of his favorites, Nevins continued: 'This [war] by which America has been projected into world leadership, with all the exhilaration and perils . . .

[1] Exceedingly suggestive on this theme and of more use to historians than its title may promise, is Edith T. Penrose, *The Theory of the Growth of the Firm* (1959).

[2] Nevins's relevant works are too voluminous to cite here, but one may note especially his *John D. Rockefeller, The Heroic Age of American Enterprise* (2 vols., 1940), and his second version of this book, retitled *Study in Power* (2 vols., 1953). Hacker's relevant work, on the other hand, largely book reviews in recent years, is too fragmentary and fugitive. For Kirkland's position, in addition to the article discussed on pp. 153–4, see his *Business in the Gilded Age* (1952); *Dream and Thought in the Business Community, 1860–1900* (1956); and *Industry Comes of Age* (1961).

of that position, will be in some fashion connected by future interpreters, with the advent of the age of mass action, mass production, and mass psychology in American life.'

C. Wright Mills, in *The Power Élite* (1956) and other books, has already made a connection. In his view, it is war and preparation for war that alone has given the 'mass production' economy its semblance of stability and growth; it is 'mass psychology', manipulated by pre-emptive propaganda, that protects the 'warlords' and the 'corporate rich' in the 'power élite' from democratic controls.

Is this the 'masculine' legacy of 'the heroes of our material growth' that today's revisionists prefer to the 'feminine idealism' that Nevins in the same speech attributed to 'our historians in the past' who 'were apologetic about our dollars, our race to wealth, our materialism'? Which historians? One would suppose, for example, that it was not the Progressives but the new apologists who peopled the millionaires' paradise with what Parrington, materialistically enough, called 'figures of earth'.

The Progressive tradition has been militant, not apologetic. The Progressive indictment, moreover, survives in the general history books because it is a true bill.

Certainly, the Progressive indictment is not the whole truth. The Beards themselves, in fact, give the 'barons' more than their Nevinsite due: 'Above all else, the new economic barons were . . . masters of the administrative art . . . Possessed of luminous imagination, they could think imperially of world-spanning operations that lifted them above the petty moralities of the village-smith or of the corner grocer.' Here, as elsewhere, even Matthew Josephson, in *The Robber Barons* (1934), follows where the Beards lead.

Nor is the indictment the truth in the only possible perspective. And here too it is a Progressive himself who offers an alternative view. In *The Growth of Large Fortunes* (1907), G. P. Watkins is at pains to make clear that objective 'economic causes'—the legal underpinning, the corporate framework, the pecuniary standard, the force of science and technology—provided a stronger impulse than the conventional

Progressive's 'malefactors of great wealth' to the latter's own accumulations. While acknowledging that 'the United States represents all the distinctive modern economic tendencies in their highest degree', Watkins nevertheless studied 'concentration' in France, England, and Germany as well, with results relevant to those found at home.

It is, moreover, down paths indicated by the Beards' generosity and Watkins's insight that the most active revisionists, besides Nevins himself, have run. The company histories sponsored by N. S. B. Gras at the Harvard Graduate School of Business Administration and its offshoot, The Business History Foundation, indeed snuggle so closely to the 'administrative art' inside the company under study that its competitors, its customers, and indeed its relation to the country itself are characteristically slighted. In his introduction to one of the early publications of this school, Ralph M. Hower's *The History of an Advertising Agency* (1939), Gras says: 'Business history written from outside material, is but the false shadow of reality.' But is the reality less falsely represented when a part pre-empts the place of the whole, and 'inside' material even on the 'administrative art' is circumscribed at the source?

Far more important work has been done along the paths indicated by Watkins: the objective 'causes', and the international comparisons. The issue of economic growth—how to start it in 'underdeveloped' lands, and how to sustain it in 'overdeveloped' ones—has given an especially strong push to the study of America's spectacular rise. The emphasis put by the economist, Joseph Schumpeter, on the signal role of the 'creative entrepreneur' in economic growth has especially directed newly sophisticated attention to the nature and nurture of Nevins's own heroes. Historians like Fritz Redlich, Thomas C. Cochran, Arthur H. Cole, and Alfred D. Chandler, Jr., have been much more interested in understanding American material success than in glorifying it. As yet, these writers have published relatively little; and that little, rather obscurely.[1] But this is not the only reason why 'the old

[1] See especially, Fritz Redlich, *History of American Business Leaders* (1940), and *The Molding of American Banking, Men and Ideas*

consensus', as Kirkland said as late as 1960, has resisted 'a new synthesis'.

In his article, 'The Robber Barons Revisited', in the *American Historical Review*, October 1960, Kirkland offered the opinion that, at best, revisionist efforts by business and economic historians 'will only shake down a little plaster'. And he added tellingly: 'Revisionism will be most fruitful if it enters the [Robber Baron] period by the gate of politics.' It was in this connection that he quoted Atkinson on 'our whole democratic organization', as the seed of a new view.

But if Nevins may complain that Progressive historians have 'forgotten', as he said, the heroic business achievements that made the country great, the Progressives may complain that Kirkland has forgotten that it was precisely through 'the gate of politics' that the tradition was established that Nevins, he, and others would revise. It was the very subordination of democratic political and legal institutions to private economic gain that prompted the whole Progressive indictment. The economic attack only overran the cup. It is true, of course, that the Progressives numbered among their adherents many who cursed Democracy for America's plight. But there were many more who turned—not without success—to more and better Democracy to set things right again.

Nevins, to paraphrase old Sumner, would promote 'The Absurd Effort to Make History Over', by having historians omit (as he largely does himself in his studies of Rockefeller) the political side of the 'Robber Baron' coin. He would 'store up in secret', consign to the Apocrypha, as it were, the very substance of the Authorized Version. But this must only make one wonder what Rockefeller was so frightened of in 1907; and it would reduce to a riddle the whole political history of the Progressive Era and the New Deal. The third American

(2 vols., 1947, 1951); Thomas C. Cochran, *Railroad Leaders 1845–1890, The Business Mind in Action* (1953); Arthur H. Cole, *Business Enterprise in its Social Setting* (1959); and Alfred D. Chandler, Jr., 'The Beginnings of "Big Business" in American Industry', in *Business History Review*, XXXIII (spring 1959), pp. 1–31. See also Chandler's contribution, and others, in William Miller, ed., *Men in Business, Essays in the History of Entrepreneurship* (1952).

revolution, after all, did occur. To hide its causes, with the hope of finding historical justification for reversing its meddling consequences, is futile. Even *Fortune*, in September 1951, warned Nevins on 'overcorrection'.

If Kirkland, in turn, had said less of revising the Progressive indictment and more of reviewing it, he would have been more helpful. If 'our whole democratic organization' justified, as he seems to argue, all the excesses of the Robber Baron breed, it also justified the Progressive attack on them. Neither the story of the excesses nor the Progressive tradition itself cries for revision. Both may profit from elaboration. To use a word so freely given by his apologists to the scene Rockefeller harmonized, has the 'chaos' of Jacksonian individualism yielded permanently to the regimentation Wilson pointed to? As a consequence of the Robber Barons' work, do Americans now have the 'mass society' that Nevins embraces so fondly? Or did the third American revolution re-establish democratic directives? Has it preserved as *political* 'units, not fractions' those who in business, as Wilson put it, may yet remain 'mere pawns in the game'? These, I think, are relevant, not revisionist, questions.

A serious shortcoming of the Progressive indictment may well be its failure, as Kirkland suggests, to see democracy whole, with all its warts and waywardness. This failure may perhaps grow in prominence as Democracy is challenged by totalitarianism, especially of a paternalistic bent. The Progressive ideal may have been a never-never land. The task of historians, however, does not include throwing away the truth because it is not the whole truth. The whole truth may be that in political life we have but a choice of tyrannies. In 'the realm of wealth', has the 'tyranny of the mob', the tyranny of Democracy, afforded the means and incentives for the continuance of Democracy? American history, read whole, will I think confirm that it has. Let us, then, reconstruct it whole.

9

THE PROGRESSIVE TRADITION

BY ARTHUR MANN

I

THE literature about social reform from the 1880's through the New Deal has grown considerably during the past twenty years and promises to become even more sizable. Not only have a great many biographies and monographs appeared, but also general narrative accounts and attempted syntheses. And not only historians, but sociologists, political scientists, economists, philosophers, and literary critics have written about what Lionel Trilling has called the liberal (or progressive) imagination.

What strikes one immediately is that much of this literature is by the leading academic writers in America today. They include Louis Hartz, Richard Hofstadter, Arthur M. Schlesinger, Jr., and at least a dozen others who deserve to be as well known abroad as they are at home. In fact, this field has attracted so many good men in recent years that there is a shortage of talent for other areas of historical research and interpretation. Yet one has only to recall the names of Frederick Jackson Turner, Carl Becker, Charles A. Beard, and Vernon L. Parrington to be reminded that, a generation and more ago, outstanding scholars did their most important work on earlier periods in American history.

A foreigner might well wonder that so concentrated an interest in one subject should come to prevail in such a sprawling profession. Pluralistic America has no academic establishment. How could it when some eighty universities grant the Ph.D., and when first-rate scholars come from no one social class, ethnic group, religion, or section of the country? Neither dress, style, nor accent unifies the large and heterogeneous membership of the American Historical Association.

Yet most writers of American history belong to the liberal intelligentsia that voted for John F. Kennedy and, before him, for Adlai E. Stevenson, Harry S. Truman, Franklin D. Roosevelt, Alfred E. Smith, Woodrow Wilson, Theodore Roosevelt, and William Jennings Bryan. These Presidents and presidential candidates have stood, in the sum of their programs, for the welfare state, the rights of labor, urban renewal, civil liberties, equal privileges and responsibilities for women, Negroes, and other minority groups, and for helping underprivileged peoples the world over. They have stood, in short, for a progressive tradition, which the massive conservatism of many Americans accepts only reluctantly.

To say that the academy since World War II has turned to the recent liberal past is really to say, then, that professors have turned to their own particular past in search of their identity. More so than specialists in earlier periods historians of the progressive tradition ask history to be relevant to themselves, their times, and their audience. They hope to know, like all good Whigs, how their present originated and evolved.

Yet this does not explain why their books and articles have proliferated during the past twenty years. Here we might formulate a law in American historiography, namely, that the historian steps in after a movement or a process peters out. Thus it was with Frederick Jackson Turner, who called attention to the frontier three years after the Census of 1890 announced that it had 'closed', and with Marcus L. Hansen, who was opening immigration as a field for historical research just about the time when Congress slammed the door shut in the Johnson-Reed Act of 1924. And so it has been for historians of the progressive tradition.

By 1952 an age of reform formally ended. President Dwight D. Eisenhower took office on the claim that progressive Republicans could administer the welfare state better than liberal Democrats. The age of consensus had arrived, when yesteryear's heterodoxy had come to be the reigning orthodoxy,

when ideas had congealed into institutions, when statesman-
ship had turned into a form of caretaking, and when political
semantics had become as tangy as pablum. But even earlier,
in the 1940's, it was clear that the New Deal, which climaxed
the humanitarian aspirations of a half-century, was expiring
as an innovating force on the domestic front.

The time had come for stocktaking. And so the academy
stepped in to describe, account for, and evaluate a creative
impulse which, though denied in the 1880's and 1890's and
turned back in the 1920's, had defined the economic and
political goals of American life from the end of Reconstruction
to the beginning of the Cold War. The process of research and
interpretation is still going on and shows no sign of falling off.

Recent historians of this seventy-year age of reform may
be divided into three groups according to the attitudes they
bring to their subject. The partisans, of whom Arthur M.
Schlesinger, Jr., is the most brilliant, have identified themselves with the reformers about whom they write. The critics,
among whom the equally brilliant Richard Hofstadter stands
out, have probed for weakness in progressive thought. The
largest number of historians are—to borrow Professor Donald
H. Sheehan's term—middleists. Critical like Hofstadter and
partisan like Schlesinger, but less so than either, the middleists
have written most of the specialized studies. But to see these
three groups clearly we must first outline the age of reform as
scholars have come to understand it.

II

A popular textbook of some twenty years ago taught that
modern American liberalism had moved in a straight line from
midwestern Populism to Progressivism to the New Deal. This
interpretation still exists and has the same appeal as the old
Whig view of English history logically progressing from Magna
Carta to the Glorious Revolution to the Reform Bill of 1832.
It is appealing because it simplifies history and absolves the
historian from asking hard questions; he only has to place the

train on track and make it travel to its appointed end. Happily, recent scholarship has been asking tougher questions about the progressive tradition.

Let us turn first to the Populists. Formed in 1891 after two decades of agricultural depression and protest, the Populist party demanded relief from political corruption, special privilege, and bottom-of-the-barrel farm prices. They proposed to make government more democratic through the initiative, referendum, recall, and the direct election of senators. They proposed to eliminate what they thought were economic parasites through postal savings banks and the public ownership of the railroads, telegraph, and telephone. They proposed to restore prosperity through government-sponsored farm-price supports and such inflationary measures as the free coinage of silver and a national currency. These and other proposals, including a graduated income tax, rested on the assumption that if the federal government expanded its functions it could banish 'oppression, injustice, and poverty . . . in the land'. In the presidential election of 1896 the Populists endorsed William Jennings Bryan, the Democratic standard bearer, who, appropriating the free silver and political reform planks, campaigned against privileged wealth ('you shall not crucify mankind upon a cross of gold') and boss politics. William McKinley, a standpat Republican, won the contest.

All this John D. Hicks described well in *The Populist Revolt*, which was published in 1931. But he misled a generation in asserting that, because many Populist planks later became law, nineteenth-century agrarian radicalism was the grandfather of twentieth-century reform. One could say just as easily that the American income tax is Marxian in origin because in 1848 Karl Marx proposed it as a levelling device, which the Populists did not (they had in mind an equitable revenue measure). To claim that social prophecy led to social policy, one must establish the connection between the two; and neither Hicks nor anyone else has done that.

Nor was he correct in making Populism out to be mainly a Midwestern farmers' experience. We now know that the agrarian South was a stronger center for the People's party than the Midwest and the plains and mountain states.[1] Moreover, the quasi-Populism of Bryan, the Great Commoner, appealed not only to farmers but to cross-roads Americans in general: to small-town merchants, lawyers, bankers, and clerks who feared the power of big business. The same fear existed in the big cities of New York and Chicago and Boston, where intellectuals attacked the theory of *laissez faire* and wrote systematic works in defense of the welfare state.[2] This is not to say that the city was more important than the farm; the point is that the demand for social reform in the 1880's and 1890's existed, and was aborted, on many fronts.

Recent scholarship has also corrected the notion that the Populist spirit reasserted itself after the Spanish-American War and, by implication, 'caused' the ensuing Progressive Era (1900–20). The truth is that higher agricultural prices quieted the countryside, whereas the cities generated their own movements for unbossed government, welfare legislation, and regulated capitalism. Even Russel B. Nye,[3] who as late as 1951 argued that Progressivism was a 'lineal descendant' of Populism, has shown by the facts in his own book that it was the urban clergyman, the urban scholar, the urban journalist, the urban social worker, the urban mayor, and the urban governor who most often led the Progressive cause.

New York's Theodore Roosevelt was the most flamboyant leader of them all. The *process* by which Roosevelt created the Progressive party in order to run for President in 1912 has been told in rich detail by George E. Mowry.[4] Here we can only

[1] See, for example, C. Vann Woodward's excellent *The Origins of the New South, 1877–1913* (1951).

[2] Robert H. Bremner, *From the Depths: The Discovery of Poverty in the United States* (1956); Sidney Fine, *Laissez Faire and the General-Welfare State: A Study of Conflict in American Thought, 1865–1901* (1956); Ray Ginger, *Altgeld's America: The Lincoln Ideals Versus Changing Realities* (1958); Arthur Mann, *Yankee Reformers in the Urban Age* (1954); and Howard H. Quint, *The Forging of American Socialism: Origins of the Modern Movement* (1953).

[3] *Midwestern Progressive Politics: A Historical Study of Its Origins and Development, 1870–1950* (1951).

[4] See his *The Era of Theodore Roosevelt, 1900–1912* (1958) and *Theodore Roosevelt and the Progressive Movement* (1947).

state that T.R. rallied round him urban reformers for clean government such as Hiram Johnson, his running mate; city intellectuals and business men who thought that regulating the giant corporations was more feasible and advisable than dissolving them; and social workers from squalid tenement house districts who wrote a plank for the party platform calling for unemployment insurance, old-age pensions, the abolition of child labor, the protection of women in industry, and minimum wage and maximum hours laws. Roosevelt called his program the New Nationalism.

His Democratic opponent in the election of 1912, which dramatized the split in American reform, was Woodrow Wilson. The latter's most recent and best biographer, Arthur S. Link,[1] has shown that Wilson was like Roosevelt only in the desire to destroy the power of the political machines. In welfare legislation he had no interest. Influenced by the agrarian and Bryanite elements in his party, advised by future Supreme Court Justice Louis D. Brandeis, and long a Cobden-Bright-free-trade-liberal, Wilson promised to dissolve the big corporations in order to restore an older, more individualistic, more competitive economy of small enterprise. This he called the New Freedom. But once in the White House Wilson reversed himself for reasons of political expediency and enacted the regulatory policy and, in a very small way, the welfare program of the New Nationalism.

Why the Progressive Era ended and gave way to the Age of Normalcy (it wasn't normal) is not altogether clear. Yet it would seem that World War I halted domestic reform and that the Paris Peace Treaties splintered the Wilson coalition. What is equally important, a humanitarian generation ran out of ideas by the second Wilson administration; and in 1924, when Senator Robert M. La Follette of Wisconsin, a veteran leader of the Progressive Era, bolted the G.O.P. to run for President on a new Progressive party, he had nothing new to say. Significantly, the only man to win election on the La Follette

[1] Link has completed three volumes of his impressive biography and more are to come. His conclusions are summarized in *Woodrow Wilson and the Progressive Era, 1910–1917* (1954).

ticket was Congressman Fiorello H. La Guardia of New York City; he was the sole spokesman in Washington, D.C., for the immigrant masses of the slums, whom only the social workers of the middle-class oriented Progressive Era had seriously noticed.[1] In the 1930's Mayor La Guardia, nominally a Republican, was to be an important political ally of the Democratic Roosevelt.

And it is here that we touch on the character of the New Deal (1932–52). Franklin D. Roosevelt and many of the men around him cut their first political teeth on the reform politics of the 1910's. Twenty years later there was a struggle within the Roosevelt inner circle over whether to adopt New-Nationalist or New-Freedom policies for big business. F.D.R. steered in both directions, first guiding the economy more thoroughly than the first Roosevelt, and then, in the 'Second New Deal', directing his congressional leaders to investigate and break up monopoly capitalism and restore competition. But despite these and other connections with the past, the New Deal was really new.

It was new because it derived from an unprecedented depression. Hard times aligned big city immigrant groups, native American whites on the farms and in the small towns, and Negroes in a coalition that kept the New Deal in office for twenty years.[2] No President before Franklin Roosevelt was able to form such a coalition (Al Smith tried in 1928 and failed); and no administration gave so much to workers (minimum wages and maximum hours), trade unionists (collective bargaining), farmers (parity prices), the elderly (social security), the unemployed (relief and·public works), and other disadvantaged groups. Unlike the New Deal, which helped those who could not help themselves, the Populists and Progressives labored to sweep away impediments in the economy that prevented the man on the make from getting ahead. Yet, in retrospect, the New Deal staged a holding action

[1] Arthur Mann, *La Guardia, A Fighter Against His Times, 1882–1933* (1959).
[2] There is a brilliant analysis of this coalition in Samuel Lubell, *The Future of American Politics* (1952).

for capitalism until World War II restored prosperity and reopened the avenues of opportunity.

Populism, Progressivism, and the New Deal rested on a common assumption, namely, that one could wring a higher standard of living out of the Industrial Revolution for all the people within the framework of constitutional government and capitalism. Because the radical left denied that assumption, it does not belong to the progressive tradition. Yet there is a considerable literature about Communist-Anarchism, Socialism, and Communism in America; in fact, owing to a project financed by the Fund for the Republic, we now know more about the Communist party than either of the two major parties. What concerns us here is why American Marxians, unlike their fellows in other countries, failed to create a major movement.

In an essay studded with neo-Augustinian allusions Daniel Bell, a former Socialist, has argued that the Marxians were moral men incapable of coping with the immoral political arena, which is only to say that they were impractical idealists. But even Socialists who built political machines, as David Shannon has written, won only a limited following. They were doomed to isolation, Louis Hartz has reminded us, because America skipped feudalism and, therefore, developed a society without the classes and class consciousness that make Marxian categories plausible. Equally important is the fact, which inheres in Oscar Handlin's books, that the industrial proletariat consisted mostly of conservative immigrants from peasant Europe who respected private property, looked up to established authority, and recoiled from the atheism and agnosticism of the radical left.[1]

We may conclude that the progressive tradition is three traditions in one. Populism, Progressivism, and the New Deal, though having obvious affinities, incorporated the resentments and aspirations of different kinds of people during

---

[1] Bell, 'The Background and Development of Marxian Socialism in the United States', in Donald D. Egbert and Stow Persons, eds., *Socialism and American Life* (1952), I, pp. 213–405; Shannon, *The Socialist Party of America: A History* (1955); Hartz, *The Liberal Tradition in America* (1955); and Handlin, *The Uprooted* (1951).

different times and different circumstances in American history. Their differences, as well as the antagonism between Progressivism and Marxism, are essential for understanding the criticism that has been directed at the progressive tradition from the 1920's through the 1950's.

III

The most abrasive writer during the 1920's, H. L. Mencken, had a savage time flaying what he called the American booboisie. Temperamentally an *enfant terrible* and philosophically a Nietzschean, he was scornful of majoritarianism, Puritanism, and uplift. In less than ten printed pages he peeled off the do-good rhetorical covering of William Jennings Bryan and Woodrow Wilson in order to reveal them as simpleminded fanatics who did harm when they meant to do well. Bryan he portrayed as a Boob from the Bible Belt, and Wilson as a Puritan evangelist with a second-rate mind. He blamed them and their kind for the imbecilities of his day: censorship, prohibition, the Nordic craze, the red scare, and religious fundamentalism.

He exaggerated, but he had a point. During Wilson's war administration the federal government muzzled the press, banned hard liquor, legislated against the allegedly inferior immigration from southern and eastern Europe, and deported radical aliens without due process of law. As for Bryan, he was the leading lay fundamentalist and prohibitionist by the 1920's. Speaking in defense of Tennessee's anti-evolution law at the world-famous Scopes Trial of 1925, he argued that to teach Darwin in the public schools was to blaspheme God, discredit the Bible, and reduce men to the level of apes. On his death in the same year an admirer hailed him as 'the greatest [Ku Klux] Klansman of our time'.

Early in the Depression, but before the advent of the New Deal, two books attacked the progressive tradition from the left position. In his *Autobiography* (1931) Lincoln Steffens, recapitulating his career as a muckraker and municipal socialist during the Progressive Era, concluded that it had been futile to try to patch up The System. By 1931 Steffens was convinced that all roads must lead to the Soviet Union. The following year John Chamberlain also bade *Farewell to Reform*. Though not yet prepared to journey to Moscow, he stated that men of good will would turn into cynics or revolutionists unless the progressive tradition (he accused it of 'preparing the ground for an American Fascism') became something more and better than a struggle by little capitalists against big capitalists. Both books found an enthusiastic audience.

But no academic historian of any reputation during the 1920's and 1930's wrote like Steffens, Chamberlain, or Mencken, who were journalists. On the contrary, scholars took the point of view of the reformers themselves, linked Populism and Progressivism to the anti-plutocratic tradition of Jefferson and Jackson, and ignored the unlovely qualities exposed by Mencken. This is the point of view of the two most influential syntheses of American history published between World War I and World War II: Vernon L. Parrington's *Main Currents in American Thought* (1927–30), and Charles A. and Mary R. Beard's *The Rise of American Civilization* (1927). The generation of Beard and Parrington, having been part and partisans of the Progressive Era, saw only the need for the crusade against big business and crooked politics, and had no second thoughts about it.

It was otherwise for many of the generation who came to write the history books in the 1940's and 1950's. Some, like Chamberlain, reduced American history to a struggle within the bourgeoisie and wondered what all the fuss had been over breaking up the trusts and letting the little fellow have his own greedy chance in the market place. Others, like Mencken, called attention to the simple certitudes, prejudices, and rigidities of the Populist-Progressive mind. Even those who thought the progressive tradition viable found fault with it. Dissecting the books by such progressive *philosophes* as Parrington and Beard, Veblen and Dewey, they discovered logical contradictions, fuzzy thinking, and moral flabbiness.

No single writer embodied all of these tendencies, and we can only speculate on the causes for the revisionist mood. But this much is clear—McCarthyism, contrary to what some have said, did not frighten professors into playing it safe by doing nasty books about liberals. Criticism of the progressive tradition began before the Senator from Wisconsin discovered the demagogic uses of the Red Peril. If anything, the McCarthyite lunacy made scholars even more aware of the Populist susceptibility to rabble-rousing.[1]

But before then the success of a liberal capitalist civilization created a mood inhospitable to progressive historiography. By 1950 even intellectuals who had made a cult of alienation were happy to call America home. There was much to be happy about: a rising standard of living, increasing opportunities for scholars, cultural pluralism, the welfare state, and a healthy balance of power between big business, big labor, and big government. Living in such a going concern, few scholars acquired the kind of compassion, resentments, and hopes for a more egalitarian society that had enabled a previous generation to identify itself with economic and political reform.

Instead, new perils to human welfare, like racism and totalitarianism, directed attention to the dark sides of reform. After the Nazi crematoria it was no longer possible to ignore the nativist phobias of the Populist-Progressive movements. And, at a time when the most dangerous enemies to humanity were the Great Simplifiers from Marx to Hitler to Mao, it was disturbing to discover that the Bryans and the Wilsons had been simplifiers too. In such an atmosphere some liberals were ready to join disillusioned Marxians in saying good-bye to ideology as they had known it.

Reinhold Niebuhr, a liberal but neo-Augustinian theologian who has been a teacher of his times largely because he is a barometer of them, summed up the new mood in *The Children of Light and the Children of Darkness* (1944). Liberals

[1] The best expression of this awareness is Daniel Bell, ed., *The New American Right* (1955). Cf. C. Vann Woodward's rebuttal, 'The Populist Heritage and the Intellectual', *The American Scholar* (winter 1959–60), pp. 55–72.

must learn, he wrote, that life is ambiguous, owing to the duality of human nature, and that only a fool can believe in final instead of 'proximate solutions' for mankind's enduring problems. What liberals need, and the world as well, is not slogans or formulas, but common sense, an appreciation for irony and paradox, and a tough-minded understanding that pride and stupidity corrupt even men of good will.

Intellectual sophistication is the one quality which the Populists and Progressives did not have, and since World War II there has been a cataloguing of their unsophistication. There is Richard Hofstadter's philosophical autopsy of Bryan's single-track brain (it went from 'the fight against gold to the fight against the ape'),[1] which would have delighted even the most savage debunker of the 1920's. There is John M. Blum's unflattering biography of Wilson as 'a nineteenth-century intelligence, obsolescing at a rapid rate, and this obsolescence the war accelerated'.[2] There are also syntheses by Hofstadter and Louis Hartz which reduce the entire liberal tradition to foolish rhetoric and mindless causes.

Blum, Hofstadter, and Hartz deserve special attention for the way they have arrived at similar conclusions from unlike starting points. The first has written from a position slightly to the right of the progressive tradition, the second from one slightly to the left of it, and the third from outside of it. They are also different in their special fields of interest. Blum's is politics as it is practised, Hofstadter's the connection between ideas and political programs, and Hartz's comparative political theory. Each man, though, is a spectator of the past, a role characteristic of so many scholars who came of professional age in the 1940's and 1950's. Their concern, in varying degrees, is with who played the best, or worst, kind of ball game.

Professor Blum, who teaches at Yale University, has an unsurpassed knowedge of twentieth-century American political history. Unlike Hofstadter and Hartz, he admires the ways of professional politicians—their lack of doctrinaireness, their

[1] *The American Political Tradition and the Men Who Made It* (1948), p. 202.
[2] *Woodrow Wilson and the Politics of Morality* (1956), p. 158.

ability to compromise, their adjustment of means to ends, their respect for institutions, and their shrewd understanding of human nature. Such men know their way around and have made an art out of getting things done without upsetting tradition. Their values are similar to those, as Blum defines the term, of responsible conservatism, to which he is inclined by temperament and intellect.

His three excellent books about the Progressive Era celebrate the virtues of the responsible conservative and professional politician at the expense of the liberal ideologue.[1] Thus, Wilson, the obsolete political theorist-moral evangelist, had himself to blame for his chief failures. The proposal to turn the hands of the economic clock back was unrealistic from the outset, while moralistic intransigence and political ineptness contributed to the Senate's rejection of the League of Nations. In contrast, the pre-1912, Republican Theodore Roosevelt, an imaginative conservative who had mastered the art of politics, was the first President (1901-9) to cope with the economic and international problems of the modern world. Blum's characterization of Roosevelt as a conservative is moot, but his main point is clear, namely, that ideology does not pay.

The obverse of this general proposition is the underlying theme of the books by Professor Hofstadter of Columbia University, though he agrees with Blum's estimate of Wilson. For more than fifteen years the most influential intellectual historian in this country, he believes in the importance of ideology. And because he does he has been disappointed by the Populist-Progressive-New Deal minds. In *The American Political Tradition and the Men Who Made It* (1948), Hofstadter put the Populists and Progressives in the same museum with fossilized Herbert Hoover; they, too, had been nostalgic in glorifying and trying to restore 'the fiercely capitalistic and individualistic' virtues of an earlier America. Franklin Roosevelt was free of this nostalgia but created no new system of thought and ruled by the force of his personality. Hofstadter, then to the left of the progressive position, concluded that a

[1] In addition to his biography of Wilson, see Blum's *Joe Tumulty and the Wilson Era* (1951) and *The Republican Roosevelt* (1955).

'corporate and consolidated society' required a political philosophy to sanction 'cohesion, centralization, and planning'.

The conclusion and spirit of Hofstadter's book were similar to those of John Chamberlain's *Farewell to Reform* of nearly twenty years before. But both men were wrong to suppose that the 'business of politics' since the founding of the Republic had been to 'protect the competitive world'. The state governments during the first sixty years or so of independence were neo-mercantilist, not *laissez faire*, in their policies; and local politics are relevant because the significant economic developments during those years took place on the state and regional, rather than national, level. More important, neither Hofstadter nor Chamberlain satisfactorily explained why American culture had been so fiercely capitalistic.

It was this problem that Professor Hartz of Harvard University explored in his provocative *The Liberal Tradition in America: An Interpretation of American Political Thought Since the Revolution* (1955). He was neither to the left of that tradition like Hofstadter nor to the right of it like Blum; he was like a foreign traveller wanting to know why America was different from Europe. This focus derived from Hartz's training under Professor Benjamin F. Wright, Jr., a political theorist and pioneer in the field of American studies, who taught his students to search for the uniqueness of America through the comparative method.

Hartz traced that uniqueness to the absence of a feudal past. Without an *ancien régime*, America did not need a revolution to become free; it was 'born free'. And without a revolutionary tradition, it was spared the Old-World struggles between reactionaries, liberals, and Marxians. If progressive historians knew European history they would make little of America's so-called social conflicts, Hartz continued; what needs emphasizing is the fact that only this country has enjoyed a 350-year-old consensus of private property, the atomistic society, popular sovereignty, and natural rights. Hamilton believed in those values as much as Jefferson, Biddle as much as Jackson, Calhoun as much as Lincoln, McKinley as much as Bryan, Taft as much as Wilson, Hoover as much as F.D.R. Intellectual descendants of John Locke, America's so-called conservatives and so-called progressives were classical liberals all. On one level, Hartz celebrated the Lockean consensus as superior to the polarities in European politics, while on another he deplored it as a strait-jacket. He agreed with Hofstadter that America was barren of ideologies because it was itself an ideology.

Hartz's America is the America discovered by Europeans in America and by Americans in Europe. It is the America of Crèvecœur and Jefferson, of De Tocqueville and Emerson, and of innumerable tourists today on both sides of the Atlantic. But Hartz deserves credit for trying to convert an old insight into a tool of analysis, and his book is indispensable to Europeans who want to understand this country in their own terms. It is less useful to Americans; for it is not about what America is, but what it is not: a Non-Europe.

One can agree that the differences between Bryan and McKinley were *not* the differences between the Dreyfusards and the anti-Dreyfusards and that as Lockeans they were *not* like Europeans. But to conclude that Bryan and McKinley should have understood their sameness is like saying that Cain and Abel should have loved each other because they were Adam's sons. Adam's descendants fought, to emphasize the positive, and so have John Locke's. What demands explanation is why, in the land of the Continuing Enlightenment, some very pugnacious men called themselves reformers and felt compelled to stand with the Lord at Armageddon against what they thought were the Devil's conservative disciples.

Professor Hofstadter turned to this problem in *The Age of Reform: From Bryan to F.D.R.*, which won the Pulitzer Prize in history for 1955. Making use of recent monographs and relevant social science theory, he traced the source of social conflict to status anxieties, ignorance, and self-deceiving images that reformers had of themselves and others. Though by 1955 more kindly disposed to the progressive tradition than in 1948, Hofstadter was, ironically, more devastating in his criticism. His analysis was also more subtle and needs to be presented in greater length.

The Populists, failing to understand that their problems derived from a world-wide agricultural depression, projected their grievances on aliens: on Easterners, Wall Street, English capitalists, and Jewish bankers who were allied in a conspiracy, according to the Populist philosophy of history, to destroy the liberty-loving, Anglo-Saxon husbandmen. This notion stemmed from self-deception. Instead of accepting himself for the agricultural capitalist he was, the Populist imagined himself to be the mythical yeoman who had been celebrated since Jefferson's day as the unspoiled child of Nature and the worthiest of all Americans.

To such attitudes Professor Hofstadter traced the isolationism, provincialism and racism inherent in the People's Crusade. The more industrialism and immigration transformed the United States, the more the Populists yearned for a golden age of Anglo-Saxon yeomen and small towners. This passionate longing for the past, and the fear of being brushed aside, gave the Ku Klux Klan its paranoia. When innocence confronted the world, it found only wickedness: the wickedness of the 'foreign' League of Nations, of Catholics, Jews, and Negroes, of city people. To grasp this illiberalism, one has only to remember that out of Populist backgrounds came Tom Watson and Cole Blease, Martin Dies, William Lemke, Huey Long—even Pat McCarran.

Hofstadter rated the Progressives more sophisticated than the Populists, but even they felt lost in the complexity of the twentieth century. Heirs of the Mugwumps, and recruited from the clergy, the bar, the new professoriat, and the old families, they inveighed against the monopolist and the political boss for sinfully choking opportunities in business and politics. Except for the professors, Progressive leaders had lost status and power to the plutocrat and the politician, a thesis that Hofstadter elaborated persuasively in perhaps the best and surely the most provocative section of the book. Resentment against the new led to a moral crusade ('the status revolution', Hofstadter called it) to restore nineteenth-century Protestant standards of merit.[1]

[1] This thesis inhered in George E. Mowry's suggestive chapter on the Progressive mind in *The California Progressives* (1951).

Seen in this light, Woodrow Wilson and Theodore Roosevelt are more important for their similarities than their differences. The one wished to smash the trusts, the other to regulate them, but neither man looked at the economy in terms of what it could produce. Earning a living was rather a test of character, and the men with the most and the best character were supposed to earn the best livings. Big business was harmful because it prevented the man on the make from proving himself in the competitive world. Political bosses and their machines were similar obstacles to a leadership of merit; by instituting direct primaries (nomination of candidates by popular election), the Progressives hoped to give good and honest men wider access to public office. As against historians who had censured the Progressives for ethical relativism, Hofstadter criticized them for moral absolutism. How else explain Wilson's passion to Americanize Europe, or the determination of the drys to legislate the wets out of existence?

One of the central theses of *The Age of Reform* is that the New Deal was not a continuation of the Populist-Progressive tradition. The New Deal developed in response to depression; Progressivism issued from an era of expansion. Populism and Progressivism agitated for the extension of entrepreneurial opportunities; the New Deal attempted to regulate an economy that was thought to have reached the limits of its growth. As important, Franklin D. Roosevelt accepted and worked with the urban bosses and, unlike the self-conscious Protestant, Anglo-Saxon Populist and Progressive leaders, welded together, for the first time, the immigrants of the city and the natives of the farms and small towns. Finally, not goals but means, not values but techniques, not crusades but organization, not slogans but manipulation—these were the values of the brain trust.

The opportunism of the New Deal troubled Hofstadter as much as the moralism of Progressivism and the primitivism of Populism. And so, in 1955 as in 1948, he bade farewell to the reform mind. But in 1955 he presented no public philosophy, which suggests that the partisan of the 1940's had become a spectator in the 1950's—the most perceptive spectator of the decade, to be sure, but ideologically homeless. Before measuring Hofstadter's influence and assessing his work we must consider another Pulitzer-Prize winner, Arthur M. Schlesinger, Jr., who has remained relatively untouched by the revisionist mood of the past twenty years.

IV

Professor Schlesinger writes history as he votes and votes as he writes. To a spectatorial age his ardent commitment to a cause has been a salutary countervailing tendency. His *Age of Roosevelt* (1957–60), now in its third volume with more to follow, promises to be the most affectionate monument to twentieth-century liberalism of this generation. It is narrative history in the grand style, written from the inside, with life, color, passion, drama, and conviction. This conviction is a family tradition. Schlesinger's father has been a well-known progressive historian for more than forty years; on his mother's side he is related to George Bancroft, the nineteenth-century New England Transcendentalist, Jacksonian Democrat, and historian of the spirit of American liberty.

Even as a young man Schlesinger showed a talent for polemics that ruled out his becoming a bystander of public life. He is as much a journalist, man of letters, and intellectual in politics as he is an historian. The past for him is a projection of the present. Columnist for the liberal New York *Post* and a founder and past president of the New Deal-ish Americans for Democratic Action; co-author of a pro-Truman-anti-General-MacArthur book and author of a tract for the times (*The Vital Center*); adviser to Adlai Stevenson in 1952 and 1956 and recently Special Assistant to the late President Kennedy, Schlesinger's career has been similar to that of his celebrated relative, George Bancroft. Yet none of this has lessened the forty-four-year-old Harvard professor's zeal for research, or his desire to tell the story as he thinks it actually happened. He has mastered a variety of manuscript collections and has read everything of importance by his colleagues.

Two related philosophical principles govern his approach to the past. The first is his belief that American history is cyclical, alternating between periods of liberal reform and conservative consolidation. Thus Jacksonian Democracy came after the hiatus that followed the Jeffersonian Revolution, the Progressive Era after the Rule of the Robber Barons, and the New Deal after the Age of Normalcy. Recently, in a nation-wide television program, Schlesinger described the New Frontier as an inevitable reaction to the Vacuous Eisenhower Years.

This theory would be as mystical and deterministic as Hegel's dialectic were it not for Schlesinger's second principle —namely, that social conflict is the generating force for the liberal-conservative cycle. 'Liberalism in America,' he has written, 'has been ordinarily the movement on the part of the other sections of society to restrain the power of the business community. This was the tradition of Jefferson and Jackson, and it has been the basic meaning of American liberalism.'

Schlesinger wrote this in the *Age of Jackson*, which won him a Pulitzer Prize in 1945 at the age of twenty-eight; and, not-withstanding the emphasis since then on consensus and con-tinuity, he has held to that position. Clearly, he is in the tradition of Parrington, Beard, and Turner, though he has rejected their dichotomies of democrat against oligarch, agrarians against capitalists, West against East, and frontier against seaboard.

The opening volume of the *Age of Roosevelt* describes the Progressive Era, the 1920's, the collapse of the old order between 1929 and 1932, and the coalition of workers, farmers, intellectuals, and liberal politicians that swept the leader of the business community out of the White House and elected Franklin D. Roosevelt President of the United States. From that point Schlesinger writes as if he were a member of the Roosevelt team and succeeds in recapturing the pragmatic spirit of the early New Deal and the crisis that faced America. Here he notes a political error, there an administrative mis-take, but with love. It is too early to say what his final con-clusion will be but already he has stated that the New Deal saved capitalism from the folly of the capitalists and prevented the United States from going fascist.

Schlesinger is characteristic of most historians in defining modern social reform as mainly a response to industrialism involving the role of the government in the economy. Yet liberals like Fiorello La Guardia, Horace Kallen, Oswald Garrison Villard, and John Dewey—to mention only a few—fought not only for a full stomach but for racial and religious democracy, the autonomy of women, free speech, and progressive education. Schlesinger is well aware of the importance of these aspects of American liberalism, but they have yet to receive the attention they deserve. There is no adequate history, for example, of the American Civil Liberties Union, the Anti-Defamation League, or the National Association for the Advancement of Colored People.

v

Where, then, do historians stand today on the age of reform? The biographies and monographs of the past fifteen years or so have altered the notion that Populism, Progressivism, and the New Deal were the same thing under different banners. Even Schlesinger, who has joined the three into a common expression against the business community, has been careful to point out their dissimilar origins and assumptions. Further, there is a growing recognition that the liberal tradition does not stop with bread-and-butter issues. In his *John Kennedy: A Political Profile* (1960), for example, James M. Burns, a political scientist, traced the growth of a ritualistic market-basket liberal into the many-sided liberal President Kennedy was.

But it is hard to say what historians *as a group* think qualitatively about social reform. Most of the specialized studies in political and intellectual history have built-in interpretations favorable to the progressive tradition. But there are no polls about the reaction of academic readers to these interpretations; and book reviewing in the scholarly journals is generally so bland that it is rarely an index to serious opinion. Nor are textbooks useful as barometers, for the authors of many of them are also the authors of the specialized studies. (These textbooks, incidentally, have had little or no influence on college students, who declared overwhelmingly for Eisenhower and Nixon in the last three presidential elections.)

It would be convenient to conclude that Schlesinger and Hofstadter represent polar positions and that members of the profession cluster around one or the other man. But Schlesinger has recently said that he and Holfstadter find each other intellectually congenial. Odd as this sounds, there is reason to believe that it is so. Hofstadter, for all his criticism, hailed the progressive achievement of extending the great American bonanza to the underprivileged. And Schlesinger, for all his celebrating this achievement, incorporated Hofstadter's criticisms into his own work. 'Our differences are a matter of emphasis,' Schlesinger has explained. Whereas Hofstadter built two books around the shortcomings of liberalism and made passing mention of its benefits, Schlesinger dedicated three volumes to its benefits and referred briefly to its shortcomings.

Most historians—if one can base a conclusion on the shop talk that goes on at the coffee tables and bars where one's colleagues gather—stand somewhere between Hofstadter and Schlesinger. Actually, the two men have concentrated on different things: Schlesinger on what the progressives did, and Hofstadter on what they thought. Hofstadter has won his point that there can be no going back to the intellectual worlds of the Populists and the Progressives. Our times are more complicated than theirs, and it is doubtful if theirs were as simple as they made them out to be. Their racism is abominated, of course. But few scholars condemn the New Deal for being 'opportunistic'. The pragmatic center was unquestionably better, as Schlesinger has reminded us, than any of the ideological solutions proposed during the depression. Historical judgment, like politics itself, is the art of choosing among alternatives.

Few historians, on the other hand, agree with Schlesinger

that social conflict in America has been merely the struggle between the People and the Business Community. As in Jacksonian Democracy, so in Populism, Progressivism, and the New Deal the desire to expand business opportunities was an important objective. And although accurate analysis of election returns is still in its infancy, it is already obvious that habit and ethnic antagonisms are often as important as economic motives in how Americans vote. The evidence in Schlesinger's third volume bears this out. In 1933 Fiorello La Guardia, though secretly loathing Fascism, was elected Mayor of New York City with the help of Italo-Americans who prized him as their own Mussolini and as an avenger of the slights they had suffered from Irish-Americans. One might add that John Fitzgerald Kennedy was elected President because he received the support of a number of blocs, among them Southern racists who voted the Democratic ticket because their ancestors have done so for more than a century, and Irish Catholics, including former McCarthyites, who wanted to avenge the defeat of Al Smith and to put one of their own kind in the White House for the first time in this predominantly Protestant country.

But Schlesinger speaks for the academy in his tribute to the progressives for what they did. They were the first to call attention to the unequitable distribution of the national income and to do something about it. They taxed, policed, lectured, and scolded big business so effectively that the power and arrogance of a J. P. Morgan is unthinkable today. They built a number of devices into the economy to cushion the shock of those who falter in the race for life. More so than any other group in America they transformed the social Darwinian jungle of some eighty years ago into the humane capitalistic society it is today.

'The place of the progressive tradition in this achievement is so secure,' wrote Hofstadter in 1955, 'that it should now be possible to indulge in some critical comments without seeming to impugn its entire value.' Therein lies the mood of the recent past. But there are signs of change. One younger historian has issued a manifesto in favor of reviving the 'deeper values' of

Parrington and Beard: 'An appreciation of the crusading spirit, a responsiveness to indignation, a sense of injustice.'[1]

These values did not perish during the 1940's and 1950's, but they were challenged. Before they can triumph, scholars will have to overcome a fear expressed by Nathaniel Hawthorne more than a hundred years ago in *The Blithedale Romance*. The New England writer published his novel about Brook Farm when a reaction was setting in against the first age of reform. He wanted to be on the side of progressive change but he was afraid that he might, like some reformers, make a fool of himself. Hawthorne concluded that the highest wisdom lay in knowing when that fear 'ought to be resisted, and when to be obeyed'.

© Arthur Mann 1962

[1] John Higham, 'The Cult of the "American Consensus": Homogenizing Our History', *Commentary* (February 1959), p. 100.

10

EMERGENCE TO WORLD POWER

BY ERNEST R. MAY

THE history of American foreign relations has engaged an increasing number of American historians. Nearly every major college and university in the United States offers a semester or a year-long course on this special subject. The number of surveys or textbooks for such courses outnumber those for economic, social, or intellectual history.

Visiting scholars from England sometimes express amusement that study of foreign affairs should be so popular in a country which only so recently admitted that it had foreign affairs. Familiar, however, with the work of Sir Charles Webster, Harold W. V. Temperley, and other specialists in British diplomatic history, they are not surprised, as visiting Europeans usually are, by the fact that the subject is taught at all. Neither Americans nor Englishmen seem usually to realize how odd and improbable a field of study is the diplomatic history of one country.

Yet the assumption that international relations can be viewed as aspects of one nation's history underlies much of the writing about past American foreign affairs. Indeed, the whole literature dealing with the last seventy years can almost be divided into two parts. On one side are works treating episodes in American history; on the other, works treating episodes in the history of international relations.

Unfortunately for any effort at simplification, the literature also lends itself to division along other lines. One can equally well separate the writings into those that ask 'What happened?' and those that ask 'What went wrong?'

More often than not the latter concentrate on occurrences in America. Assuming that some event, such as the annexation of the Philippines or intervention in one of the World Wars, was a tragic and avoidable mistake, they seek out forces or individuals in America upon whom to lay the blame. The coincidence has been by no means perfect. For example, in a detailed two-volume study of Soviet-American relations from 1917 to 1920, Ambassador George F. Kennan scrutinizes the American and Russian governments, the American and Allied embassies in Russia, and inter-Allied agencies in Paris.[1] Yet his evident purpose is to discover what Americans might have done to prevent Soviet-American antagonism. His work proves that a historian can look at a topic from several national perspectives but still ask, 'What went wrong?'

Works on American foreign relations can thus be described as either national or multi-national in approach and also as either Rankean or Actonian in intent. The writers have looked at only one side or at several, and they have had either Ranke's aim of finding out what actually happened or Acton's of sitting as a hanging judge.

To illustrate how these pairs of tendencies have interlaced in writing about American diplomacy, it is simplest to isolate three crucial episodes, summarize the facts in each case, and then glance at the major works dealing with them.

The first such episode, if the term can be applied to a series of events running through more than a decade, was the emergence of the United States as a great power. Up to the 1890's the nation had not been generally so regarded. European diplomats and political analysts coupled it with such states as Sweden, the Netherlands, Belgium, and Spain. By the early twentieth century, on the other hand, some of the very same people had begun to say in all seriousness that Europe was in danger from America. The distinguished French historian, Henri Hauser, for example, asserted in a little volume on American imperialism in 1905 that the principal topic of conversation in France was the so-called 'American peril'. In little more than a decade the United States had

[1] *Russia Leaves the War* (1956); *The Decision to Intervene* (1958).

moved from among the second-rate powers to a front rank among first-rate powers.

This change in America's reputation was obviously due in part to changes in the United States itself. The country had grown in population. Whereas in the 1850's it had fewer people than France or Austria-Hungary, by the 1890's it had more than any European state except Russia. At the same time, its economy expanded. It became not only the world's leading grower of wheat and other foodstuffs but also by 1900 the foremost producer of coal, iron, and steel. By that time, too, its banks and exchanges did almost as much business as those of Britain. Perhaps more important, it possessed a navy equal to Germany's and was building warships at a rate that threatened soon to make it a rival of France and Britain. The United States had become physically as strong as the so-called great powers, and its fleet gave it the capacity to influence events in distant parts of the globe.

Not even all of these changes, however, would have sufficed to transform the nation's reputation had it not been for the altered behavior of the American government and people. Reacting in 1889–90 to an apparent German threat to American rights in the Samoan Islands, Congress virtually threatened war. In 1893 President Benjamin Harrison endeavored to annex the Hawaiian Islands. Though his successor, Grover Cleveland, refused to carry out the project, the domestic controversy roused an imperialist movement comparable to those in Britain, France, Germany, and Russia. At about the same time a significant number of Americans showed that they were eager for the government to use its strength in support of Christian missionaries in such faraway places as China and Armenia.

Then at the end of 1895 President Cleveland startled the world by suddenly threatening a war against Britain. He had urged the British to submit to arbitration a boundary dispute between their Guiana colony and the republic of Venezuela. When the British government refused, Cleveland declared that the United States would itself mark out the frontier and force both parties to accept it. Though he eventually accepted a compromise, the United States still seemed successfully to have challenged the then greatest of the great powers.

In 1898 Cleveland's successor, William McKinley, actually took the country into a war. It was not with one of the great states of Europe, it is true, but rather with Spain, a nation plainly inferior in resources, and it grew out of events close to the American homeland. Spain's colony, Cuba, had revolted. In three years of fighting the Spanish government had been unable to subdue the rebels. Conditions on the island had grown worse and worse. It was estimated, indeed, that a third of the population had been killed by hunger or disease. Partly at America's urging, the Spaniards attempted every palliative, including an offer to give Cuba self-government comparable to Canada's. Not even this drastic step checked the rebellion. McKinley pleaded with the Spanish government to concede independence. When it refused, he asked Congress for power to intervene in the name of humanity in order to bring the struggle to an end.

Hostilities ensued, and in three months' time American forces utterly destroyed the Spanish navy, conquered eastern Cuba, and compelled the Spanish government to surrender. Even though there had been some danger that European powers might support Spain, American public opinion had frenziedly demanded war. The President had assumed the risk. During the war, furthermore, he authorized a bold attack on Spain's Philippine colony, near which the British, the French, and others had important interests; he revived the Hawaiian project and annexed the islands; he then insisted that Spain give up the Philippines to the United States. All in all, the American government and people showed themselves audacious, ambitious, aggressive, bumptious, and covetous. These were the supposed attributes of a great power.

For a time after the Spanish-American war, moreover, the nation continued to behave in appropriate fashion. It marked out the Caribbean area as its exclusive domain, annexing Puerto Rico, establishing a protectorate over Cuba, and endeavoring, at this time unsuccessfully, to buy the Virgin Islands from Denmark. Exploiting the preoccupation of

Britain with the Boer War and with the growing German menace, the government also extorted the cancellation of a half-century-old Anglo-American treaty and secured for the United States the exclusive right to build and fortify a canal through Central America.

Before even these first steps were completed McKinley was assassinated, and his place was taken by the Vice-President, Theodore Roosevelt. A flamboyant personality and a man of vast learning and energy, Roosevelt had been a conspicuous imperialist and, before the Spanish war, a violent jingo. He later identified himself with the motto, 'Speak softly and carry a big stick'. As President, however, he was not loath to rattle a sabre, and he was even more determined than McKinley that the Caribbean should be American-controlled.

In 1905 he pronounced what came to be called the 'Roosevelt corollary' to the Monroe doctrine. Since the United States would not permit European states to punish Latin-American governments, he said, it had a duty to police the conduct of these governments. They were in effect to be America's wards. Acting upon this doctrine, he and his successors on occasion sent in American officials and forces to manage finances in Latin-American states or, for long or short periods, to govern them.

Roosevelt also carried on the effort to create a canal. After much controversy the isthmus of Panama had been selected as the best site. Though Colombia would not sell a right of way, Roosevelt waited impatiently until the Panamanians proclaimed a revolution for independence. He then instructed American naval forces to prevent Colombia from landing forces to retake the isthmus. He recognized the rebel government and immediately obtained from it permission to proceed with the canal. He later boasted, 'I took the Canal Zone.' And with this step and the subsequent Roosevelt corollary declaration he succeeded in effect in turning the Caribbean into an American lake.

At the same time Roosevelt and his predecessor displayed marked interest in the Far East. In 1899 Secretary Hay gratuitously asked the various European powers to guarantee the maintenance of an 'open door' in China. He asked that, even if China were partitioned, commerce there should remain free. In 1900, after the so-called Boxer rebellion erupted, Hay went further and called for the preservation of China's territorial and administrative integrity. McKinley meanwhile authorized American warships and troops to participate in an international expedition to rescue foreign diplomats in Peking. Even before Roosevelt came to office the United States entered into Far Eastern politics as one of the great powers.

Roosevelt, indeed, added little to McKinley's policy. Faced with evidence that Russia wished to absorb Manchuria and Korea, he did what he could to dissuade them. At the same time he tried to make it clear that the United States would never go so far as to fight for this distant territory. Then, when Russia did become involved in war with Japan, he preserved a scrupulous neutrality. Though he privately expressed hope that neither side would achieve overwhelming victory and that the outcome would leave in Asia 'balanced antagonism', when asked to mediate he agreed only after long hesitation. In the negotiations that took place at Portsmouth, New Hampshire, he declined to intervene until the very last moment, when it was clear that he alone could propose compromises acceptable to both parties.

In 1907 Roosevelt did send the American navy around Cape Horn and on a cruise of the Far East, thus demonstrating that the United States retained interest in the area. At the same time, however, he also negotiated with Tokyo a series of agreements designed to reassure the Japanese that the United States would not stand in their way. Under McKinley and Roosevelt, America played an important role in the Far East, but played it cautiously.

The nation had won recognition as a power, even outside the Western Hemisphere and Asia. The proof came during the so-called first Moroccan crisis of 1905–6. Roosevelt himself endeavored to avoid involvement. When compelled to send a delegate to the international conference at Algeçiras, he instructed his emissary to play as small a part as possible. Nevertheless, from beginning to end, the Germans on one side and

the French and British on the other treated the American as
if he had a deciding voice—as if by supporting either party he
could force a settlement in its favor. Clearly the diplomatists
of Europe had come to look upon America as a formidable
factor in the diplomatic balance. The nation had won almost
universal recognition as a major power. To this transformation there is no parallel in modern history except perhaps that
of Communist China in the 1950's.

The earliest historians of these events were much struck by
this change. Contributing the final volume to Albert Bushnell
Hart's *American Nation* series, Johns Hopkins professor John H.
Latané in 1907 chose the title, *America as a World Power, 1897–
1907*. In 1908 Archibald Cary Coolidge of Harvard published
The United States as a World Power. And this or some similar
phrase became a standard chapter heading in textbooks.

Not until the 1930's did historians begin to examine in
detail the episodes that occurred during this period of change.
And those who did were mostly descendants, literally or meta-
phorically, of intellectuals who, at the time of the Spanish war,
had opposed both the war and the annexation of the Philippines. In 1931 Walter Millis of the New York *Herald Tribune*
in *The Martial Spirit* documented the case which the *Nation*
and other liberal journals had been consistently putting forward. He charged that public opinion had been wrought up
in 1898 by circulation-hungry publishers of 'yellow' journals
and that this artificial hysteria had been exploited by opportunistic imperialists such as Roosevelt and Senator Henry
Cabot Lodge. Although the real interest of the United States
lay in preserving its own peace and its non-involvement in
international politics, a weak-willed President had allowed
himself to be forced into war and into assuming colonial
burdens.

These theses were reiterated by Charles A. Beard in 1934
in *The Idea of National Interest*, and further documented in
monographs on American newspaper opinion. One scholar
did go well beyond these generalizations. Julius W. Pratt in
1937 in *Expansionists of 1898* explored the enthusiasm for annexing Hawaii and the Philippines and found it rooted in

contemporary social Darwinism and in the missionary zeal of churchmen. He disputed by implication the thesis that a handful of newspapers deserved all blame, but he did not disagree with the view that expansionism and jingoism had been wrongheaded movements. So prevalent did these interpretations become that in 1936 Samuel Flagg Bemis of Yale, in his careful, scholarly *Diplomatic History of the United States*, entitled a chapter on the taking of the Philippines 'The Great Aberration', and he kept that heading in revised editions through more than two decades.

Expressive of the quasi-pacifism that characterized so much post-World War I thought, a similar blend of cynicism and outrage appeared in writing on other aspects of McKinley's and Roosevelt's diplomacy. Another New York newspaperman, Henry F. Pringle, published in 1931 a biography of Theodore Roosevelt. In it he mocked not only Roosevelt's jingoism and imperialism in the 1890's but also the policies he advocated and pursued afterward. Portraying Roosevelt as a poseur and blusterer, Pringle described his behavior as blameworthy in the Panama affair and ridiculous in most other instances.

As had been the case with Millis's theses, so with Pringle's; supporting evidence soon came from writers of monographs. Though most of these scholars were less ungenerous than Pringle, their judgments tended to reinforce that of one of Roosevelt's contemporaries. The British diplomat, Cecil Spring-Rice, had written a friend, 'You must remember that the President is about six'.

On the Far Eastern policies of the two administrations, historians were even more severe. Tyler Dennett, a historian working in the State Department, published in 1933 a biography of John Hay. Though generally kindly toward Hay, he suggested that the Secretary had been prompted toward his Open Door declarations by an excess of Anglophilia and that the doctrine had proved an embarrassment even at the time. In 1938 A. Whitney Griswold of Yale dredged from Hay's manuscripts and those of his contemporaries evidence that the notes had actually originated with an Englishman, an official of the Chinese customs service, and, little changed, become the famous circular of 1899—a statement of policy which, in Griswold's view, remained a danger to America's peace.[1] Wherever they looked in the decades from 1890 to 1914 students found disorder, error, and mischief.

It gradually became evident, however, that most of these writers had been excessively influenced by their changing times—by the climate of opinion that had also given rise to the 'outlawry of war' movement and the neutrality acts. After the Munich crisis of 1938, some Americans began to regain the sense of danger, the belief in the possible appropriateness of war, which had informed the diplomacy of both McKinley and Roosevelt. Scholarly writers in the 1940's began to suggest that both Presidents might have been prudently concerned with America's safety.

Roosevelt's reputation in particular gained. Political scientist Hans Morgenthau in *In Defense of the National Interest* in 1950 praised him as one of the few realists in American history. An associate of Morgenthau's at the University of Chicago Center for the Study of American Foreign Policy, Robert E. Osgood, wrote in 1953 *Ideals and Self-Interest in America's Foreign Relations.* In it he contrasted Roosevelt, a man who understood power politics, with Wilson and other idealists, who did not. Even Howard K. Beale of the University of Wisconsin, an avowed pacifist, praised Roosevelt's perception and insight. In *Theodore Roosevelt and America's Rise to World Power* in 1959 he portrayed the President as almost a second Bismarck. Recent textbooks have presented Roosevelt in much this light.

The change did not come entirely from change in the Zeitgeist, for it was due also to the introduction of other perspectives. One early investigator, Alfred L. P. Dennis of Clark University, had seen events of the McKinley and Roosevelt administrations as other than comic blunders. A specialist in European history and a writer on Russian affairs, he had endeavored in *Adventures in American Diplomacy, 1896–1906* in 1928 to show American policies as rational responses

[1] *The Far Eastern Policy of the United States* (1938).

to problems with which the two administrations had had to deal. In 1935 Alfred Vagts published two huge volumes in German on German-American relations from 1809 to 1906. In them he showed Harrison, Cleveland, McKinley, and Roosevelt working amid powerful domestic and international forces, all of which tended to draw the United States into conflict with other powers. Dexter Perkins made the same point in a volume on the Monroe doctrine.[1] In 1938 Lionel Gelber of the University of Toronto printed *The Rise of Anglo-American Friendship, 1898–1906*. Elaborating on a theme suggested by Dennis, he pointed out that these had been years in which America and Britain had dissolved old controversies and established an informal entente. In 1946 in *American-Russian Rivalry in the Far East, 1895–1914*, E. H. Zabriskie demonstrated that the Open Door note and subsequent American diplomacy in East Asia had been called forth by actions of the Tsarist government and had in turn had profound effects in St Petersburg. Together, Vagts, Perkins, Gelber, and Zabriskie made it clear that the McKinley-Roosevelt era was that in which German-American rivalry, Anglo-American friendship, and Russian-American antagonism had their origins. It was, as had been said earlier by Latané and Coolidge, a crucial formative period in America's history as a great power. As such it is now being reanalyzed in depth by newer historians and political scientists.

Our second episode is the intervention of the United States in the First World War. The essential facts are better known. When the war opened in 1914, few observers in either Europe or America imagined that the United States would take part. After the first six weeks, as the combatants settled down for prolonged hostilities, the British did realize that they would probably become dependent on overseas supplies and hence could not afford a rift with America, but no other members of the Allied coalition had similar insight. And the

[1] *Deutschland und die Vereinigten Staaten in der Weltpolitik* (1935); *The Monroe Doctrine, 1867–1907* (1937). In two preceding volumes Perkins traced the Monroe doctrine from its inception in 1823 to 1867.

Central Powers were so indifferent to the United States that in February 1915 they announced a submarine campaign against neutral shipping, even though recognizing that it would stir anger in Washington.

These attitudes were in part justified, for President Wilson and his advisers were themselves determined that the United States would remain a neutral. For over two years they bent much effort toward avoiding friction with Britain, fearing a repetition of the events that had brought on war in 1812. The President even appealed to the public to be neutral in thought as well as deed.

When the Germans opened their submarine campaign Wilson nevertheless spoke out. In solemn language he warned that the United States would hold Germany to 'strict accountability' for any American ships or lives lost. Though the government in Berlin then modified its decrees, several incidents soon occurred. In May 1915 a torpedo sank the British liner *Lusitania*, killing 124 Americans. Again the President felt constrained to protest, even though conscious that refusal by Germany to modify its submarine campaign might well result in war. Time after time new incidents occurred, new protests went out from Washington, and new apologies came from Berlin. In Europe the war wore on hungrily and bloodily, and the German public and the leaders of Germany's armed forces became ever more fearful that if they did not conquer soon they would eventually be wasted away.

In January 1917 the Kaiser's government finally decided to make full use of the U-boat, even though certain that the result would be to make the United States a belligerent. An unrestricted submarine campaign was proclaimed. Wilson, consistently with his earlier threats, severed diplomatic relations. Ship after ship went down, and in early April the President went before Congress to call for a war that would 'make the world safe for democracy'.

During the era of the Great Depression a large number of works dealt with this event or aspects of it, among them *Why We Fought* in 1929 by C. Hartley Grattan, a journalist, *The Road to War* in 1935 by Walter Millis, and *America Goes to*

War in 1939 by Professor Charles Callan Tansill of George-
town. These and similar works all proceeded from the premise
that intervention had been a tragic mistake. Their authors
asked wonderingly how such a madcap mistake had been made.

With minor variations all of them offered the same
answers. In the first place, they asserted, Wilson and his
advisers had let themselves be influenced by pro-British and
anti-German propaganda. They had been taken in by an
illusion that there was some moral difference between the
Allies and the Central Powers.

In the second place the Wilson administration had been
excessively tender toward industrialists and bankers who
wanted to make money out of supplying the Allies. It had let
trade in arms and munitions grow to such an extent that the
Germans had had to find some means of cutting it off. And
the public had developed a financial as well as an emotional
interest in the war's outcome.

In the third place the administration had been mistakenly
eager for the United States to have some influence in world
affairs. Wilson had erred in thinking that the United States
had some duty to preserve international law and speak out for
international morality.

And finally the administration had been carried along by
public feeling, itself whipped up by Allied propagandists,
munitions-makers, and opportunistic politicians.

Had the government not been so misled, indicated all of
these historians, it would have prevented Americans from
giving such extensive material support to one belligerent. It
would also have taken issue with the British more frequently
over their measures to halt Central European trade, while at
the same time protesting less vigorously and certainly less
belligerently against Germany's use of the submarine. By these
means the United States could have kept out of the war.

That the interpretations advanced by these writers were
influential was suggested by the fact that their formulae were
incorporated in the successive neutrality acts of 1935 to 1939.
Congress thus sought to ensure that the nation would not
again become embroiled in the war of 1914–18.

Again, however, there was another group of scholars which endeavored to reconstruct what had happened either in broader perspective or in less self-critical terms. Charles Seymour, subsequently the President of Yale, did so in 1934 and 1937 in two volumes, *American Diplomacy during the World War* and *American Neutrality, 1914–1917*. So did Arthur S. Link of Princeton, the biographer of Wilson, in his 1954 survey, *Woodrow Wilson and the Progressive Era*, and his 1957 lectures, *Wilson the Diplomatist*. So did I in 1959 in *The World War and American Isolation*.

All of us saw Wilson's efforts to avoid conflict with the British and to prevent a German U-boat campaign as not only rational but almost inevitable responses to problems with which the President had to deal. The trade loss resulting from the Allied blockade was negligible. The gain from Allied war buying, on the other hand, meant the difference between prosperity and depression. Moreover, long before propaganda could have had any effect, Wilson estimated that 90 per cent of the public was pro-Ally. When confronting the first German submarine decree, he had to recognize that it threatened the American economy. He also had to take account of the fact that a significant part of the public already felt outraged against Germany not just because of atrocity stories but also because of such acts as the violation of Belgian neutrality and the bombing of open cities.

Seymour and Link and I all stressed the importance of seeing Wilson's actions in perspective against those of the Allies and especially of the Germans. We pointed out that the British deliberately endeavored to keep American goodwill while the German government always discussed submarine operations in terms of war or peace with the United States. We endeavored to show, as Vagts and Perkins and Gelber and Zabriskie had for the earlier period, that the American government was not making a series of absolute moral judgments but was choosing among the unsatisfactory alternatives available to it at given moments of time.

Our final episode is American intervention in World War II. Again the basic facts are relatively simple. Most of the American people had become isolationist during the 1930's. They had also become convinced, paradoxically, that Mussolini and Hitler were wicked men and that the British and French governments were endeavoring to maintain peace. When the Germans struck at Poland in 1939 and thus opened a general war, the public, Congress, and the administration united in believing the United States should stay out. At the same time a substantial number felt that moral and material support could not be withheld from nations that were victims of aggression. The neutrality Acts were promptly repealed, and a trickle of supplies and volunteers started across the ocean.

In 1940, when France fell, President Franklin Roosevelt and a significant part of the public became convinced that Americans should not let Britain fall. Quite apart from wishing that evil would not triumph over good, they feared that the result would be to endanger the Western Hemisphere. The Führer would be sure to make the Americas one of his next targets, and he would then have to be fought on home ground rather than overseas.

Calculation and emotion thus combined to bring the President's appeal to the country in June 1940 to become 'the arsenal of democracy', his trade of fifty destroyers to Britain in September 1940 in exchange for naval bases in the Caribbean, and his Lend-Lease program in 1941 for unlimited aid to the United Kingdom and subsequently to Russia. At the same time, however, calculation and emotion also combined to draw from Roosevelt such declarations as that with which he concluded his third-term campaign in 1940: 'while I am talking to you mothers and fathers, I give you one more assurance . . . Your boys are not going to be sent into any foreign wars.'

As Germany drove deep into Russia and at the same time threatened to cut the Suez lifeline with her Afrika-korps and the trans-Atlantic sealanes with her U-boats, the American government resorted to more and more warlike expedients. Destroyers were sent out to patrol the western Atlantic and broadcast the position of German submarines. Subsequently, on a trumpery pretext, these warships were given orders to shoot on sight. Some were detailed to convoy duty. A number of American officials and at least a significant minority of the public agreed that the nation should go beyond such undeclared naval hostilities and actually declare war and dispatch expeditionary forces to Europe. The President may have concurred. If so, however, he was in no hurry to act.

Before he had to make up his mind, events in the Far East took the decision out of his hands. Ever since the outbreak of the European war the Japanese had been exploiting the opportunity given them. They had demanded from the defeated French extensive concessions in northern Indo-China. As time passed, they pressed harder and harder for further concessions elsewhere in French and Dutch Asiatic colonies.

The British, drawing off forces from Singapore, Malaya, Australia, and New Zealand, asked the United States to help prevent a Japanese attack on these territories. Already sympathetic to the Chinese and conscious that the Japanese were co-operating with Germany and Italy, Roosevelt agreed. By word and gesture he tried to create in Tokyo a belief that any further aggression would mean war with the United States. In the summer of 1941 he resorted to stopping exports of American oil, thus cutting off from Japan a resource which was indispensable to her if she were to continue her four-year-old war with China. Roosevelt and his advisers reasoned that only if the Japanese were shocked into realization of their weakness would they abandon dreams of vast conquests. And lest any conciliatory American act reduce the pain of this discovery, the President declined Japanese proposals for a 'summit' conference, and he and his Secretary of State rigidly refused to discuss any compromise.

Faced with a choice between diplomatic surrender and war, the Japanese chose the latter. On 7 December 1941 they bombed the American naval base at Pearl Harbor. The Germans and Italians joined them in declaring war, and the United States thus found its dilemma resolved.

Scarcely was the conflict over in 1945 before certain historians began to lament these events, much as they had those of 1914–17. In two acid volumes in 1946 and 1948, *American Foreign Policy, 1932–1940* and *President Roosevelt and the Coming of the War, 1941,* Charles A. Beard charged Roosevelt with having lied to the public and with having secretly maneuvered not only to make the United States an ally of Britain but also to inveigle the Japanese into striking Pearl Harbor. Tansill, in *Back Door to War* (1952), went back to World War I and the Manchurian crisis to trace a pattern of anti-German and anti-Japanese conspiracy. A few other writers followed suit.

By the early 1950's, however, scholars had had opportunity to look over not only the documents examined by Beard and Tansill but also captured German and Japanese records. Herbert Feis, former Economic Adviser in the State Department, brought out *The Road to Pearl Harbor* in 1950 and William L. Langer of Harvard and S. Everett Gleason, formerly of Amherst, collaborated on two massive volumes, *The Challenge to Isolation, 1937–1940* and *The Undeclared War, 1940–1941,* which were published in 1952 and 1953. In these works Feis and Langer and Gleason pointed out instances of error and miscalculation. Feis suggested, for example, that the oil embargo might in fact have forced Japan's hand and that a different policy might at least have won some further delay. But he and Langer and Gleason endeavored to make it clear that the government had faced issues requiring decisions, that it had made those decisions as carefully and conscientiously as possible, but that it had never been able either to guarantee that they would have the desired effects or that other and graver issues would not follow.

Major writings on all three episodes fall conveniently into two pairings among our original four categories. Those historians who concerned themselves exclusively with American events tended also to be those who were on the hunt for villains. Those viewing occurrences from more than one perspective were less interested in alleging mistakes and apportioning blame. In these three groups of books there was a linkage between parochialism and Actonism.

Despite Kennan's example to the contrary, this linkage

seems natural. Historians who really saw all sides in an international controversy were more apt to realize that one side was rarely able to control or determine the actions of others. Seeing how often there was a wide gap between intention and effect, they were more likely to be charitable, humble, and perhaps fatalistic.

In current writing, both the multi-national approach and the Rankean attitude are on the rise. The surprises of the Cold War have made Americans increasingly conscious that their own government does not make all the decisions that are made in the world. Work is still done, to be sure, on purely American aspects of the nation's involvement in world affairs. Some writers still seek out devils—if not among individuals then at least among ideas or institutions. In *American Diplomacy, 1900–1950* (1951) Kennan ascribed to traditions of 'moralism' and 'legalism' many of the country's past woes. Nevertheless, in the total output in the field the proportion of studies endeavoring merely to describe what happened on the several sides has been steadily increasing.

To say this is not necessarily to conclude with a loud hosannah. In the past works of this kind have generally been far superior. On the other hand the Rankean approach may tend to cause a suspension of judgment. The historian may find himself justifying what has happened. As A. J. P. Taylor remarks of those who obey the canons of Sir Herbert Butterfield's 'technical history', they may end up saying: 'The Nazis sent millions of Jews to the gas-chamber. They did a fine job according to their lights.' But this point still seems far away. For the time being the approach seems likely to yield a more durable understanding of the life that the United States has lived within its international community.

11

THE QUEST FOR
THE NATIONAL CHARACTER

BY DAVID M. POTTER

UNLIKE most nationality groups in the world today, the people of the United States are not ethnically rooted in the land where they live. The French have remote Gallic antecedents; the Germans, Teutonic; the English, Anglo-Saxon; the Italians, Roman; the Irish, Celtic; but the only people in America who can claim ancient American origins are a remnant of Red Indians. In any deep dimension of time, all other Americans are immigrants. They began as Europeans (or in the case of 10 per cent of the population, as Africans), and if they became Americans it was only, somehow, after a relatively recent passage westbound across the Atlantic.

It is, perhaps, this recency of arrival which has given to Americans a somewhat compulsive preoccupation with the question of their Americanism. No people can really qualify as a nation in the true sense unless they are united by important qualities or values in common. If they share the same ethnic, or linguistic, or religious, or political heritage, the foundations of nationality can hardly be questioned. But when their ethnic, religious, linguistic, and political heritage is mixed, as in the case of the American people, nationality can hardly exist at all unless it takes the form of a common adjustment to conditions of a new land, a common commitment to shared values, a common esteem for certain qualities of character, or a common set of adaptive traits and attitudes. It is partly for this reason that Americans, although committed to the principle of freedom of thought, have nevertheless placed such heavy emphasis upon the obligation to accept certain undefined tenets of 'Americanism'. It is for this same reason, also, that Americans have insisted upon their distinctiveness from the Old World from which they are derived. More than two centuries ago Hector St John de Crèvecœur asked a famous question, 'What then is the American, this new man?' He simply assumed, without arguing the point, that the American is a new man, and he only inquired wherein the American is different. A countless array of writers, including not only careful historians and social scientists but also professional patriots, hit-and-run travellers, itinerant lecturers, intuitive-minded amateurs of all sorts, have been repeating Crèvecœur's question and seeking to answer it ever since.

A thick volume would hardly suffice even to summarize the diverse interpretations which these various writers have advanced in describing or explaining the American character. Almost every trait, good or bad, has been attributed to the American people by someone,[1] and almost every explanation, from Darwinian selection to toilet-training, has been advanced to account for the attributed qualities. But it is probably safe to say that at bottom there have been only two primary ways of explaining the American, and that almost all of the innumerable interpretations which have been formulated can be grouped around or at least oriented to these two basic explanations, which serve as polar points for all the literature.

The most disconcerting fact about these two composite images of the American is that they are strikingly dissimilar and seemingly about as inconsistent with one another as two interpretations of the same phenomenon could possibly be. One depicts the American primarily as an individualist and an idealist, while the other makes him out as a conformist and a materialist. Both images have been developed with great

[1] Lee Coleman, 'What is American: a Study of Alleged American Traits', in *Social Forces*, XIX (1941), surveyed a large body of the literature on the American character and concluded that 'almost every conceivable value or trait has at one time or another been imputed to American culture by authoritative observers'.

detail and elaborate explanation in extensive bodies of literature, and both are worth a close scrutiny.

For those who have seen the American primarily as an individualist, the story of his evolution as a distinctive type dates back possibly to the actual moment of his decision to migrate from Europe to the New World, for this was a process in which the daring and venturesome were more prone to risk life in a new country while the timid and the conventional were more disposed to remain at home. If the selective factors in the migration had the effect of screening out men of low initiative, the conditions of life in the North American wilderness, it is argued, must have further heightened the exercise of individual resourcefulness, for they constantly confronted the settler with circumstances in which he could rely upon no one but himself, and where the capacity to improvise a solution for a problem was not infrequently necessary to survival.

In many ways the colonial American exemplified attitudes that were individualistic. Although he made his first settlements by the removal of whole communities which were transplanted bodily—complete with all their ecclesiastical and legal institutions—he turned increasingly, in the later process of settlement, to a more and more individualistic mode of pioneering, in which one separate family would take up title to a separate, perhaps an isolated, tract of land, and would move to this land long in advance of any general settlement, leaving churches and courts and schools far behind. His religion, whether Calvinistic Puritanism or emotional revivalism, made him individually responsible for his own salvation, without the intervention of ecclesiastical intermediaries between himself and his God. His economy, which was based very heavily upon subsistence farming, with very little division of labor, also impelled him to cope with a diversity of problems and to depend upon no one but himself.

With all of these conditions at work, the tendency to place a premium upon individual self-reliance was no doubt well developed long before the cult of the American as an individualist crystallized in a conceptual form. But it did crystallize, and it took on almost its classic formulation in the thought of Thomas Jefferson.

It may seem paradoxical to regard Jefferson as a delineator of American national character, for in direct terms he did not attempt to describe the American character at all. But he did conceive that one particular kind of society was necessary to the fulfillment of American ideals, and further that one particular kind of person, namely the independent farmer, was a necessary component in the optimum society. He believed that the principles of liberty and equality, which he cherished so deeply, could not exist in a hierarchical society, such as that of Europe, nor, indeed, in any society where economic and social circumstances enabled one set of men to dominate and exploit the rest. An urban society or a commercial society, with its concentration of financial power into a few hands and its imposition of dependence through a wage system, scarcely lent itself better than an aristocracy to his basic values. In fact, only a society of small husbandmen who tilled their own soil and found sustenance in their own produce could achieve the combination of independence and equalitarianism which he envisioned for the ideal society. Thus, although Jefferson did not write a description of the national character, he erected a model for it, and the model ultimately had more influence than a description could ever have exercised. The model American was a plain, straightforward agrarian democrat, an individualist in his desire for freedom for himself, and an idealist in his desire for equality for all men.

Jefferson's image of the American as a man of independence, both in his values and in his mode of life, has had immense appeal to Americans ever since. They found this image best exemplified in the man of the frontier, for he, as a pioneer, seemed to illustrate the qualities of independence and self-reliance in their most pronounced and most dramatic form. Thus in a tradition of something like folklore, half-legendary figures like Davy Crockett have symbolized America as well as symbolizing the frontier. In literature, ever since J. Fenimore Cooper's Leatherstocking tales, the frontier scout, at home under the open sky, free from the trammels of an organized and stratified society, has been cherished as an incarnation of American qualities.[1] In American politics the voters showed such a marked preference for men who had been born in log cabins that many an ambitious candidate pretended to pioneer origins which were in fact fictitious.

The pioneer is, of course, not necessarily an agrarian (he may be a hunter, a trapper, a cowboy, a prospector for gold), and the agrarian is not necessarily a pioneer (he may be a European peasant tilling his ancestral acres), but the American frontier was basically an agricultural frontier, and the pioneer was usually a farmer. Thus it was possible to make an equation between the pioneer and the agrarian, and since the pioneer evinced the agrarian traits in their most picturesque and most appealing form there was a strong psychological impulse to concentrate the diffused agrarian ideal into a sharp frontier focus. This is, in part, what Frederick Jackson Turner did in 1893 when he wrote *The Significance of the Frontier in American History*. In this famous essay Turner offered an explanation of what has been distinctive in American history, but it is not as widely realized as it might be that he also penned a major contribution to the literature of national character. Thus Turner affirmed categorically that 'The American intellect owes its striking characteristics to the frontier. That coarseness and strength, combined with acuteness and acquisitiveness; that practical inventive turn of mind, quick to find expedients; that masterful grasp of material things, lacking in the artistic but powerful to effect great ends; that restless, nervous energy; that dominant individualism, working for good and for evil; and withal, that buoyancy and exuberance which comes with freedom—these are traits of the frontier, or traits called out elsewhere because of the existence of the frontier.'[2]

[1] Henry Nash Smith, *Virgin Land: the American West as Symbol and Myth* (1950), brilliantly analyzes the power which the image of the Western pioneer has had upon the American imagination.

[2] Frederick J. Turner, *The Frontier in American History* (Henry Holt and Co., 1920), p. 37.

A significant but somewhat unnoticed aspect of Turner's treatment is the fact that, in his quest to discover the traits of the American character, he relied for proof not upon descriptive evidence that given traits actually prevailed, but upon the argument that given conditions in the environment would necessarily cause the development of certain traits. Thus the cheapness of land on the frontier would make for universal land-holding which in turn would make for equalitarianism in the society. The absence of division of labor on the frontier would force each man to do most things for himself, and this would breed self-reliance. The pitting of the individual man against the elemental forces of the wilderness and of nature would further reinforce this self-reliance. Similarly, the fact that a man had moved out in advance of society's institutions and its stratified structure would mean that he could find independence, without being overshadowed by the institutions, and could enjoy an equality unknown to stratified society. All of this argument was made without any sustained effort to measure exactly how much recognizable equalitarianism and individualism and self-reliance actually were in evidence either on the American frontier or in American society. There is little reason to doubt that most of his arguments were valid or that most of the traits which he emphasized did actually prevail, but it is nevertheless ironical that Turner's interpretation, which exercised such vast influence upon historians, was not based upon the historian's kind of proof, which is from evidence, but upon an argument from logic which so often fails to work out in historical experience.

But no matter how he arrived at it, Turner's picture reaffirmed some by-now-familiar beliefs about the American character. The American was equalitarian, stoutly maintaining the practices of both social and political democracy; he had a spirit of freedom reflected in his buoyance and exuberance; he was individualistic—hence 'practical and inventive', 'quick to find expedients', 'restless, nervous, acquisitive'. Turner was too much a scholar to let his evident fondness for the frontiersman run away with him entirely, and he took pains to point out that this development was not without its sordid aspects. There was a marked primitivism about the frontier, and with it, to some extent, a regression from civilized standards. The buoyant and exuberant frontiersman sometimes emulated his Indian neighbors in taking the scalps of his adversaries. Coarse qualities sometimes proved to have more survival value than gentle ones. But on the whole this regression was brief, and certainly a rough-and-ready society had its compensating advantages. Turner admired his frontiersman, and thus Turner's American, like Jefferson's American, was partly a realistic portrait from life and partly an idealized model from social philosophy. Also, though one of these figures was an agrarian and the other was a frontiersman, both were very much the same man—democratic, freedom-loving, self-reliant, and individualistic.

An essay like this is hardly the place to prove either the validity or the invalidity of the Jeffersonian and Turnerian conception of the American character. The attempt to do so would involve a review of the entire range of American historical experience, and in the course of such a review the proponents of this conception could point to a vast body of evidence in support of their interpretation. They could argue, with much force, that Americans have consistently been zealous to defend individualism by defending the rights and the welfare of the individual, and that our whole history is a protracted record of our government's recognizing its responsibility to an ever broader range of people—to men without property, to men held in slavery, to women, to small enterprises threatened by monopoly, to children laboring in factories, to industrial workers, to the ill, to the elderly, and to the unemployed. This record, it can further be argued, is also a record of the practical idealism of the American people, unceasingly at work.

But without attempting a verdict on the historical validity of this image of the American as individualist and idealist, it is important to bear in mind that this image has been partly a portrait, but also partly a model. In so far as it is a portrait

—a likeness by an observer reporting on Americans whom he knew—it can be regarded as authentic testimony on the American character. But in so far as it is a model—an idealization of what is best in Americanism, and of what Americans should strive to be, it will only be misleading if used as evidence of what ordinary Americans are like in their everyday lives. It is also important to recognize that the Jefferson-Turner image posited several traits as distinctively American, and that they are not all necessarily of equal validity. Particularly, Jefferson and Turner both believed that love of equality and love of liberty go together. For Jefferson the very fact, stated in the Declaration of Independence, that 'all men are created equal', carried with it the corollary that they are all therefore 'entitled to [and would be eager for] life, liberty, and the pursuit of happiness'. From this premise it is easy to slide imperceptibly into the position of holding that equalitarianism and individualism are inseparably linked, or even that they are somehow the same thing. This is, indeed, almost an officially sanctioned ambiguity in the American creed. But it requires only a little thoughtful reflection to recognize that equalitarianism and individualism do not necessarily go together. Alexis de Tocqueville understood this fact more than a century ago, and out of his recognition he framed an analysis which is not only the most brilliant single account of the American character, but is also the only major alternative to the Jefferson-Turner image.

After travelling the length and breadth of the United States for ten months at the height of Andrew Jackson's ascendancy, Tocqueville felt no doubt of the depth of the commitment of Americans to democracy. Throughout two volumes which ranged over every aspect of American life, he consistently emphasized democracy as a pervasive factor. But the democracy which he wrote about was far removed from Thomas Jefferson's dream.

'Liberty,' he observed of the Americans, 'is not the chief object of their desires; equality is their idol. They make rapid and sudden efforts to obtain liberty, and if they miss their aim resign themselves to their disappointment; but nothing can satisfy them without equality, and they would rather perish than lose it.'[1]

This emphasis upon equality was not, in itself, inconsistent with the most orthodox Jeffersonian ideas, and indeed Tocqueville took care to recognize that under certain circumstances equality and freedom might 'meet and blend'. But such circumstances would be rare, and the usual effects of equality would be to encourage conformity and discourage individualism, to regiment opinion and to inhibit dissent. Tocqueville justified this seemingly paradoxical conclusion by arguing that:

'When the inhabitant of a democratic country compares himself individually with all those about him, he feels with pride that he is the equal of any one of them; but when he comes to survey the totality of his fellows, and to place himself in contrast with so huge a body, he is instantly overwhelmed by the sense of his own insignificance and weakness. The same equality that renders him independent of each of his fellow citizens, taken severally, exposes him alone and unprotected to the influence of the greater number. The public, therefore, among a democratic people, has a singular power, which aristocratic nations cannot conceive; for it does not persuade others to its beliefs, but it imposes them and makes them permeate the thinking of everyone by a sort of enormous pressure of the mind of all upon the individual intelligence.'[2]

At the time when Tocqueville wrote, he expressed admiration for the American people in many ways, and when he criticized adversely his tone was abstract, bland, and free of the petulance and the personalities that characterized some critics, like Mrs Trollope and Charles Dickens. Consequently, Tocqueville was relatively well received in the United States,

[1] Alexis de Tocqueville, *Democracy in America*, edited by Phillips Bradley (Alfred A. Knopf, 1946), I, pp. 53–4.
[2] *Ibid.*, II, p. 94; II, p. 10.

and we have largely forgotten what a severe verdict his observations implied. But, in fact, he pictured the American character as the very embodiment of conformity, of conformity so extreme that not only individualism but even freedom was endangered. Because of the enormous weight with which the opinion of the majority pressed upon the individual, Tocqueville said, the person in the minority 'not only mistrusts his strength, but even doubts of his right; and he is very near acknowledging that he is in the wrong when the greater number of his countrymen assert that he is so. The majority do not need to force him; they convince him.' 'The principle of equality', as a consequence, had the effect of 'prohibiting him from thinking at all', and 'freedom of opinion does not exist in America'. Instead of reinforcing liberty, therefore, equality constituted a danger to liberty. It caused the majority 'to despise and undervalue the rights of private persons', and led on to the pessimistic conclusion that 'Despotism appears . . . peculiarly to be dreaded in democratic times'.[1]

Tocqueville was perhaps the originator of the criticism of the American as conformist, but he also voiced another criticism which has had many echoes, but which did not originate with him. This was the condemnation of the American as a materialist. As early as 1805 Richard Parkinson had observed that 'all men there [in America] make it [money] their pursuit', and in 1823 William Faux had asserted that 'two selfish gods, pleasure and gain, enslave the Americans'. In the interval between the publication of the first and second parts of Tocqueville's study, Washington Irving coined his classic phrase concerning 'the almighty dollar, that great object of universal devotion throughout the land'.[2] But it remained for Tocqueville, himself, to link materialism with equality, as he had already linked conformity.

[1] *Ibid.*, II, p. 261; II, p. 11; I, p. 265; II, p. 326; II, p. 322.
[2] Richard Parkinson, *A Tour in America in 1798–1800* (2 vols., 1805), vol. II, p. 652; William Faux, *Memorable Days in America* (1823), p. 417; Washington Irving, 'The Creole Village', in *The Knickerbocker Magazine*, November 1836.

'Of all passions,' he said, 'which originate in or are fostered by equality, there is one which it renders peculiarly intense, and which it also infuses into the heart of every man: I mean the love of well-being. The taste for well-being is the prominent and indelible feature of democratic times. . . . The effort to satisfy even the least wants of the body and to provide the little conveniences of life is uppermost in every mind.'

He described this craving for physical comforts as a 'passion', and affirmed that 'I know of no country, indeed, where the love of money has taken stronger hold on the affections of men'.[1]

For more than a century we have lived with the contrasting images of the American character which Thomas Jefferson and Alexis de Tocqueville visualized. Both of these images presented the American as an equalitarian and therefore as a democrat, but one was an agrarian democrat while the other was a majoritarian democrat; one an independent individualist, the other a mass-dominated conformist; one an idealist, the other a materialist. Through many decades of self-scrutiny Americans have been seeing one or the other of these images whenever they looked into the mirror of self-analysis.

The discrepancy between the two images is so great that it must bring the searcher for the American character up with a jerk, and must force him to grapple with the question whether these seemingly antithetical versions of the American can be reconciled in any way. Can the old familiar formula for embracing opposite reports—that the situation presents a paradox—be stretched to encompass both Tocqueville and Jefferson? Or is there so grave a flaw somewhere that one must question the whole idea of national character and call to mind all the warnings that thoughtful men have uttered against the very concept that national groups can be distinguished from one another in terms of collective group traits.

[1] Tocqueville, *Democracy in America*, II, p. 26; II, p. 128; II, p. 129; I, p. 51.

Certainly there is a sound enough basis for doubting the validity of generalizations about national character. To begin with, many of these generalizations have been derived not from any dispassionate observation or any quest for truth, but from superheated patriotism which sought only to glorify one national group by invidious comparison with other national groups, or from a pseudoscientific racism which claimed innately superior qualities for favored ethnic groups. Further, the explanations which were offered to account for the ascribed traits were as suspect as the ascriptions themselves. No one today will accept the notions which once prevailed that such qualities as the capacity for self-government are inherited in the genes, nor will anyone credit the notion that national character is a unique quality which manifests itself mystically in all the inhabitants of a given country. Between the chauvinistic purposes for which the concept of national character was used, and the irrationality with which it was supported, it fell during the 1930's into a disrepute from which it has by no means fully recovered.

Some thinkers of a skeptical turn of mind had rejected the idea of national character even at a time when most historians accepted it without question. Thus, for instance, John Stuart Mill as early as 1849 observed that 'of all vulgar modes of escaping from the consideration of the effect of social and moral influences on the human mind, the most vulgar is that of attributing diversities of character to inherent natural differences'. Sir John Seely said, 'no explanation is so vague, so cheap, and so difficult to verify'.[1]

But it was particularly at the time of the rise of Fascism and Naziism, when the vicious aspects of extreme nationalism and of racism became glaringly conspicuous, that historians in general began to repudiate the idea of national character and to disavow it as an intellectual concept, even though they sometimes continued to employ it as a working device in their treatment of the peoples with whose history they were con-

[1] Mill, *The Principles of Political Economy* (1849), I, p. 390; Seely, quoted by Boyd C. Shafer, 'Men are More Alike', in *American Historical Review*, LVII (1952), p. 606.

cerned. To historians whose skepticism had been aroused, the conflicting nature of the images of the American as an individualistic democrat or as a conformist democrat would have seemed simply to illustrate further the already demonstrated flimsiness and fallacious quality of all generalizations about national character.

But to deny that the inhabitants of one country may, as a group, evince a given trait in higher degree than the inhabitants of some other country amounts almost to a denial that the culture of one people can be different from the culture of another people. To escape the pitfalls of racism in this way is to fly from one error into the embrace of another, and students of culture—primarily anthropologists, rather than historians—perceived that rejection of the idea that a group could be distinctive, along with the idea that the distinction was eternal and immutable in the genes, involved the ancient logical fallacy of throwing out the baby along with the bath. Accordingly, the study of national character came under the special sponsorship of cultural anthropology, and in the 'forties a number of outstanding workers in this field tackled the problem of national character, including the American character, with a methodological precision and objectivity that had never been applied to the subject before. After their investigations, they felt no doubt that national character was a reality—an observable and demonstrable reality. One of them, Margaret Mead, declared that 'In every culture, in Samoa, in Germany, in Iceland, in Bali, and in the United States of America, we will find consistencies and regularities in the way in which new born babies grow up and assume the attitudes and behavior patterns of their elders—and this we may call "character formation". We will find that Samoans may be said to have a Samoan character structure and Americans an American character structure.'[1] Another, the late Clyde Kluckhohn, wrote: 'The statistical prediction can safely be made that a

[1] Margaret Mead, *And Keep Your Powder Dry* (William Morrow and Co., 1942), p. 21. Miss Mead also says, 'The way in which people behave is all of a piece, their virtues and their sins, the way they slap the baby, handle their court cases, and bury their dead.'

hundred Americans, for example, will display certain defined characteristics more frequently than will a hundred Englishmen comparably distributed as to age, sex, social class, and vocation.'[1]

If these new students were correct, it meant that there was some kind of identifiable American character. It might conform to the Jeffersonian image; it might conform to the Tocquevillian image; it might conform in part to both; or it might conform to neither. But in any event discouraged investigators were enjoined against giving up the quest with the conclusion that there is no American character. It has been said that a philosopher is a blind man in a dark room looking for a black cat that isn't there; the student of national character might also, at times, resemble a blind man in a dark room, looking for a black cat, but the cultural anthropologists exhorted him to persevere in spite of the problems of visibility, for the cat was indubitably there.

Still confronted with the conflicting images of the agrarian democrat and the majoritarian democrat, the investigator might avoid an outright rejection of either by taking the position that the American character has changed, and that each of these images was at one time valid and realistic, but that in the twentieth century the qualities of conformity and materialism have grown increasingly prominent, while the qualities of individualism and idealism have diminished. This interpretation of a changing American character has had a number of adherents in the last two decades, for it accords well with the observation that the conditions of the American culture have changed. As they do so, of course the qualities of a character that is derived from the culture might be expected to change correspondingly. Thus, Henry S. Commager, in his *The American Mind* (1950), portrayed in two contrasting chapters 'the nineteenth-century American' and 'the twentieth-century American'. Similarly, David Riesman, in *The Lonely Crowd* (1950), significantly sub-titled *A Study of the Changing American Character*, pictured two types of Americans, first an

[1] Clyde Kluckhohn and Henry A. Murray, *Personality in Nature, Society, and Culture* (Alfred A. Knopf, 1949), p. 36.

'inner-directed man', whose values were deeply internalized and who adhered to these values tenaciously, regardless of the opinions of his peers (clearly an individualist), and second an 'other-directed man', who subordinated his own internal values to the changing expectations directed toward him by changing peer groups (in short, a conformist).

Although he viewed his inner-directed man as having been superseded historically by his other-directed man, Riesman did not attempt to explain in historical terms the reason for the change. He made a rather limited effort to relate his stages of character formation to stages of population growth, but he has since then not used population phase as a key. Meanwhile, it is fairly clear, from Riesman's own context, as well as from history in general, that there were changes in the culture which would have accounted for the transition in character. Most nineteenth-century Americans were self-employed; most were engaged in agriculture; most produced a part of their own food and clothing. These facts meant that their well-being did not depend on the goodwill or the services of their associates, but upon their resourcefulness in wrestling with the elemental forces of Nature. Even their physical isolation from their fellows added something to the independence of their natures. But most twentieth-century Americans work for wages or salaries, many of them in very large employee groups; most are engaged in office or factory work; most are highly specialized, and are reliant upon many others to supply their needs in an economy with an advanced division of labor. Men now do depend upon the goodwill and the services of their fellows. This means that what they achieve depends less upon stamina and hardihood than upon their capacity to get along with other people and to fit smoothly into a co-operative relationship. In short the culture now places a premium upon the qualities which will enable the individual to function effectively as a member of a large organizational group. The strategic importance of this institutional factor has been well recognized by William H. Whyte, Jr., in his significantly titled book *The Organization Man* (1956)—for the conformity of Whyte's bureaucratized individual results from the fact that he lives under an imperative to succeed in a situation where promotion and even survival depend upon effective inter-action with others in an hierarchical structure.

Thus, by an argument from logic (always a treacherous substitute for direct observation in historical study), one can make a strong case that the nineteenth-century American should have been (and therefore must have been) an individualist, while the twentieth-century American should be (and therefore is) a conformist. But this formula crashes headlong into the obdurate fact that no Americans have ever been more classically conformist than Tocqueville's Jacksonian democrats—hardy specimens of the frontier breed, far back in the nineteenth century, long before the age of corporate images, peer groups, marginal differentiation, and status frustration. In short, Tocqueville's nineteenth-century American, whether frontiersman or no, was to some extent an other-directed man. Carl N. Degler has pointed out this identity in a very cogent paper not yet published, in which he demonstrates very forcibly that most of our easy assumptions about the immense contrast between the nineteenth-century American and the twentieth-century American are vulnerable indeed.[1]

This conclusion should, perhaps, have been evident from the outset, in view of the fact that it was Tocqueville who, in the nineteenth century, gave us the image which we now frequently identify as the twentieth-century American. But in any case, the fact that he did so means that we can hardly resolve the dilemma of our individualist democrat and our majoritarian democrat by assuming that both are historically valid but that one replaced the other. The problem of determining what use we can make of either of these images, in view of the fact that each casts doubt upon the other, still remains. Is it possible to uncover common factors in these apparently contradictory images, and thus to make use of them both in our quest for a definition of the national character? For no matter whether either of these versions of the American is realistic as a type or image, there is no doubt that

[1] Delivered on 30 December 1960, at the annual meeting of the American Historical Association in New York.

both of them reflect fundamental aspects of the American experience.

There is no purpose, at this point in this essay, to execute a neat, pre-arranged sleight-of-hand by which the individualist democrat and the conformist democrat will cast off their disguises and will reveal themselves as identical twin Yankee Doodle Dandies, both born on the fourth of July. On the contrary, intractable, irresolvable discrepancies exist between the two figures, and it will probably never be possible to go very far in the direction of accepting the one without treating the other as a fictitious image, to be rejected as reflecting an anti-democratic bias and as at odds with the evidence from actual observation of the behavior of *Homo americanus* in his native haunts. At the same time, however, it is both necessary to probe for the common factors, and legitimate to observe that there is one common factor conspicuous in the extreme —namely the emphasis on equality, so dear both to Jefferson's American and to Tocqueville's. One of these figures, it will be recalled, has held no truth to be more self-evident than that all men are created equal, while the other has made equality his 'idol', far more jealously guarded than his liberty.

If the commitment to equality is so dominant a feature in both of these representations of the American, it will perhaps serve as a key to various facets of the national character, even to contradictory aspects of this character. In a society as complex as that of the United States, in fact, it may be that the common factors underlying the various manifestations are all that our quest should seek. For it is evident that American life and American energy have expressed themselves in a great diversity of ways, and any effort to define the American as if nearly two hundred million persons all corresponded to a single type would certainly reduce complex data to a blunt, crude, and oversimplified form. To detect what qualities Americans share in their diversity may be far more revealing than to superimpose the stereotype of a fictitious uniformity. If this is true, it means that our quest must be to discover the varied and dissimilar ways in which the commitment to equality expresses itself--the different forms which it takes in different individuals—rather than to regard it as an undifferentiated component which shows in all individuals in the same way. Figuratively, one might say that in seeking for what is common, one should think of the metal from which Americans are forged, no matter into how many shapes this metal may be cast, rather than thinking of a die with which they all are stamped into an identical shape. If the problem is viewed in this way, it will be readily apparent that Tocqueville made a pregnant statement when he observed that the idea of equality was 'the fundamental fact from which all others seem to be derived'.

The term 'equality' is a loose-fitting garment and it has meant very different things at very different times. It is very frequently used to imply parity or uniformity. The grenadiers in the King of Prussia's guard were equal in that they were all, uniformly, over six feet six inches tall. Particularly, it can mean, and often does mean in some social philosophies, uniformity of material welfare—of income, of medical care, etc. But people are clearly not uniform in strength or intelligence or beauty, and one must ask, therefore, what kind of uniformity Americans believed in. Did they believe in an equal sharing of goods? Tocqueville himself answered this question when he said, 'I know of no country . . . where a profounder contempt is expressed for the theory of the permanent equality of property'.[1]

At this point in the discussion of equality, someone, and very likely a business man, is always likely to break in with the proposition that Americans believe in equality of opportunity —in giving everyone what is called an equal start, and in removing all handicaps such as illiteracy and all privileges such as monopoly or special priority, which will tend to give one person an advantage over another. But if a person gains the advantage without having society give it to him, by being more clever or more enterprising or even just by being stronger than someone else, he is entitled to enjoy the benefits that accrue from these qualities, particularly in terms of possessing more property or wealth than others.

[1] Tocqueville, *Democracy in America*, I, p. 57–8.

Historically, equality of opportunity was a particularly apt form of equalitarianism for a new, undeveloped frontier country. In the early stages of American history, the developed resources of the country were so few that an equality in the division of these assets would only have meant an insufficiency for everyone. The best economic benefit which the government could give was to offer a person free access in developing undeveloped resources for his own profit, and this is what America did offer. It was an ideal formula for everyone: for the individual it meant a very real chance to gain more wealth than he would have secured by receiving an equal share of the existing wealth. For the community, it meant that no one could prosper appreciably without activities which would develop undeveloped resources, at a time when society desperately needed rapid economic development. For these reasons, equality of opportunity did become the most highly sanctioned form of equalitarianism in the United States.

Because of this sanction, Americans have indeed been tolerant of great discrepancies in wealth. They have approved of wealth much more readily when they believed that it had been earned—as in the case, for instance, of Henry Ford—than when they thought it had been acquired by some special privilege or monopoly. In general, however, they have not merely condoned great wealth; they have admired it. But to say that the ideal of equality means only equality of opportunity is hardly to tell the whole story. The American faith has also held, with intense conviction, the belief that all men are equal in the sense that they share a common humanity—that all are alike in the eyes of God—and that every person has a certain dignity, no matter how low his circumstances, which no one else, no matter how high *his* circumstances, is entitled to disregard. When this concept of the nature of man was translated into a system of social arrangements, the crucial point on which it came to focus was the question of rank. For the concept of rank essentially denies that all men are equally worthy and argues that some are better than others—that some are born to serve and others born to command. The American creed not only denied this view, but even condemned it and placed a taboo upon it. Some people, according to the American creed, might be more fortunate than others, but they must never regard themselves as better than others. Pulling one's rank has therefore been the unforgivable sin against American democracy, and the American people have, accordingly, reserved their heartiest dislike for the officer class in the military, for people with upstage or condescending manners, and for anyone who tries to convert power or wealth (which are not resented) into overt rank or privilege (which are). Thus it is permissible for an American to have servants (which is a matter of function), but he must not put them in livery (which is a matter of rank); permissible to attend expensive schools, but not to speak with a cultivated accent; permissible to rise in the world, but never to repudiate the origins from which he rose. The most palpable and overt possible claim of rank is, of course, the effort of one individual to assert authority, in a personal sense, over others, and accordingly the rejection of authority is the most pronounced of all the concrete expressions of American beliefs in equality.

In almost any enterprise which involves numbers of people working in conjunction, it is necessary for some people to tell other people what to do. This function cannot be wholly abdicated without causing a breakdown, and in America it cannot be exercised overtly without violating the taboos against authority. The result is that the American people have developed an arrangement which skillfully combines truth and fiction, and maintains that the top man does not rule, but leads; and does not give orders, but calls signals; while the men in the lower echelons are not underlings, but members of the team. This view of the relationship is truthful in the sense that the man in charge does depend upon his capacity to elicit the voluntary or spontaneous co-operation of the members of his organization, and he regards the naked use of authority to secure compliance as an evidence of failure; also, in many organizations, the members lend their support willingly, and contribute much more on a voluntary basis than authority could ever exact from them. But the element of fiction sometimes enters, in terms of the fact that both sides understand that in many situations authority would have to be invoked if voluntary compliance were not forthcoming. This would be humiliating to all parties—to the top man because it would expose his failure as a leader and to the others because it would force them to recognize the carefully concealed fact that in an ultimate sense they are subject to coercion. To avoid this mutually undesirable exploration of the ultimate implications, both sides recognize that even when an order has to be given, it is better for it to be expressed in the form of a request or a proposal, and when compliance is mandatory, it should be rendered with an appearance of consent.

It is in this way that the anti-authoritarian aspect of the creed of equality leads to the extraordinarily strong emphasis upon permissiveness, either as a reality or as a mere convention in American life. So strong is the taboo against authority that the father, once a paternal authority, is now expected to be a pal to his children, and to persuade rather than to command. The husband, once a lord and master, to be obeyed under the vows of matrimony, is now a partner. And if, perchance, an adult male in command of the family income uses his control to bully his wife and children, he does not avow his desire to make them obey, but insists that he only wants them to be co-operative. The unlimited American faith in the efficacy of discussion as a means of finding solutions for controversies reflects less a faith in the powers of rational persuasion than a supreme reluctance to let anything reach a point where authority will have to be invoked. If hypocrisy is the tribute that vice pays to virtue, permissiveness is, to some extent, the tribute that authority pays to the principle of equality.

When one recognizes some of these varied strands in the fabric of equalitarianism it becomes easier to see how the concept has contributed to the making, both of the Jeffersonian American and the Tocquevillian American. For as one picks at the strands they ravel out in quite dissimilar directions. The strand of equality of opportunity, for instance, if followed out, leads to the theme of individualism. It challenged each individual to pit his skill and talents in a competition against the skill and talents of others and to earn the individual rewards which talent and effort might bring. Even more, the imperatives of the competitive race were so compelling that the belief grew up that everyone had a kind of obligation to enter his talents in this competition and to 'succeed'. It was but a step from the belief that ability and virtue would produce success to the belief that success was produced by—and was therefore an evidence of—ability and virtue. In short, money not only represented power, it also was a sign of the presence of admirable qualities in the man who attained it. Here, certainly, an equalitarian doctrine fostered materialism, and if aggressiveness and competitiveness are individualistic qualities, then it fostered individualism also.

Of course, neither American individualism nor American materialism can be explained entirely in these terms. Individualism must have derived great strength, for instance, from the reflection that if all men are equal, a man might as well form his own convictions as accept the convictions of someone else no better than himself. It must also have been reinforced by the frontier experience, which certainly compelled every man to rely upon himself. But this kind of individualism is not the quality of independent-mindedness, and it is not the quality which Tocqueville was denying when he said that Americans were conformists. A great deal of confusion has resulted, in the discussion of the American character, from the fact that the term individualism is sometimes used (as by Tocqueville) to mean willingness to think and act separately from the majority, and sometimes (as by Turner) to mean capacity to get along without help. It might be supposed that the two would converge, on the theory that a man who can get along by himself without help will soon recognize that he may as well also think for himself without help. But in actuality, this did not necessarily happen. Self-reliance on the frontier was more a matter of courage and of staying power than of intellectual resourcefulness, for the struggle with the wilderness challenged the body rather than the mind, and a man might be supremely effective in fending for himself, and at the same time supremely conventional in his ideas. In this sense, Turner's

individualist is not really an antithesis of Tocqueville's conformist at all.

Still, it remains true that Jefferson's idealist and Tocqueville's conformist both require explanation, and that neither
can be accounted for in the terms which make Jefferson's
individualist and Tocqueville's materialist understandable.
As an explanation of these facets of the American character,
it would seem that the strand of equalitarianism which
stresses the universal dignity of all men, and which hates rank
as a violation of dignity, might be found quite pertinent. For
it is the concept of the worth of every man which has stimulated a century and a half of reform, designed at every step
to realize in practice the ideal that every human possesses
potentialities which he should have a chance to fulfill. Whatever
has impeded this fulfillment, whether it be lack of education,
chattel slavery, the exploitation of the labor of unorganized
workers, the hazards of unemployment, or the handicaps of
age and infirmity, has been the object, at one time or another,
of a major reforming crusade. The whole American commitment to progress would be impossible without a prior belief in
the perfectibility of man and in the practicability of steps to
bring perfection nearer. In this sense, the American character
has been idealistic. And yet its idealism is not entirely irrecon-
cilable with its materialism, for American idealism has often
framed its most altruistic goals in materialistic terms—for
instance of raising the standard of living as a means to a better
life. Moreover, Americans are committed to the view that
materialistic means are necessary to idealistic ends. Franklin
defined what is necessary to a virtuous life by saying 'an empty
sack cannot stand upright', and Americans have believed that
spiritual and humanitarian goals are best achieved by instru-
mentalities such as universities and hospitals which carry
expensive price tags.

If the belief that all men are of equal worth has contributed
to a feature of American life so much cherished as our tradition
of humanitarian reform, how could It at the same time have
contributed to a feature so much deplored as American
conformity? Yet it has done both, for the same respect of the

American for his fellow men, which has made many a reformer think that his fellow citizens are worth helping, has also made many another American think that he has no business to question the opinions that his neighbors have sanctioned. True, he says, if all men are equal, each ought to think for himself, but on the other hand, no man should consider himself better than his neighbors, and if the majority have adopted an opinion on a matter, how can one man question their opinion, without setting himself up as being better than they. Moreover, it is understood that the majority are pledged not to force him to adopt their opinion. But it is also understood that in return for this immunity he will voluntarily accept the will of the majority in most things. The absence of a formal compulsion to conform seemingly increases the obligation to conform voluntarily. Thus, the other-directed man is seen to be derived as much from the American tradition of equalitarianism as the rugged individualist, and the compulsive seeker of an unequally large share of wealth as much as the humanitarian reformer striving for the fulfillment of democratic ideals.

To say that they are all derived from the same tradition is by no means to say that they are, in some larger, mystic sense, all the same. They are not, even though the idealism of the reformer may seek materialistic goals, and though men who are individualists in their physical lives may be conformists in their ideas. But all of them, it may be argued, do reflect circumstances which are distinctively American, and all present manifestations of a character which is more convincingly American because of its diversity than any wholly uniform character could possibly be. If Americans have never reached the end of their quest for an image that would represent the American character, it may be not because they failed to find one image but because they failed to recognize the futility of attempting to settle upon one, and the necessity of accepting several.

FOR FURTHER READING*

I

The Construction of American History

The most up-to-date survey of four centuries of American historiography is Harvey Wish's *The American Historian* (1960). Michael Kraus presents a more factually comprehensive treatment in *The Writing of American History* (revised ed., 1953), and David D. Van Tassel adds information on many minor figures in *Recording America's Past, 1607–1884* (1960). There are some striking insights in an almost forgotten little book by J. Franklin Jameson, *The History of Historical Writing in America* (1891).

On Puritan history, no substantial study exists, but Kenneth Murdock has a sensible chapter in his *Literature and Theology in Colonial New England* (1949). Richard S. Dunn points out significant contrasts among 'Seventeenth-Century English Historians of America' in *Seventeenth-Century America*, ed. James Morton Smith (1959), pp. 195–225. For the eighteenth-century historians there are, in addition to the general surveys, only scattered biographical articles, one of the best of which is Page Smith's 'David Ramsay and the Causes of the American Revolution', *William and Mary Quarterly*, XVII (1960), pp. 51–77.

Merrill Peterson throws much light on the whole sweep of historical thought in the nineteenth and twentieth centuries in *The Jefferson Image in the American Mind* (1960). David Levin's fine study of the ideas and literary achievement of the great mid-nineteenth-century historians, *History as Romantic Art* (1959), should be supplemented with a sociological report:

* This very selective bibliography supplements—it does not repeat —titles mentioned in the text and footnotes.

George H. Callcott, 'Historians in Early Nineteenth-Century America', *New England Quarterly*, XXXII (1959), pp. 496–520. On the transition at the end of the nineteenth century, William A. Dunning makes some perceptive comments in 'A Generation of American Historiography', American Historical Association *Report*, 1917, pp. 347–54. Among the many biographical critiques of the leading historians of this period, one of the best is J. C. Levenson's *The Mind and Art of Henry Adams* (1957).

We have many appraisals of twentieth-century scholarship, most of them topical in nature. A general review, now somewhat out of date, from a British perspective is in H. Hale Bellot's *American History and American Historians* (1952). For a severe American appraisal, see Oscar Handlin, 'The Central Themes of American History', *Relazioni del X Congresso Internazionale di Scienze Storiche* (1955), I, pp. 139–66. Cushing Strout's *The Pragmatic Revolt in American History* (1958) discusses the efforts of Carl Becker and Charles A. Beard to break away from scientific history.

For bibliographical guidance to any aspect of American culture, a good starting point is a selective, descriptive list of books edited by Donald H. Mugridge and Blanche P. McCrum, *A Guide to the Study of the United States of America* (1960). The *Harvard Guide to American History*, ed. Oscar Handlin et al. (1954), offers a more comprehensive bibliography of specifically historical material.

2

The Puritan Strain

A complete list of modern writings on Puritanism can be found in the bibliographies of Perry Miller and Thomas H. Johnson, *The Puritans* (1938), and the annual bibliographies published in the *New England Quarterly* (1928 to the present). The *New England Quarterly* also has excellent reviews of the principal books published since 1928.

Miller and Johnson, *The Puritans*, is also the principal collection of Puritan documents and has transformed the study of Puritanism in American colleges and universities. Unfortunately, it has been allowed to go out of print and the paperbook reprint (Perry Miller, *The American Puritans*, 1956), which omits much of the original, is not a satisfactory substitute. Other important Puritan writings easily available in modern editions are William Bradford, *History of Plymouth Plantations*, John Winthrop, *Journal*, Cotton Mather, *Magnalia Christi Americana*, Kenneth B. Murdock, *Selections from Cotton Mather* (1926), Perry Miller, *Roger Williams* (1953), and the *Diaries* of Cotton Mather and Samuel Sewall. Special mention should be made of the poems of Edward Taylor, the one really important poet of early New England, whose forgotten and unpublished works were discovered by Thomas H. Johnson in 1937; a complete edition of the poems, edited by Donald E. Stanford, is now available (1960).

Other important modern books about Puritanism are G. L. Kittredge, *Witchcraft in Old and New England* (1929); Herbert W. Schneider, *The Puritan Mind* (1930), which contains the best account of the Puritan tradition in later America; Edmund S. Morgan, *The Puritan Family* (1944); Carl Bridenbaugh, *Cities in the Wilderness* (1938); D. J. Boorstin, *The Americans: The Colonial Experience* (1958); and George L. Haskins, *Law and Authority in Early Massachusetts* (1960). *The Cultural Life of the American Colonies* (1957) is the most recent of the many works by Louis B. Wright which deal in part with colonial New England.

3

The Revolutionary Era

Curiously, George Bancroft's *History of the United States* remains the fullest comprehensive account of the Revolutionary era yet written by an American historian. Claude H. Van Tyne in

1922 published *The Causes of the War of Independence* as the first part of a projected three-volume *History of the Founding of the American Republic*. With the publication in 1929 of the second volume, *The War of Independence, American Phase*, which carried the story to the French alliance of 1778, it was announced that the work would be completed in four volumes, but death prevented execution of the plan. Consequently, the reader must depend, except for the great biographies mentioned before, upon shorter studies of particular parts of the general subject.

The fullest and best account of the Revolution itself is John Miller's *The Triumph of Freedom, 1775–1783* (1948), which follows in sequence upon his *Origins of the American Revolution* (1944). Much more recent is Bernhard Knollenberg, *Origin of the American Revolution: 1759–1766* (1960). Lawrence H. Gipson, *The Coming of the Revolution, 1763–1775* (1954), a volume in the New American Nation Series, tells the story from the point of view of the imperial school. In the same series, John R. Alden's *The American Revolution, 1775–1783* (1954), is especially strong on the military side of the story. His *The South in the Revolution, 1763–1789* (1957) is a unique study for that area and this period. Merrill Jensen's *The New Nation; a History of the United States During the Confederation, 1781–1789* (1950) quickly became the standard authority for the post-war years.

On the Constitution, mention should be given to the older works of Robert L. Schuyler, *The Constitution of the United States* (1923), and of Charles Warren, *The Making of the Constitution* (1929), together with Carl Van Doren's more recent *The Great Rehearsal* (1948). Carl Becker's *The Declaration of Independence* (1922; reissued in 1951) is a classic account. Samuel F. Bemis, *The Diplomacy of the American Revolution* (1935) is the standard study. Several helpful studies have been made for individual states, but there is no substitute for Allan Nevins, *The American States During and After the Revolution, 1775–1789* (1924). Edmund C. Burnett, *The Continental Congress* (1941), is full and detailed. Ralph Barton Perry's *Puritanism and Democracy* (1944) is an imaginative and thoroughly readable discussion by an eminent philosopher of two of the main streams which have been joined in the American historical tradition.

1

The Changing West

Some indication of the growth of the literature of Western-American history since Turner's retirement appears in the difference between the bibliographical footnotes in Frederic L. Paxson's *History of the American Frontier* (1924) and the appendices in Ray A. Billington's *Westward Expansion* (2d ed., 1959). None of the general accounts is significantly more interpretative than the first, and some are less. The best known of the many articles about Turner's interpretations of American history and about Turner himself are conveniently listed in Billington, *Westward Expansion* and *The American Frontier* (Service Center for Teachers of History pamphlet, American Historical Association, 1958).

Some of the most significant works published since 1920 and not mentioned above are Verner W. Crane, *The Southern Frontier, 1670–1732* (1928); Stanley Elkins and Eric McKitrick, 'A Meaning for Turner's Frontier', *Political Science Quarterly*, LXIX (September, December 1954), pp. 321–53, 565–602; Paul W. Gates, *The Illinois Central Railroad and its Colonization Work* (1934), *Frontier Landlords and Pioneer Tenants* (1945); Colin B. Goodykoontz, *Home Missions on the American Frontier* (1939); John D. Hicks, *The Populist Revolt* (1931); Charles A. Johnson, *The Frontier Camp Meeting* (1955); James C. Malin, *The Grassland of North America: Prolegomena to its History* (1947); Frederick Merk, *Fur Trade and Empire* (1931); Ernest S. Osgood, *The Day of the Cattleman* (1929); Rodman W. Paul, *California Gold* (1947); Frederic L. Paxson, *When the West is Gone* (1930); Clark C. Spence, *British Investments and the American Mining Frontier* (1958); William W. Sweet, *Religion on the American Frontier, 1783–1840* (4 vols., 1931–46); Robert Taft, *Artists and Illustrators of the Old West: 1850–1900* (1953); Frederick J. Turner, *The Significance of Sections in American History* (1932) and *The United States, 1830–1850* (1935); Walter P. Webb, *The*

Great Frontier (1952) and *An Honest Preface* (1959); Louis B. Wright, *Culture on the Moving Frontier* (1955).

Among useful essays on the literature and prospects of Western history are some in Merrill Jensen, ed., *Regionalism in America* (1951); see also Allan G. Bogue, 'Social Theory and the Pioneer', *Agricultural History*, XXXIV (January 1960), pp. 21–34, 100; Earl Pomeroy, 'Toward a Reorientation of American History: Continuity and Environment', *Mississippi Valley Historical Review*, XLI (March 1955), pp. 579–600, and 'Old Lamps for New: The Cultural Lag in Pacific Coast Historiography', *Arizona and the West*, II (summer 1960), pp. 107–26.

5

The Age of the Common Man

An excellent and fuller discussion of the recent scholarship on the Jacksonian period is Charles Grier Sellers, Jr., 'Andrew Jackson Versus the Historians', *Mississippi Valley Historical Review*, XLIV (March 1958), pp. 615–48. There are two convenient collections of primary sources: Joseph L. Blau, ed., *Social Theories of Jacksonian Democracy, Representative Writings of the Period 1825–1850* (1947); Harold C. Syrett, *Andrew Jackson, His Contribution to the American Tradition* (1953). Leonard D. White, *The Jacksonians, A Study in Administrative History, 1829–1861* (1954), is a fine treatment of its subject.

George Rogers Taylor, ed., *The Turner Thesis Concerning the Role of the Frontier in American History* (1949), one of the paper pamphlets in the Amherst 'Problems in American Civilization' series, provides Turner's two most important essays, plus a sampling of sentiment pro and con, and a good brief bibliography; Louis Hacker's critical remarks which I have quoted from the *Nation* are included. David M. Potter, *People of Plenty: Economic Abundance and the American Character* (1954), suggests that 'the frontier was only one form in which America offered abundance' and goes beyond the Turner thesis to suggest that abundance itself has been a major force in the shaping of the American character.

Herbert Croly, *The Promise of American Life* (1909), gives a major statement of the problem that the tradition of the common man raised for twentieth-century political action. In the same regard, see Mosei Ostrogorski, *Democracy and the Party System* (1910), which, by including only material relevant to the American experience, is an abridgment of his famous, two-volume study, *Democracy and the Organization of Political Parties* (1902).

Edward Pessen, 'The Workingmen's Movement of the Jacksonian Era', *Mississippi Valley Historical Review*, XLIII (December 1956), pp. 428–43, gives a good summary of the 'wage-earner' thesis and his notes provide a valuable bibliography of both the primary sources and the scholarship. One should also consult volume two of Joseph Dorfman, *The Economic Mind in American Civilization* (1946). Alice Felt Tyler, *Freedom's Ferment, Phases of American Social History to 1860* (1944), is a good narration of the many social and utopian reform movements of the period.

For particular studies, we have many fine biographies of key figures in the early nineteenth century. Two of the best are Charles Grier Sellers, *James K. Polk, Jacksonian: 1795–1843* (1957), and Elbert B. Smith, *Magnificent Missourian: The Life of Thomas Hart Benton* (1958). We have not fared so well at the general level. The most recent account, which is largely straight political history, is Glyndon G. Van Deusen, *The Jacksonian Era, 1828–1848* (1959), which has an excellent bibliography. Although it is a classic, with all the uncritical use made of classics, perhaps the best general treatment of early nineteenth-century America is still Alexis de Tocqueville, *Democracy in America*, available in many editions, the best of which is Phillips Bradley's (1948).

6

Disunion and Reunion

Two important historiographical studies not previously mentioned are Howard K. Beale, 'What Historians Have Said about the Causes of the Civil War', Social Sciences Research Council Bulletin 54, *Theory and Practice in Historical Study* (1946); and Thomas N. Bonner, 'Civil War Historians and the "Needless War" Doctrine', *Journal of the History of Ideas*, XVII (1956), pp. 193–216. Changing interpretations of the event that opened the final phase of the sectional controversy are summarized in Roy F. Nichols, 'The Kansas-Nebraska Act: A Century of Historiography', *Mississippi Valley Historical Review*, XLIII (1956–7), pp. 187–212. Basic readings are brought together in Kenneth M. Stampp, ed., *The Causes of the Civil War* (Spectrum paperback, 1959); and in two Amherst paperback 'Problems in American Civilization', edited by Edwin C. Rozwenc: *The Causes of the American Civil War* (1961); *Reconstruction in the South* (1952).

For the antislavery movement see Dwight L. Dumond, *Antislavery Origins of the Civil War in the United States* (1939); and Louis Filler, *The Crusade Against Slavery, 1830–1860* (1960). The progress of the South toward secession is covered in Avery O. Craven, *The Growth of Southern Nationalism, 1848–1861* (1953). The best one-volume life of Lincoln is Benjamin P. Thomas, *Abraham Lincoln* (1952). T. Harry Williams, *Lincoln and the Radicals* (1941), stresses the conflict within the Republican party. Two popular histories of Reconstruction whose authors show more restraint than Bowers are Robert S. Henry, *The Story of Reconstruction* (1938); and Hodding Carter, *The Angry Scar: the Story of Reconstruction* (1959). W. E. Burghardt Du Bois, *Black Reconstruction* (1935), is the work of a Negro Marxist. W. J. Cash, *The Mind of the South* (1941), is a perceptive and influential study.

7

The Working Class

The works cited in the text come from a vast literature on various aspects of labor. Recent brief bibliographies may be found in Henry J. Pelling, *American Labor* (1960); Maldwyn Allen Jones, *American Immigration* (1960); and John Hope Franklin, *From Slavery to Freedom* (revised edition, 1956): three books which are also the best surveys of their respective fields.

The standard histories of the major labor organizations are (on the Knights of Labor) Norman F. Ware, *The Labor Movement in the United States* (1929); Lewis L. Lorwin, *The American Federation of Labor* (1933); and Philip A. Taft, *The A. F. of L.* (2 vols., 1957–9). There are competent biographies of several labor leaders, notably Jonathan Grossman, *William Sylvis: Pioneer of American Labor* (1945); Hyman Weintraub, *Andrew Furuseth: Emancipator of the Seamen* (1959); and Elsie Glück, *John Mitchell: Miner* (1929). Strikes and violence have attracted due attention: J. Walter Coleman, *The Molly Maguire Riots* (1936); Henry David, *History of the Haymarket Affair* (1936); Donald L. McMurry, *The Great Burlington Strike of 1888* (1956); and Vernon H. Jensen, *Heritage of Conflict* (1950).

Local history has proved a useful approach to labor, and especially to the immigrant working class, in Caroline Ware, *The Early New England Cotton Manufacture* (1931); Vera Shlakman, *Economic History of a Factory Town* (1935); Hannah Josephson, *The Golden Threads* (1949); Robert Ernst, *Immigrant Life in New York City* (1949); and William A. Sullivan, *The Industrial Worker in Pennsylvania* (1955). Other important topics are covered by Helene S. Zahler, *Eastern Workingmen and National Land Policy* (1941); Charlotte Erickson, *American Industry and the European Immigrant* (1957); and Marc Karson, *American Labor Unions and Politics* (1958).

Immigration history as such consists almost entirely of studies of the various ethnic groups. Among the better ones are Ian C. C. Graham, *Colonists from Scotland* (1956); Jacob R. Marcus, *Early American Jewry* (2 vols., 1951–2); William F. Adams, *Ireland and Irish Emigration to the New World from 1815 to the Famine* (1932); Henry S. Lucas, *Netherlanders in America* (1955); John A. Hawgood, *The Tragedy of German America* (1940); Marcus Lee Hansen, *The Mingling of the Canadian and American People* (1940); and Yamato Ichihashi, *Japanese in the United States* (1932).

For Negro slavery Lewis C. Gray, *History of Agriculture in the Southern United States to 1860* (1933), provides the essential context, while Lorenzo J. Greene, *The Negro in Colonial New England* (1942), is representative of other sections of the country. Herbert Aptheker, *American Negro Slave Revolts* (1943), deals with a clandestine sort of labor movement, and Charles H. Wesley, *Negro Labor in the United States* (1927), with the more normal kind since emancipation.

I have suggested an American social history comprehending labor and other classes in 'The American Social Order: A Conservative Hypothesis', *American Historical Review* (April 1960).

8

The Realm of Wealth

A useful review of the recent literature on a central theme of this essay is Hal Bridges, 'The Robber Baron Concept in American History', *Business History Review*, vol. XXXII, number 1 (spring 1958), pp. 1–13. Valuable also is Edward N. Saveth, 'What Historians Teach About Business', *Fortune* (April 1952), pp. 118 ff. Thomas C. Cochran and William Miller, *The Age of Enterprise, A Social History of Industrial America* (1942), is a standard work, with an extensive bibliography brought up to date in 1961.

Works more specifically on 'the realm of wealth' include John Moody, *The Masters of Capital* (1919), and *The Railroad*

Builders (1919); and Stewart H. Holbrook, *The Age of the Moguls* (1953). The New York *Tribune* list of millionaires is reproduced and analyzed in Sidney Ratner, *New Light on the History of Great American Fortunes* (1953). The peculations of the rich are classically recorded in Gustavus Myers, *History of the Great American Fortunes* (3 vols., 1909); their peccadillos in Dixon Wecter, *The Saga of American Society, A Record of Social Aspiration 1607–1937* (1937). One of the themes projected in recent years by Fritz Redlich is the activity of the aristocracy in business, a theme which suggests the universality of certain drives that did in fact flower in the Gilded Age. See his excellent article, 'European Aristocracy and Economic Development', in *Explorations in Entrepreneurial History*, vol. VI, number 2 (December 1953), pp. 78–91. A related theme is business men in the aristocracy, which suggests that social climbing was as vigorous elsewhere as in the United States. See, for example, Ralph E. Pumphrey, 'The Introduction of Industrialists into the British Peerage', *American Historical Review*, vol. LXV, no. 1 (October 1959), pp. 1–16.

Most valuable bibliographically and otherwise on the problem of the poor is Robert H. Bremner, *From the Depths, The Discovery of Poverty in the United States* (1956). A penetrating survey of the Progressive tradition from Emerson to Theodore Roosevelt is Daniel Aaron, *Men of Good Hope* (1951).

9

The Progressive Tradition

For different interpretations from this essay, see George E. Mowry, *The Progressive Movement, 1900–1920: Recent Ideas and New Literature* (Service Center for Teachers of History pamphlet, American Historical Association, 1958), and the appropriate chapters in Donald H. Sheehan and Harold C. Syrett, eds., *Essays in American Historiography* (1960). Also see the bibliographical essay in Samuel P. Hays's able synthesis, *The*

Response to Industrialism, 1885–1914 (1957). This book is characteristic of the recent tendency to reject the validity of writing history from the point of view of the reformers

Intellectual history has boomed as an academic discipline since World War II. In addition to the works previously cited by Fine, Ginger, Quint, and Mann, the following critical but sympathetic books are important and readable: Daniel Aaron, *Men of Good Hope* (1951); Henry Steele Commager, *The American Mind* (1950); Eric F. Goldman, *Rendezvous With Destiny* (1952); Henry F. May, *The End of American Innocence* (1959); and Morton G. White, *Social Thought in America* (1949). Contrast Louis Filler's euphoric *Crusaders for American Liberalism* (1939) with David W. Noble's labored attack, *The Paradox of Progressive Thought* (1958). Two useful studies, with 'old' and 'new' points of view, about the role of the Protestant clergy in social reform are Charles H. Hopkins, *The Rise of the Social Gospel in American Protestantism, 1865–1915* (1940), and Paul A. Carter, *The Decline and Revival of the Social Gospel, 1920–1940* (1954).

Perhaps the most pleasant way of getting at reformers is through biography and autobiography. For the years before the New Deal, one might start with Charles A. Barker, *Henry George* (1955); C. Vann Woodward, *Tom Watson: Agrarian Rebel* (1938); Walter Johnson, *William Allen White's America* (1947); Robert M. La Follette, *La Follette's Autobiography* (1913); and Theodore Roosevelt, *An Autobiography* (1921). Contrast this last with Blum's *Republican Roosevelt* and Henry F. Pringle, *Theodore Roosevelt* (1931). For the liberal leader of the Democratic party during the 1920's, see Oscar Handlin's sympathetic *Al Smith and His America* (1958). The best single-volume biography of F.D.R. is James M. Burns, *Roosevelt: The Lion and the Fox* (1956), but no student should deny himself the pleasure of reading Frank Freidel's monumental *Franklin D. Roosevelt*, which is still in progress and of which three volumes have been published: *The Apprenticeship* (1952), *The Ordeal* (1954), and *The Triumph* (1956).

Emergence to World Power

On general writings concerning American diplomacy, a useful survey is Alexander De Conde, *New Interpretations in American Foreign Policy* (American Historical Association, 1957), which is pamphlet number two issued by the Service Center for Teachers of History. A more interpretive rundown is F. H. Soward, 'American Foreign Policy: Research, Reflection, and Recrimination', *International Journal*, XIII (summer 1958).

There are no essays on the historiography of America's emergence as a power. There are several, however, on American entry into the two wars, notably Richard W. Leopold, 'The Problem of American Intervention, 1917', *World Politics*, II (summer 1950); Louis Morton, 'Pearl Harbor in Perspective: A Bibliographical Survey', *Proceedings of the United States Naval Institute*, LXXXI (April 1955); and Wayne S. Cole, 'American Entry into World War II: A Historiographical Appraisal', *Mississippi Valley Historical Review*, XLIII (March 1957). Robert H. Ferrell, 'Pearl Harbor and the Revisionists', *Historian*, XVII (spring 1955), deals with some of the more extreme anti-Roosevelt writers. William A. Williams, 'Reflections on the Historiography of American Entry into World War II', *Oregon Historical Quarterly*, LVII (September 1956), treats of an alleged third force. My *American Intervention: 1917 and 1941* (American Historical Association, 1960), which is pamphlet number thirty from the Service Center for Teachers of History, describes the controversies in somewhat greater detail.

The Quest for the National Character

In addition to the titles by Turner, Tocqueville, Mead, Commager, Riesman, and Whyte, mentioned in the text, the following all provide incisive interpretations of the American character: James Truslow Adams, *The American* (1943); Jacques Barzun, *God's Country and Mine* (1954); Denis W. Brogan, *The American Character* (1944); James, Lord Bryce, *The American Commonwealth* (2 vols., 1888); Alastair Cooke, *One Man's America* (1953); James Fenimore Cooper, *The American Democrat* (1838); Geoffrey Gorer, *The American People* (1948); Francis L. K. Hsu, *Americans and Chinese: Two Ways of Life* (1953); Louis Kronenberger, *Company Manners: A Cultural Inquiry into American Life* (1954); Max Lerner, *America as a Civilization* (1957), chaps. II, IX, XI; Ralph Barton Perry, *Characteristically American* (1949); George Santayana, *Character and Opinion in the United States* (1920); Arthur M. Schlesinger, Sr., 'What, then, is the American, this new man?' in his *Paths to the Present* (1949).

For an excellent summary of recent literature with valuable bibliography, see Clyde Kluckhohn, 'Have There Been Discernible Shifts in American Values during the Past Generation', in Elting E. Morison, ed., *The American Style* (1958).

A series of anthropological interpretations appeared in the *American Anthropologist*, LVII (1955), including especially a basic contribution by Cora Du Bois, 'The Dominant Value Profile of American Culture'.

Historians of nationalism usually give some attention to the question of national character. Hans Kohn, *American Nationalism* (1957), is perhaps the best example.

For a discussion both of the theoretical problem of national character and of certain aspects of the American character, see David M. Potter, *People of Plenty* (1954).

The literature of travellers is a rich source. Much of this has been well anthologized in Henry S. Commager, *America in Perspective* (1947); Allan Nevins, *America Through British Eyes* (1948); Oscar Handlin, *This Was America* (1949); and Warren S. Tryon, *A Mirror for Americans* (3 vols., 1952).

INDEX

1. People

Aaron, D., 231, 232
Abernethy, T. P., 73, 74
Adams, H., 13, 17–18, 93
Adams, James T., 30–1, 32, 37, 43, 44, 234
Adams, John, 12, 56
Adams, W. F., 230
Albion, R. G., 138
Alden, J. R., 224
Alvord, C. W., 69
Andrews, C. M., 19, 29, 48–52, 59
Andrews, W., 139
Aptheker, H., 230
Arrington, L. J., 78
Astor, J. J., 137, 138
Astor, W. B., 139
Atkinson, E., 151, 155

Bailyn, B., 45
Bancroft, G., 12, 16–17, 19, 46–8, 52, 55, 57, 85, 90, 151, 174, 223
Bancroft, H. H., 67, 69
Barker, C. A., 232
Barry, C. J., 133
Barzun, J., 234
Beach, M. Y., 137, 138, 141, 150
Beale, H. K., 114–15, 116, 188, 228
Beard, C. A., 20, 21, 22, 23, 48, 51, 52–4, 55, 56, 57, 58, 71, 72, 109–10, 111, 115, 117, 147, 153, 154, 157, 166, 175, 179, 186, 195, 222
Beard, M. R., 147, 153, 154, 166
Becker, C., 18, 22, 54–5, 157, 222, 224
Beer, G. L., 48–52, 54
Bell, D., 164, 167
Bellot, H. Hale, 222

Bemis, S. F., 187, 224
Bennett, J. G., 139
Benson, L., 58, 95, 96
Benton, T. H., 227
Berlin, I., 41
Berthoff, R., 23, 131, 230
Billington, R. A., 225
Blau, J. L., 226
Blegen, T. C., 129
Blum, J. M., 168–9, 170, 232
Bogue, A., 77, 226
Bogue, M., 77
Bolton, H. E., 69, 70
Bonner, T. N., 228
Boorstin, D., 59, 60, 223
Bowers, C. G., 108
Boyd, J. P., 56
Bradford, W., 12, 37, 223
Bradley, P., 205, 227
Brandeis, L. D., 150, 162
Brant, I., 18, 56–7, 60
Bremner, R. H., 161, 231
Bridenbaugh, C., 124, 223
Bridges, H., 230
Brody, D., 132
Brogan, D. W., 234
Brown, R. E., 58, 61
Browne, H. J., 133
Bryan, W. J., 158, 160, 161, 162, 165, 168, 171
Bryce, J., 67, 234
Buchanan, J., 111
Buck, P. H., 108
Burgess, J. W., 106–7, 108
Burnett, E. C., 224
Burns, J. M., 176, 232

Calhoun, J. C., 100
Callcott, G. H., 222

2. Subjects

Revised January, 1970

ḥarper ✦ ꞇorchbooks

---

† The New American Nation Series, edited by Henry Steele Commager and Richard B. Morris.
‡ American Perspectives series, edited by Bernard Wishy and William E. Leuchtenburg.
a History of Europe series, edited by J. H. Plumb.
§ The Library of Religion and Culture, edited by Benjamin Nelson.
‖ Researches in the Social, Cultural, and Behavioral Sciences, edited by Benjamin Nelson.
ᵡ Harper Modern Science Series, edited by James A. Newman.
° Not for sale in Canada.
+ Documentary History of the United States series, edited by Richard B. Morris.
# Documentary History of Western Civilization series, edited by Eugene C. Black and Leonard W. Levy.
ʌ The Economic History of the United States series, edited by Henry David et al.
¶ European Perspectives series, edited by Eugene C. Black.
** Contemporary Essays series, edited by Leonard W. Levy.
* The Stratum Series, edited by John Hale.

ROBERT L. HEILBRONER: The Future as History: *The Historic Currents of Our Time and the Direction in Which They Are Taking America* TB/1386

ROBERT L. HEILBRONER: The Great Ascent: *The Struggle for Economic Development in Our Time* TB/3030

FRANK H. KNIGHT: The Economic Organization TB/1214

DAVID S. LANDES: Bankers and Pashas: *International Finance and Economic Imperialism in Egypt. New Preface by the Author* TB/1412

ROBERT LATOUCHE: The Birth of Western Economy: *Economic Aspects of the Dark Ages* TB/1290

ABBA P. LERNER: Everbody's Business: *A Reexamination of Current Assumptions in Economics and Public Policy* TB/3051

W. ARTHUR LEWIS: Economic Survey, 1919-1939 TB/1446

W. ARTHUR LEWIS: The Principles of Economic Planning. *New Introduction by the Author°* TB/1436

ROBERT GREEN MC CLOSKEY: American Conservatism in the Age of Enterprise TB/1137

PAUL MANTOUX: The Industrial Revolution in the Eighteenth Century: *An Outline of the Beginnings of the Modern Factory System in England°* TB/1079

WILLIAM MILLER, Ed.: Men in Business: *Essays on the Historical Role of the Entrepreneur* TB/1081

GUNNAR MYRDAL: An International Economy. *New Introduction by the Author* TB/1445

HERBERT A. SIMON: The Shape of Automation: *For Men and Management* TB/1245

PERRIN STRYER: The Character of the Executive: *Eleven Studies in Managerial Qualities* TB/1041

RICHARD S. WECKSTEIN, Ed.: Expansion of World Trade and the Growth of National Economies ** TB/1373

Education

JACQUES BARZUN: The House of Intellect TB/1051

RICHARD M. JONES, Ed.: Contemporary Educational Psychology: *Selected Readings* ** TB/1292

CLARK KERR: The Uses of the University TB/1264

Historiography and History of Ideas

HERSCHEL BAKER: The Image of Man: *A Study of the Idea of Human Dignity in Classical Antiquity, the Middle Ages, and the Renaissance* TB/1047

J. BRONOWSKI & BRUCE MAZLISH: The Western Intellectual Tradition: *From Leonardo to Hegel* TB/3001

EDMUND BURKE: On Revolution. Ed. by Robert A. Smith TB/1401

WILHELM DILTHEY: Pattern and Meaning in History: *Thoughts on History and Society.° Edited with an Intro. by H. P. Rickman* TB/1075

ALEXANDER GRAY: The Socialist Tradition: *Moses to Lenin°* TB/1375

J. H. HEXTER: More's Utopia: *The Biography of an Idea. Epilogue by the Author* TB/1195

H. STUART HUGHES: History as Art and as Science: *Twin Vistas on the Past* TB/1207

ARTHUR O. LOVEJOY: The Great Chain of Being: *A Study of the History of an Idea* TB/1009

JOSE ORTEGA Y GASSET: The Modern Theme. *Introduction by Jose Ferrater Mora* TB/1038

RICHARD H. POPKIN: The History of Scepticism from Erasmus to Descartes. *Revised Edition* TB/1391

G. J. RENIER: History: *Its Purpose and Method* TB/1209

MASSIMO SALVADORI, Ed.: Modern Socialism # HR/1374

GEORG SIMMEL et al.: Essays on Sociology, Philosophy and Aesthetics. *Edited by Kurt H. Wolff* TB/1234

BRUNO SNELL: The Discovery of the Mind: *The Greek Origins of European Thought* TB/1018

W. WARREN WAGER, ed.: European Intellectual History Since Darwin and Marx TB/1297

W. H. WALSH: Philosophy of History: In Introduction TB/1020

History: General

HANS KOHN: The Age of Nationalism: *The First Era of Global History* TB/1380

BERNARD LEWIS: The Arabs in History TB/1029

BERNARD LEWIS: The Middle East and the West ° TB/1274

History: Ancient

A. ANDREWS: The Greek Tyrants TB/1103

ERNST LUDWIG EHRLICH: A Concise History of Israel: *From the Earliest Times to the Destruction of the Temple in A.D. 70 °* TB/128

ADOLF ERMAN, Ed.: The Ancient Egyptians: *A Sourcebook of their Writings. New Introduction by William Kelly Simpson* TB/1233

THEODOR H. GASTER: Thespis: *Ritual Myth and Drama in the Ancient Near East* TB/1281

MICHAEL GRANT: Ancient History ° TB/1190

A. H. M. JONES, Ed.: A History of Rome through the Fiftgh Century # Vol. I: *The Republic* HR/1364

Vol. II *The Empire:* HR/1460

SAMUEL NOAH KRAMER: Sumerian Mythology TB/1055

NAPHTALI LEWIS & MEYER REINHOLD, Eds.: Roman Civilization Vol. I: *The Republic* TB/1231

Vol. II: *The Empire* TB/1232

History: Medieval

MARSHALL W. BALDWIN, Ed.: Christianity Through the 13th Century # HR/1468

MARC BLOCH: Land and Work in Medieval Europe. *Translated by J. E. Anderson* TB/1452

HELEN CAM: England Before Elizabeth TB/1026

NORMAN COHN: The Pursuit of the Millennium: *Revolutionary Messianism in Medieval and Reformation Europe* TB/1037

G. G. COULTON: Medieval Village, Manor, and Monastery HR/1022

HEINRICH FICHTENAU: The Carolingian Empire: *The Age of Charlemagne. Translated with an Introduction by Peter Munz* TB/1142

GALBERT OF BRUGES: The Murder of Charles the Good: *A Contemporary Record of Revolutionary Change in 12th Century Flanders. Translated with an Introduction by James Bruce Ross* TB/1311

F. L. GANSHOF: Feudalism TB/1058

F. L. GANSHOF: The Middle Ages: *A History of International Relations. Translated by Rémy Hall* TB/1411

W. O. HASSALL, Ed.: Medieval England: *As Viewed by Contemporaries* TB/1205

DENYS HAY: The Medieval Centuries ° TB/1192

DAVID HERLIHY, Ed.: Medieval Culture and Socitey # HR/1340

4

J. M. HUSSEY: The Byzantine World   TB/1057
ROBERT LATOUCHE: The Birth of Western Economy: *Economic Aspects of the Dark Ages* °   TB/1290
HENRY CHARLES LEA: The Inquisition of the Middle Ages. || *Introduction by Walter Ullmann*   TB/1456
FERDINARD LOT: The End of the Ancient World and the Beginnings of the Middle Ages. *Introduction by Glanville Downey*   TB/1044
H. R. LOYN: The Norman Conquest   TB/1457
ACHILLE LUCHAIRE: Social France at the time of Philip Augustus. *Intro. by John W. Baldwin*   TB/1314
GUIBERT DE NOGENT: Self and Society in Medieval France: *The Memoirs of Guibert de Nogent.* || Edited by John F. Benton TB/1471
MARSILIUS OF PADUA: The Defender of Peace. *The Defensor Pacis. Translated with an Introduction by Alan Gewirth*   TB/1310
CHARLES PETET-DUTAILLIS: The Feudal Monarchy in France and England: *From the Tenth to the Thirteenth Century* °   TB/1165
STEVEN RUNCIMAN: A History of the Crusades
Vol. I: *The First Crusade and the Foundation of the Kingdom of Jerusalem. Illus.*   TB/1143
Vol. II: *The Kingdom of Jerusalem and the Frankish East 1100-1187. Illus.*   TB/1243
Vol. III: *The Kingdom of Acre and the Later Crusades. Illus.*   TB/1298
J. M. WALLACE-HADRILL: The Barbarian West: *The Early Middle Ages, A.D. 400-1000*   TB/1061

History: Renaissance & Reformation

JACOB BURCKHARDT: The Civilization of the Renaissance in Italy. *Introduction by Benjamin Nelson and Charles Trinkaus. Illus.*
Vol. I TB/40;   Vol. II TB/41
JOHN CALVIN & JACOPO SADOLETO: A Reformation Debate. *Edited by John C. Olin*   TB/1239
FEDERICO CHABOD: Machiavelli and the Renaissance   TB/1193
THOMAS CROMWELL: Thomas Cromwell on Church and Commonwealth,: *Selected Letters 1523-1540.* ¶ *Ed. with an Intro. by Arthur J. Slavin*   TB/1462
R. TREVOR DAVIES: The Golden Century of Spain, 1501-1621 °   TB/1194
J. H. ELLIOTT: Europe Divided, 1559-1598 a °   TB/1414
G. R. ELTON: Reformation Europe, 1517-1559 ° a   TB/1270
DESIDERIUS ERASMUS: Christian Humanism and the Reformation: *Selected Writings. Edited and Translated by John C. Olin*   TB/1166
DESIDERIUS ERASMUS: Erasmus and His Age: *Selected Letters. Edited with an Introduction by Hans J. Hillerbrand. Translated by Marcus A. Haworth*   TB/1461
WALLACE K. FERGUSON et al.: Facets of the Renaissance   TB/1098
WALLACE K. FERGUSON et al.: The Renaissance: *Six Essays. Illus.*   TB/1084
FRANCESCO GUICCIARDINI: History of Florence. *Translated with an Introduction and Notes by Mario Domandi*   TB/1470
WERNER L. GUNDERSHEIMER, Ed.: French Humanism, 1470-1600. * *Illus.*   TB/1473
MARIE BOAS HALL, Ed.: Nature and Nature's Laws: *Documents of the Scientific Revolution* #   HR/1420
HANS J. HILLERBRAND, Ed., The Protestant Reformation #   HR/1342
JOHAN HUIZINGA: Erasmus and the Age of Reformation. *Illus.*   TB/19

JOEL HURSTFIELD: The Elizabethan Nation   TB/1312
JOEL HURSTFIELD, Ed.: The Reformation Crisis   TB/1267
PAUL OSKAR KRISTELLER: Renaissance Thought: *The Classic, Scholastic, and Humanist Strains*   TB/1048
PAUL OSKAR KRISTELLER: Renaissance Thought II: *Papers on Humanism and the Arts*   TB/1163
PAUL O. KRISTELLER & PHILIP P. WIENER, Eds.: Renaissance Essays   TB/1392
DAVID LITTLE: Religion, Order and Law: *A Study in Pre-Revolutionary England.* § *Preface by R. Bellah*   TB/1418
NICCOLO MACHIAVELLI: History of Florence and of the Affairs of Italy: *From the Earliest Times to the Death of Lorenzo the Magnificent. Introduction by Felix Gilbert* TB/1027
ALFRED VON MARTIN: Sociology of the Renaissance. ° *Introduction by W. K. Ferguson*   TB/1099
GARRETT MATTINGLY et al.: Renaissance Profiles. *Edited by J. H. Plumb*   TB/1162
J. E. NEALE: The Age of Catherine de Medici °   TB/1085
J. H. PARRY: The Establishment of the European Hegemony: 1415-1715: *Trade and Exploration in the Age of the Renaissance* TB/1045
J. H. PARRY, Ed.: The European Reconnaissance: *Selected Documents* #   HR/1345
BUONACCORSO PITTI & GREGORIO DATI: Two Memoirs of Renaissance Florence: *The Diaries of Buonaccorso Pitti and Gregorio Dati. Edited with Intro. by Gene Brucker. Trans. by Julia Martines*   TB/1333
J. H. PLUMB: The Italian Renaissance: *A Concise Survey of Its History and Culture*   TB/1161
A. F. POLLARD: Henry VIII. *Introduction by A. G. Dickens.* °   TB/1249
RICHARD H. POPKIN: The History of Scepticism from Erasmus to Descartes   TB/139
PAOLO ROSSI: Philosophy, Technology, and the Arts, in the Early Modern Era 1400-1700. || *Edited by Benjamin Nelson. Translated by Salvator Attanasio*   TB/1458
FERDINAND SCHEVILL: The Medici. *Illus.* TB/1010
FERDINAND SCHEVILL: Medieval and Renaissance Florence. *Illus. Vol. I: Medieval Florence*   TB/1090
Vol. II: *The Coming of Humanism and the Age of the Medici*   TB/1091
R. H. TAWNEY: The Agrarian Problem in the Sixteenth Century. *Intro. by Lawrence Stone*   TB/1315
H. R. TREVOR-ROPER: The European Witch-craze of the Sixteenth and Seventeenth Centuries and Other Essays °   TB/1416
VESPASIANO: Rennaissance Princes, Popes, and XVth Century: *The Vespasiano Memoirs. Introduction by Myron P. Gilmore. Illus.*   TB/1111

History: Modern European

RENE ALBRECHT-CARRIE, Ed.: The Concert of Europe #   HR/1341
MAX BELOFF: The Age of Absolutism, 1660-1815   TB/1062
OTTO VON BISMARCK: Reflections and Reminiscences. *Ed. with Intro. by Theodore S. Hamerow* ¶   TB/1357
EUGENE C. BLACK, Ed.: British Politics in the Nineteenth Century #   HR/1427

5

W. J. BATE: From Classic to Romantic: *Premises of Taste in Eighteenth Century England* TB/1036

VAN WYCK BROOKS: Van Wyck Brooks: The Early Years: *A Selection from his Works, 1908-1921* Ed. with Intro. by Claire Sprague TB/3082

ERNST R. CURTIUS: European Literature and the Latin Middle Ages. *Trans. by Willard Trask* TB/2015

RICHMOND LATTIMORE, Translator: The Odyssey of Homer TB/1389

JOHN STUART MILL: On Bentham and Coleridge. *Introduction by F. R. Leavis* TB/1070

SAMUEL PEPYS: The Diary of Samual Pepys. ° *Edited by O. F. Morshead. 60 illus. by Ernest Shepard* TB/1007

ROBERT PREYER, Ed.: Victorian Literature ** TB/1302

ALBION W. TOURGEE: A Fool's Errand: *A Novel of the South during Reconstruction. Intro. by George Fredrickson* TB/3074

BASIL WILEY: Nineteenth Century Studies: *Coleridge to Matthew Arnold* ° TB/1261

RAYMOND WILLIAMS: Culture and Society, 1780-1950 ° TB/1252

Philosophy

HENRI BERGSON: Time and Free Will: *An Essay on the Immediate Data of Consciousness* ° TB/1021

LUDWIG BINSWANGER: Being-in-the-World: *Selected Papers. Trans. with Intro. by Jacob Needleman* TB/1365

H. J. BLACKHAM: Six Existentialist Thinkers: *Kierkegaard, Nietzsche, Jaspers, Marcel, Heidegger, Sartre* ° TB/1002

J. M. BOCHENSKI: The Methods of Contemporary Thought. *Trans. by Peter Caws* TB/1377

CRANE BRINTON: Nietzsche. *Preface, Bibliography, and Epilogue by the Author* TB/1197

ERNST CASSIRER: Rousseau, Kant and Goethe. *Intro. by Peter Gay* TB/1092

FREDERICK COPLESTON, S. J.: Medieval Philosophy TB/376

F. M. CORNFORD: From Religion to Philosophy: *A Study in the Origins of Western Speculation* § TB/20

WILFRID DESAN: The Tragic Finale: *An Essay on the Philosophy of Jean-Paul Sartre* TB/1030

MARVIN FARBER: The Aims of Phenomenology: *The Motives, Methods, and Impact of Husserl's Thought* TB/1291

MARVIN FARBER: Basic Issues of Philosophy: *Experience, Reality, and Human Values* TB/1344

MARVIN FARBER: Phenomenology and Existence: *Towards a Philosophy within Nature* TB/1295

PAUL FRIEDLANDER: Plato: *An Introduction* TB/2017

MICHAEL GELVEN: A Commentary on Heidegger's "Being and Time" TB/1464

J. GLENN GRAY: Hegel and Greek Thought TB/1409

W. K. C. GUTHRIE: The Greek Philosophers: *From Thales to Aristotle* ° TB/1008

G. W. F. HEGEL: On Art, Religion Philosophy: *Introductory Lectures to the Realm of Absolute Spirit.* || *Edited with an Introduction by J. Glenn Gray* TB/1463

G. W. F. HEGEL: Phenomenology of Mind. ° || *Introduction by George Lichtheim* TB/1303

MARTIN HEIDEGGER: Discourse on Thinking. *Translated with a Preface by John M. Anderson and E. Hans Freund. Introduction by John M. Anderson* TB/1459

F. H. HEINEMANN: Existentialism and the Modern Predicament TB/28

WERER HEISENBERG: Physics and Philosophy: *The Revolution in Modern Science. Intro. by F. S. C. Northrop* TB/549

EDMUND HUSSERL: Phenomenology and the Crisis of Philosophy. § *Translated with an Introduction by Quentin Lauer* TB/1170

IMMANUEL KANT: Groundwork of the Metaphysic of Morals. *Translated and Analyzed by H. J. Paton* TB/1159

IMMANUEL KANT: Lectures on Ethics. § *Introduction by Lewis White Beck* TB/105

WALTER KAUFMANN, Ed.: Religion From Tolstoy to Camus: *Basic Writings on Religious Truth and Morals* TB/123

QUENTIN LAUER: Phenomenology: *Its Genesis and Prospect. Preface by Aron Gurwitsch* TB/1169

MAURICE MANDELBAUM: The Problem of Historical Knowledge: *An Answer to Relativism* TB/1338

GEORGE A. MORGAN: What Nietzsche Means TB/1198

H. J. PATON: The Categorical Imperative: *A Study in Kant's Moral Philosophy* TB/1325

MICHAEL POLANYI: Personal Knowledge: *Towards a Post-Critical Philosophy* TB/1158

KARL R. POPPER: Conjectures and Refutations: *The Growth of Scientific Knowledge* TB/1376

WILLARD VAN ORMAN QUINE: Elementary Logic *Revised Edition* TB/577

WILLARD VAN ORMAN QUINE: From a Logical Point of View: *Logico-Philosophical Essays* TB/566

JOHN E. SMITH: Themes in American Philosophy: *Purpose, Experience and Community* TB/1466

MORTON WHITE: Foundations of Historical Knowledge TB/1440

WILHELM WINDELBAND: A History of Philosophy *Vol. I: Greek, Roman, Medieval* TB/38 *Vol. II: Renaissance, Enlightenment, Modern* TB/39

LUDWIG WITTGENSTEIN: The Blue and Brown Books ° TB/1211

LUDWIG WITTGENSTEIN: Notebooks, 1914-1916 TB/1441

Political Science & Government

C. E. BLACK: The Dynamics of Modernization: *A Study in Comparative History* TB/1321

KENNETH E. BOULDING: Conflict and Defense: *A General Theory of Action* TB/3024

DENIS W. BROGAN: Politics in America. *New Introduction by the Author* TB/1469

CRANE BRINTON: English Political Thought in the Nineteenth Century TB/1071

ROBERT CONQUEST: Power and Policy in the USSR: *The Study of Soviet Dynastics* ° TB/1307

ROBERT A. DAHL & CHARLES E. LINDBLOM: Politics, Economics, and Welfare: *Planning and Politico-Economic Systems Resolved into Basic Social Processes* TB/1277

HANS KOHN: Political Ideologies of the 20th Century TB/1277

ROY C. MACRIDIS, Ed.: Political Parties: *Contemporary Trends and Ideas* ** TB/1322

ROBERT GREEN MC CLOSKEY: American Conservatism in the Age of Enterprise, 1865-1910 TB/1137

MARSILIUS OF PADUA: The Defender of Peace. *The Defensor Pacis. Translated with an Introduction by Alan Gewirth* TB/1310

KINGSLEY MARTIN: French Liberal Thought in the Eighteenth Century: *A Study of Political Ideas from Bayle to Condorcet* TB/1114

BARRINGTON MOORE, JR.:Political Power and
Social Theory: *Seven Studies* || TB/1221
BARRINGTON MOORE, JR.: Soviet Politics—The
Dilemma of Power: *The Role of Ideas in
Social Change* || TB/1222
BARRINGTON MOORE, JR.: Terror and Progress—
USSR: *Some Sources of Change and Stability*
JOHN B. MORRALL: Political Thought in Medieval
Times TB/1076
KARL R. POPPER. The Open Society and Its
Enemies *Vol. I: The Spell of Plato* TB/1101
*Vol. II: The High Tide of Prophecy: Hegel,
Marx, and the Aftermath* TB/1102
CONYERS READ, Ed.: The Constitution Recon-
sidered. *Revised Edition, Preface by Richard
B. Morris* TB/1384
JOHN P. ROCHE, Ed.: Origins of American Po-
litical Thought: *Selected Readings* TB/1301
JOHN P. ROCHE, Ed.: American Political
Thought: *From Jefferson to Progressivism*
TB/1332
HENRI DE SAINT-SIMON: Social Organization, The
Science of Man, and Other Writings. ||
*Edited and Translated with an Introduction
by Felix Markham* TB/1152
CHARLES SCHOTTLAND, Ed.: The Welfare State **
TB/1323
JOSEPH A. SCHUMPETER: Capitalism, Socialism
and Democracy TB/3008
PETER WOLL, Ed.: Public Administration and
Policy: *Selected Essays* TB/1284

Psychology

ALFRED ADLER: The Individual Psychology of
Alfred Adler: *A Systematic Presentation in
Selections from His Writings. Edited by
Heinz L. & Rowena R. Ansbacher* TB/1154
ALFRED ADLER: Problems of Neurosis: *A Book
of Case Histories. Introduction by Heinz L.
Ansbacher* TB/1145
LUDWIG BINSWANGER: Being-in-the-World: *Se-
lected Papers. || Trans. with Intro. by Jacob
Needleman* TB/1365
ARTHUR BURTON & ROBERT E. HARRIS: Clinical
Studies of Personality Vol. I TB/3075
Vol. II TB/3076
HADLEY CANTRIL: The Invasion from Mars: *A
Study in the Psychology of Panic* || TB/1282
MIRCEA ELIADE: Cosmos and History: *The Myth
of the Eternal Return* § TB/2050
MIRCEA ELIADE: Myth and Reality TB/1369
MIRCEA ELIADE: Myths, Dreams and Mysteries:
*The Encounter Between Contemporary Faiths
and Archaic Realities* § TB/1320
MIRCEA ELIADE: Rites and Symbols of Initiation:
The Mysteries of Birth and Rebirth § TB/1236
HERBERT FINGARETTE: The Self in Transforma-
tion: *Psychoanalysis, Philosophy and the Life
of the Spirit* || TB/1177
SIGMUND FREUD: On Creativity and the Uncon-
scious: *Papers on the Psychology of Art,
Literature, Love, Religion. § Intro. by Ben-
jamin Nelson* TB/45
J. GLENN GRAY: The Warriors: *Reflections on
Men in Battle. Introduction by Hannah
Arendt* TB/1294
WILLIAM JAMES: Psychology: *The Briefer
Course. Edited with an Intro. by Gordon
Allport* TB/1034
C. G. JUNG: Psychological Reflections. *Ed. by
J. Jacobi* TB/2001
KARL MENNINGER, M.D.: Theory of Psychoan-
alytic Technique TB/1144
JOHN H. SCHAAR: Escape from Authority: *The
Perspectives of Erich Fromm* TB/1155

MUZAFER SHERIF: The Psychology of Social
Norms. *Introduction by Gardner Murphy*
TB/3072
HELLMUT WILHELM: Change: *Eight Lectures on
the I Ching* TB/2019

Religion: Ancient and Classical, Biblical and Judaic Traditions

W. F. ALBRIGHT. The Biblical Period from Abra-
ham to Ezra TB/102
SALO W. BARON: Modern Nationalism and Re-
ligion TB/818
C. K. BARRETT, Ed.: The New Testament Back-
ground: *Selected Documents* TB/86
MARTIN BUBER: Eclipse of God: *Studies in the
Relation Between Religion and Philosophy*
TB/12
MARTIN BUBER: Hasidism and Modern Man.
Edited and Translated by Maurice Friedman
TB/839
MARTIN BUBER: The Knowledge of Man. *Edited
with an Introduction by Maurice Friedman.
Translated by Maurice Friedman and Ronald
Gregor Smith* TB/135
MARTIN BUBER: Moses. *The Revelation and the
Covenant* TB/837
MARTIN BUBER: The Origin and Meaning of
Hasidism. *Edited and Translated by Maurice
Friedman* TB/835
MARTIN BUBER: The Prophetic Faith TB/73
MARTIN BUBER: Two Types of Faith: *Interpene-
tration of Judaism and Christianity* °
TB/75
MALCOLM L. DIAMOND: Martin Buber: *Jewish
Existentialist* TB/840
M. S. ENSLIN: Christian Beginnings TB/5
M. S. ENSLIN: The Literature of the Christian
Movement TB/6
ERNST LUDWIG EHRLICH: A Concise History of
Israel: *From the Earliest Times to the De-
struction of the Temple in A.D. 70* ° TB/128
HENRI FRANKFORT: Ancient Egyptian Religion:
An Interpretation TB/77
MAURICE S. FRIEDMAN: Martin Buber: *The Life
of Dialogue* TB/64
ABRAHAM HESCHEL: The Earth Is the Lord's &
The Sabbath. *Two Essays* TB/828
ABRAHAM HESCHEL: God in Search of Man: *A
Philosophy of Judaism* TB/807
ABRAHAM HESCHEL: Man Is not Alone: *A Phil-
osophy of Religion* TB/838
ABRAHAM HESCHEL: The Prophets: *An Introduc-
tion* TB/1421
T. J. MEEK: Hebrew Origins TB/69
JAMES MUILENBURG: The Way of Israel: *Bibli-
cal Faith and Ethics* TB/133
H. J. ROSE: Religion in Greece and Rome
TB/55
H. H. ROWLEY: The Growth of the Old Testa-
ment TB/107
D. WINTON THOMAS, Ed.: Documents from Old
Testament Times TB/85

Religion: General Christianity

ROLAND H. BAINTON: Christendom: *A Short
History of Christianity and Its Impact on
Western Civilization. Illus.*
Vol. I TB/131; Vol. II TB/132
JOHN T. MCNEILL: Modern Christian Move-
ments. *Revised Edition* TB/1402
ERNST TROELTSCH: The Social Teaching of the
Christian Churches. *Intro. by H. Richard
Niebuhr* Vol. TB/71; Vol. II TB/72

9